World Bank Group Impact Evaluations

Relevance and Effectiveness

IEG WORLD BANK | IFC | MIGA

INDEPENDENT EVALUATION GROUP

World Bank Group Impact Evaluations

Relevance and Effectiveness

Contents

BOXES

FIGURES

TABLES

Acknowledgments

This study was prepared by a team led by Javier Baez and Izlem Yenice. The core team includes Andaleeb Alam, Jacqueline Andrieu, Carmen Domingues, and Tu Chi Nguyen; Alberto Abadie advised the team on the framework and process to assess the quality of all the impact evaluations reviewed for this study. Background papers were prepared by Michael Mertaugh and Andrew Warner. Yezena Yimer and Viktoriya Yevsyeyeva assisted the team.

The team thanks Martha Ainsworth, Radu Ban, Maria Isabel Beltran, Bertha Briceno, Subrata Dhar, Ariel Fiszbein, Scott Guggenheim, Florence Kondylis, Ariana Legovini, Oscar Raul Antezana Malpartida, Maria M. Nuñez, Cuong Hung Pham, Laura Rawlings, Adam Ross, Carlos Asenjo Ruiz, Garima Sahai, Renos Vakis, and Almud Weitz for providing relevant material, sharing thoughtful insights, and facilitating the conduct of the country case studies. The team is also grateful to all task team leaders, monitoring and evaluation specialists, and evaluators who responded to the electronic surveys. The team greatly appreciates the time and insights of chief economists, directors, sector managers, business line leaders, World Bank Group country staff, government officials, and local researchers who were interviewed.

The work was conducted under the general guidance of Mark Sundberg (Manager) and Stoyan Tenev (Manager). The team is grateful for the extensive and excellent advice provided by its peer reviewers, David McKenzie and Howard White.

Overview

The use of impact evaluation (IE) to assess causal effects of development interventions and complement other evaluation approaches has expanded rapidly over the past decade, as the development community has focused more sharply on measuring results. Consistent with this trend, the production of IEs at the World Bank Group has also grown rapidly, from an average of 16 initiated per year in the period 1999–2004 to an average of 62 per year in 2005–10. In parallel, the role of IEs in furthering the learning and knowledge agenda has received increased corporate attention, particularly at the World Bank, starting with the creation of the Development Impact Evaluation Initiative (DIME) in 2005. More recently, the replenishment discussions for the International Development Association (IDA) recommended institutionalizing IEs at the World Bank under a strategic framework.

In the study, the Independent Evaluation Group (IEG) examines the relevance, quality, and influence of World Bank and International Finance Corporation (IFC) IEs on operational, institutional, and knowledge priorities by examining their experience throughout the IE production cycle, from initiation to implementation to dissemination and uptake.

IEG finds that the Bank Group portfolio of IEs is largely aligned with project objectives and sector strategies. In particular, World Bank IEs initiated more recently are better integrated with operations and cover a broader range of sector and knowledge priorities than earlier ones. Still, some areas for improvement need to be addressed, in particular in consideration of the relatively high cost of producing IEs.

Strategic IE selection and coordination has been improving over time at the World Bank, led by DIME and the Spanish Impact Evaluation Trust Fund (SIEF). Through SIEF, for example, a systematic approach to identifying and financing IEs has been rolled out, most widely in the Human Development Network (HDN). Other initiatives, such as the creation of new IE thematic programs and the adoption of the programmatic model by an increasing number of IE programs, have improved strategic prioritization of IE topics as well as coordination between DIME and project teams in the initiation of IEs. In IFC, where the use of IE is relatively more recent and much smaller than in the World Bank, the selection of IEs has not yet been guided by a strategic framework, though a new Evaluation Strategy—approved in FY12—moves in this direction. Across the World Bank Group, issues related to funding, staff capacity, and incentives still constrain the scope and coverage of IEs.

Most World Bank IEs meet either medium or high technical quality standards, and about half of IFC IEs did. With some exceptions, notably SIEF-financed IEs, there are at present no *formal* and *standardized* mechanisms at the World Bank to ensure that all evaluations go through similar quality controls. A more formal process could guarantee that individual evaluations receive the feedback and scrutiny needed to ensure high quality. The lower technical quality of IFC IEs partly reflects the early developmental stage of IE use, limited staff capacity, and absence of a standardized mechanism to review and supervise IE quality.

This study found also that there are opportunities for more systematic use of IEs in the World Bank Group. Varied sources point to IE influence on aspects of development practice and to real benefits from IEs, and many development professionals espouse a belief in their potential to increase development effectiveness through better evidence. At the World Bank, the feedback loop between IE production and project operations and learning is modest. Notable examples of IE influence on development practice include their contribution to project assessment and to decisions to design and sustain evaluated and future projects, raising the profile of certain types of interventions, informing policy dialogue and institutional strategies, and building local monitoring and evaluation capabilities. But in some instances, even when IEs have been relevant and of good quality, they appear to have had limited use and influence for various reasons: poor timing, underdeveloped operational linkages, failure to engage project teams and decision makers, or lack of dissemination.

There are signs of improvement, including, for example, dedicated SIEF support for results dissemination, concerted capacity building efforts, and closer collaboration with operations and clients in design and implementation of ongoing IEs. At IFC, IEs have been primarily used by project teams to assess project impacts. There are examples of use beyond the project, such as informing dialogue with clients, but these are not common.

IEG makes five recommendations for the World Bank and IFC to strengthen the relevance, quality, and usefulness of future IEs: (i) consistently apply mechanisms for strategic identification and prioritization of IEs to balance learning and results measurement objectives; (ii) coordinate fragmented external funding with core funds to strategically finance the production of IEs; (iii) improve integration of IEs into the design and review of projects to sharpen the focus of project operations on results; (iv) adopt and consistently apply good practice quality standards to the conduct of all IEs, including independent peer review and data availability for replication; and (v) regularly incorporate, where feasible, analytical elements such as cost-benefit analysis to enhance the operational relevance of IEs.

IE has grown more popular as a method for identifying the causal links between interventions and outcomes. This is largely because of innovations in statistical methods and econometrics and because demand is increasing for evaluations that can measure development results. That demand has caught the attention of academia and the research community and encouraged global collaboration and the creation of national institutions dedicated to IE. The result is a sizable increase in the number of IEs produced.

The World Bank Group is the largest producer of IEs among all development institutions, with 460 IEs completed or in progress. In addition to conducting them in-house, the Bank Group is also supporting countries in carrying out IEs of their programs, strengthening monitoring and evaluation (M&E) frameworks to provide data for IEs, and facilitating global learning activities to promote these evaluations and their results. These increased efforts aim to contribute to the results and knowledge agendas at the Bank Group, which identify IE as a tool that helps improve decision making by generating project performance information and adding to global knowledge about development effectiveness.

This report assesses the relevance, quality, and use of Bank Group IEs, including both experimental and non-experimental IEs. Because this type of evaluation is a product of analytic and advisory activity, this evaluation follows IEG's goal of evaluating the explicit and implicit objectives of such activity and answers three questions: (i) *Relevance:* To what extent and why (or why not) are IEs aligned with the operational and strategic priorities of the World Bank Group and its clients and relevant to closing knowledge gaps? (ii) *Quality:* To what extent and why (or why not) do IEs meet expected quality standards? (iii) *Use and influence:* To what extent and why are IEs used (or not used) to influence development practice?

This evaluation does not provide answers to questions about the "impact" and cost effectiveness of IEs, the contribution of IEs relative to other evaluation approaches or forms of knowledge production, or the strategic scope of the Bank Group's IE work. The study also does not formally evaluate specific IE initiatives or models of IE conduct at the World Bank Group.

The results of the evaluation are based on triangulation of evidence from different sources of information. These source include a desk review of the reports and/or project documents related to all completed World Bank and IFC IEs linked to a lending, advisory service or nonlending project code (119 World Bank and 26 IFC IEs), a random sample of 21 completed World Bank IEs not linked to a lending or nonlending project code, a random sample of 54 ongoing World Bank IEs, and all four ongoing IFC IEs; electronic surveys of evaluators and World Bank Group task leaders of evaluated projects; field-based case studies in five countries and seven desk-based country case studies; one sector case study in education; and interviews with Bank Group managers and staff.

Background: Impact Evaluations at the World Bank Group

IEs assess the causal effects (impacts) attributable to an intervention by comparing the outcomes of interest (short, medium, or long term) with what would have happened without the program—a counterfactual. There is a long tradition in evaluation of defining the term "impact" as long-term effects of a development intervention. By this token, any evaluation that refers to impact indicators is an IE. However, in the IE community, including at the World Bank Group, impact denotes causal effect of a program on outcomes, whether immediate, intermediate, or final. Consistent with the terminology used in the IE community and at the Bank Group, this report uses the term impact to mean causal effects of an intervention, irrespective of the time dimension of the outcomes of interest.

A challenge of any IE is that the counterfactual cannot be observed for the same program participants at the same point in time. These evaluations seek to overcome this challenge by creating a control group that is similar to the group that receives the intervention (treatment group). In experimental approaches, generating a robust counterfactual involves randomly assigning units to control and treatment groups before program implementation. When randomization is not possible, quasi-experimental techniques are used to create counterfactuals that aim for statistical equivalence with the treatment group.

Over the past decade, especially since 2005, the World Bank has established several initiatives to raise and coordinate IE production. In 2005, the Bank's Office of the Chief Economist created DIME with the objective of generating knowledge on selected policies. Also in 2005, IE programs were started in the Africa Region and in the HDN, which served as DIME's implementation backbone. In 2006, Operations Policy and Country Services established IE as a new analytic and advisory activity product line, and in 2008, the managing director responsible for knowledge and networks transformed DIME into a Bank-wide decentralized program with its own governance structure.

In 2009–10, and following Bank-wide consultations to identify IE topics based on the network portfolio and operational agenda, several new IE programs along thematic lines were created that supplemented the eight that were already active. Several of these thematic IE programs have now developed a coordinated approach—also referred to as the programmatic model—and assumed responsibility for programmatic and country-specific activities. In addition to conducting IEs, DIME and HDN (among other networks and units) are also undertaking efforts to build IE capacity and facilitate global learning through workshops, clinics, methodology notes, meta-analyses, and data sharing.

More recently, the deputies at the IDA16 Replenishment discussions requested the World Bank to prepare a strategic selection framework for IEs, with associated financing and implementation plans, to be applied at the outset of the IDA16 period. In addition, the discussion participants recommended that the number of IEs be included in the IDA16 Results Measurement System and the IDA Report Card as an indicator of operational effectiveness, with measurable targets.

IFC began using the IE tool in 2005, in response to growing demand from stakeholders, to evaluate its advisory services, which provide advice and training to governments and private sector firms on improving investment climate, infrastructure, access to finance, and sustainable business practices. Examples of advisory service projects include simplification of the business licensing procedures in Lima and supervisory skills training programs in Cambodian garment factories.

The World Bank and IFC differ on the level of their IE production, motivation, and capacity. IE efforts are new in IFC, and IEs are primarily conducted to supplement project assessments. Unlike the World Bank, where IE is a corporate priority and structures with an exclusive IE focus have been established, IFC has had limited resources to facilitate IE production—one IE specialist and no specific budget allocation.

The aforementioned IE initiatives have been associated with an increase in the production of IEs at the World Bank over the past decade. Figure A shows that the annual production of IEs at the World Bank increased markedly after 2005, from an average of 16 initiated per year in the 1999–2004 period to an average of 57 per year in 2005–10. Since the creation of DIME in 2005, the advent of other notable IE initiatives has further accelerated IE production at the World Bank. The IE agenda at IFC is in its early developmental stage, producing 26 completed IEs between 2005 and 2010.

The proportion of World Bank IEs assessing lending operations has also grown over time, from 59 percent of IEs initiated in 2005–08 to 75 percent initiated in 2009–10. Most IFC IEs evaluate advisory service projects, which are similar to some of the interventions being evaluated by World Bank IEs (for example, training, microfinance, and reform support). More recently, two investment operations have been subject to an IE.

At the World Bank, there is also an increasing trend toward IEs adopting a randomized design, consistent with the focus of initiatives like DIME and SIEF. For instance, more than 80 percent of IEs initiated in 2007–10 use randomization, compared with 57 percent in 2005–06 and a modest 19 percent in the years before (figure 1).

The increase in the number of IEs and the introduction of new IE initiatives at the World Bank is associated with broader regional and sector coverage. Until 2005, most World Bank IEs were in the Latin America and the Caribbean Region and in the education, local development (mainly social funds), and social protection sectors. Since then, IEs have greatly expanded in the Africa region, in part due to IE efforts targeted to the region, such as the Africa Impact Evaluation Initiative. In addition, recent IEs have started to cover new themes, such as malaria, and have rapidly grown in areas where IE work was scarce, such as agriculture, HIV, finance and private sector development, in part because of the advent of IE thematic programs in these areas.

These trends notwithstanding, few IEs have been conducted in some regions (such as the Middle East and North Africa and Europe and Central Asia) and on some topics (for example, energy and transport). Meanwhile, IFC IEs have been concentrated in the Latin America and the Caribbean, Europe and Central Asia, and South Asia Regions, and in the Sustainable Business and Access to Finance business lines.

Client involvement in different stages of IE production has been modest, but it is increasing. The increase in proportion of World Bank IEs *initiated* by the government or borrower (defined as the client) has been small, but there is evidence of growing *involvement* of the client in the design of IEs. A survey of World Bank staff found that three-fifths of the IEs initiated in 2007–10 *involved* the client in the design stage compared with 40 percent in 2005–06, and 22 percent in the years before. Clients have been less active in the review and discussion of findings (39 percent of completed IEs), based on survey data. However, evidence also suggests that among completed IEs, those initiated in

Figure 1

Figure 1 — Total IEs at the World Bank and IEs Using Randomization by Initiation Year

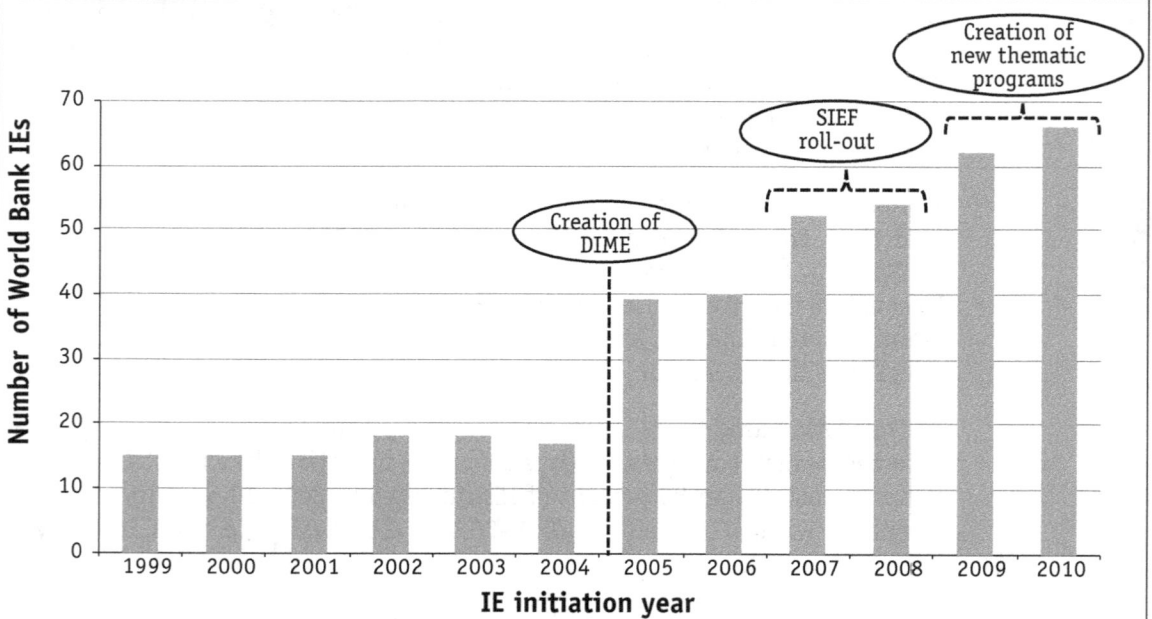

Source: IEG.

Note: Based on 411 of 430 World Bank IEs. The remaining 16 IEs were initiated before 1999 period; for three IEs, the start year could not be identified. IE data for 2010 are partial because the IE database did not include new IEs initiated in the second half of 2010. For 15 ongoing IEs, the IE design was not specified in DIME database; these are excluded from the count of IEs using randomization. The information on IE design for completed IEs is drawn from IE reports; the source of information for design of ongoing World Bank IEs is the DIME database.

2005 or later were more often reviewed by the client at the final stage versus those that had been initiated earlier.

World Bank and IFC IEs and evaluated projects have different cost profiles. DIME estimates indicate that the average cost of World Bank IEs is around $500,000, about 1.4 percent of the total cost of the evaluated interventions and 0.5 percent of the cost of the projects of which those interventions are a part. At IFC, the medium cost of an IE relative to the project budget is about 7 percent. However, it would be misleading to compare the cost ratios between the two institutions because the expenditures on both the IE and the project being evaluated are different. The median cost of an IFC advisory service project that has been subject to an IE is $564,000, whereas the median expenditure on IE is $60,000.

Funding for IEs at the World Bank Group is fragmented and has become increasingly dependent on external sources. World Bank IEs initiated before 2005 primarily relied on project budget or government funds and on budget of the unit supporting the project. IEs initiated since then have increasingly come to depend on trust funds and/or trust-funded IE initiatives in the World Bank for financing (63 percent of IEs initiated in 2005–10 versus 10 percent of IEs initiated before 2005). In IFC, the Results Measurements Unit's M&E budget has been the main source of funding for IEs, leveraging project budget and donor funding. Increasingly, however, IFC IEs are being conducted with more resources from regional or business line budgets and donor funding, and less from the Results Measurement Unit's budget.

Relevance of World Bank Group Impact Evaluations to Operational, Institutional, and Knowledge Priorities

The usefulness of IEs depends largely on the extent to which the information they provide is aligned with the questions asked by their potential users. For the World Bank Group, those users include operational staff, management, governments or private sector clients, and the development community. Hence, in its evaluation, IEG examined the relevance of Bank Group IEs for *project operations, institutional strategies,* and *knowledge generation.*

With regard to project operations, the majority of questions addressed by World Bank Group IEs have been well aligned with project development objectives and results frameworks. Based on a comparison of the questions addressed by completed IEs with the development objectives of the evaluated projects, almost all Bank Group IEs were found to investigate outcomes that, if influenced by the intervention, would contribute to the project development objectives. Because development objectives tend to be defined broadly (for example, poverty reduction or human capital accumulation), IE questions were also compared against outcomes articulated in the project results framework. For 70 percent of completed World Bank and IFC IEs, all or at least some of the outcome indicators were mentioned in the results framework of the project.

Recent IEs at the World Bank are more likely to be part of the project plan than earlier ones, and are also better integrated into project M&E. For 25 percent of completed IEs linked to World Bank lending operations, the appraisal document mentioned plans for an IE and baseline data collection. In contrast, the project documents for 50 percent of ongoing World Bank IEs mentioned such plans. This is consistent with the push for more prospective IEs at the World Bank in the past few years, as well as for increased coordination between operational teams and DIME in the design stage. The increase in the linkages between IE and project plans is statistically significant for IEs initiated in 2007–10 compared with IEs for projects initiated in earlier years.

The average short-term effects of a program are just one issue among many worth investigating with IEs. Among these other issues are long-term program effects, differential effects of separate program designs, and the efficiency of programs. Yet these have received less attention than short-term effects:

- Seventy-nine percent of completed World Bank IEs and 35 percent of completed IFC IEs estimated the *distribution of program impacts* across some subset of beneficiaries, based on characteristics such as age, gender, or income.

- Twenty-seven percent of completed Bank Group IEs measured the *contribution to impacts of individual components* of a program's design. However, World Bank IEs initiated in recent years pay more attention to testing treatment variations and supplementary project components for improving beneficiary outcomes.

- Twenty-one percent of completed World Bank and 46 percent of completed IFC IEs did an efficiency analysis, such as a simple comparison of costs with benefits, cost-benefit analysis, economic rate of return, or cost effectiveness analysis across treatment types or programs. Some efforts are now being made at the World Bank to address the issue of lack of efficiency analysis in IEs. For instance, the HDN is developing tools for incorporating cost-benefit analysis into IE.

- Eleven percent of completed World Bank IEs and 20 percent of completed IFC IEs attempted to evaluate medium- and longer-term outcomes.

With regard to institutional strategies, Bank Group IE questions have fit the priorities identified in the sector strategies, but coverage has been uneven. The review of completed World Bank Group IEs reveals that they are well aligned with the priorities identified in corresponding sector strategies. These strategies are generally broad, encompassing a wide range of activities that the Bank Group deems relevant to the sector.

However, some sector priorities have received more attention by completed IEs than others. In sectors and business lines with fewer IEs, such as energy, evaluations covered fewer priority areas identified in the corresponding sector strategies. Even in sectors where there were a large number of completed IEs, such as social protection and sustainable business advisory services, these IEs were concentrated in few of the priority areas.

At the World Bank, recent IEs are covering broader sector priorities, especially priorities that were previously underevaluated. Although there are still more World Bank IEs in some sectors than others, recent IE initiatives have led to more IEs being undertaken in sectors and sector priority areas that did not have an IE or were scarcely evaluated, including energy efficiency, malaria, investment climate, land management, and agrimarkets. Even in sectors where IE presence before 2005 was substantial, World Bank IEs in recent years have been initiated in sector priorities with fewer IEs, such as active labor markets and health systems.

Still, a few sectors and sector priority areas where IEs can have significant learning potential have not received much attention. These include transport (excepting rural roads), environmental health, small and medium enterprise finance, and housing markets, among others.

With regard to *knowledge generation,* World Bank IEs have advanced knowledge about the impacts of a large variety of interventions, especially their role in small-scale testing and determining whether results can be generalized to different settings. Surveys suggest that 80 percent of evaluators and task team leaders think that IEs have contributed, or are anticipated to contribute, to the global knowledge of "what works." Based on survey data from World Bank staff and evaluators and an external assessment of knowledge priorities, IEs initiated in recent years (2007–10) appear better targeted to filling global knowledge gaps.

At IFC, with a few exceptions, IEs are not deliberately selected to close global knowledge gaps. Compared with other sectors, fewer IEs have been done in the private sector, and there are several private sector development topics where there is a knowledge gap (for example, financial literacy and business training). IFC IEs for the most part have been chosen primarily to supplement self-assessment of projects rather than to fill global knowledge gaps, although the two are not mutually exclusive. Indeed, IFC staff who responded to the IEG survey perceive that IFC IEs contributed to the global knowledge of what works. In a recent effort to contribute more to the private sector knowledge base and IFC's business, IFC has partnered with academia and provided grants for implementing innovative IEs.

Factors that affect the scope and relevance of IEs at the World Bank Group include IE selection and coordination, operational linkages, funding, staff capacity, and incentives. In particular, issues related to the last three of those factors persist and can inhibit the Bank Group's IE initiatives from realizing their full potential:

- Interviews with senior management of the World Bank revealed that the selection of IEs in non-human development sectors is considered to be opportunistic, whereas the human development sectors are perceived to have adopted a more systematic approach to identification of IEs. Indeed, the roll-out of SIEF has improved strategic IE selection and financing, most widely in the human development sectors. Meanwhile, other IE initiatives, such as the creation of IE thematic programs and the adoption of the programmatic model by a growing number of IE programs both in human development and non-human development, has improved prioritization of IE topics and strategic coordination between DIME and project teams in IE design. At IFC, where the use of IE as a tool is not as developed as in the World Bank, the selection of IEs has not been guided by a strategic framework; however, the recent IFC Evaluation Strategy, approved in FY12, moves in this direction.

- IEs that are not a formal part of the project and M&E plan are less likely to be used as an integral part of the project M&E. This holds true even if the IE is randomized and/or planned before the intervention is implemented. At the World Bank, the weak integration of IEs with project and M&E plans was more prevalent in older IEs. For instance, less than one-fourth of completed IEs were a formal part of project and M&E design, compared with more than a half of ongoing IEs, and newer IEs are more often reported to be integral to project M&E than older ones.

- World Bank Group staff sometimes face incentives that constrain the scope and relevance of IE(s). This includes incentives to assess interventions that are "easier" to evaluate, limited understanding of the tool, or fear of negative results.

- At the World Bank, in the context of the flat budget environment, limited project funding for IEs, and their high relative cost, most evaluations initiated in recent years have come to rely heavily on trust funds. Many IEs rely on multiple trust fund sources. Although access to multiple sources of financing eases the budget constraint, this fragmentation adds to staff transaction costs. Trust fund resources are not necessarily detrimental to IE relevance, but they are less flexible than Bank budget in terms of where and how to allocate resources, as donor preferences must also be considered.

The Quality of World Bank Group Impact Evaluations

To distinguish IEs that produce reliable findings (*medium* and *high* quality) from those that require significant additional analytical work to be credible (*low* quality), IEG used a quality assessment framework that was developed from a well-established literature on IE and independently validated by an IE specialist. Four key aspects of quality were assessed: data, data measurement, evaluation design, and robustness of findings. The framework was applied to 166 completed IEs (140 Bank and 26 IFC IEs).

At the World Bank, 94 percent of IEs completed in 2000–10 meet medium or high quality standards. This prevalence of IEs meeting quality standards is consistent with the perception of senior management at the World Bank. Overall, these medium and high-quality IEs assessed well-defined and relevant outcomes, used reliable data, and applied some checks for selection bias. More specifically, the majority of IEs used baseline data, conducted their own surveys (including collecting longitudinal information), and relied less on retrospective data.

The outcome indicators measured by these IEs were well defined, separate enough from the inputs of the projects, and achievable within the evaluated time frame. Most IEs tested the validity of their methods and conducted some form of robustness check; however, the scope and rigor of these analyses varied, particularly among those employing quasi-experimental methods and those of medium quality. For instance, 80 percent of IEs using quasi-experimental methods tested at least one identification assumption associated with the evaluation method, but less than one-third of them checked all the key identification assumptions.

The technical quality of completed World Bank IEs has improved over time. For instance, 51 percent of completed IEs that were initiated in 2000–04 met high quality standards and 90 percent met at least medium quality standards. This compares with 71 percent of completed World Bank IEs initiated in 2005 or later that met high quality standards and 98 percent that met at least medium quality standards.

About half of IFC IEs meet medium or high-quality standards. The quality of the data and outcome indicators in these IEs is similar to that of World Bank IEs. However, their evaluation design—fundamental for identifying causal effects—is often weak: many IFC IEs did not carefully construct counterfactuals, and a few adequately addressed the issue of selection bias and other methodological issues that can affect the validity of the evaluation. In addition, the quantitative analysis in many IEs relied on samples that were too small to measure impacts with sufficient statistical confidence. However, the design of ongoing IFC IEs that were reviewed is stronger, as they pay careful attention to issues of sample size and selection bias.

The constraints to maintaining high technical quality are related to review processes and staff capacity. In the World Bank, with some exceptions, there are currently no *formal* and *standardized* mechanisms to ensure that all evaluations go through similar quality controls. Recent IE initiatives like SIEF have established formal quality review procedures that are uniformly applied to all SIEF IEs. Although it is too early to assess these products for their quality, IEG finds that IEs initiated under this approach are more likely to be subject to specialist review at the concept stage. A more formal process could guarantee that individual IEs undergo rigorous scrutiny and receive feedback to ensure high quality. IFC does not have a streamlined review mechanism, and the process is more ad hoc.

In addition, staff capacity to implement and supervise for IE is inadequate in many units of the World Bank, and even more so at IFC, where it also limits the ability to discern the credibility and quality of IE findings.

The Influence of World Bank Group Impact Evaluations on Operational Decisions, Policy Dialogue, Institutional Strategies, and Evaluation Promotion

In assessing the influence of World Bank Group IEs, IEG documented the incidences of IE use, including their role in demonstrating program impacts, informing decisions about a project's future, supporting policy dialogue, defining strategic priorities, and building evaluation capacity and culture.

The use of World Bank IEs to provide evidence of program impact or to inform *operational* decisions is modest. At the project level, this tool is intended to credibly measure impact and provide evidence for project decisions. The findings of less than half (47 percent) of completed World Bank IEs were mentioned in the project completion documents to demonstrate project impact. Similarly, IE findings were cited in one-fifth of project evaluations that IEG did. At IFC, country case studies and survey responses indicate the frequent use of IEs at project level.

The incidence of World Bank IEs being used for decisions to continue, expand, scale down, or cancel the evaluated project or to initiate and refine the design of follow-on projects is also sporadic, ranging from 22 to 33 percent, depending on the source of information (evaluated project completion reports or follow-on project appraisal reports). In addition, the use of completed World Bank IEs that tested pilots and treatment variations was often limited.

Some IEs have influenced projects beyond the ones they evaluated. For instance, the positive IE findings and lessons of a pioneer conditional cash transfer (CCT) program in Mexico *(Progresa/Oportunidades)* inspired other countries in the region (Colombia, Ecuador, El Salvador, Jamaica, Nicaragua, and Peru) to adopt similar instruments. CCTs now have been implemented in more than 30 countries in most regions of the world.

IEs are perceived to be useful for World Bank Group staff in *policy* dialogue with clients and donors. According to a survey of evaluators and project leaders, around half of World Bank IEs were used to influence policy dialogue with a client government. Country case studies support this finding with examples of IEs that have been instrumental in raising political support for effective programs and in influencing policy decisions. Examples include:

- The positive impacts of the *Familias en Accion* CCT in Colombia on consumption, schooling, and health demonstrated by a set of IEs helped convince the new government not only to continue and expand the programs but also to broaden eligibility to include more children.
- IE results of nutrition interventions in Madagascar and Senegal contributed to maintaining political support for the programs.
- Results from IEs empowered managers of the Rural Roads Rehabilitation Program in Peru to make a stronger argument to the Ministry of Finance to ensure financial sustainability for the program.

Institutional strategies at the World Bank Group have benefitted from IEs in areas where there is a large body of evidence. For instance, in education and social protection, where there are many relevant and good-quality IEs and the IE evidence has been synthesized, the sector strategies of the World Bank reflect IE influence. Similarly, in regions with a large concentration of IEs, such as Africa and Latin America, the Bank's Country Assistance Strategies cite their contribution. It has also been found that Bank Group IEs raise the profile of, and draw resources toward, certain interventions (such as CCTs, school feeding, scholarships, and teacher incentives in the World Bank, and business regulation simplification at IFC).

Overall, the direct contribution of World Bank IEs in promoting evaluation capacity and culture has been modest but is now increasing. One-third of completed World Bank IEs were considered by the surveyed team leaders and evaluators to help improve World Bank staff/client (or other institution) capacity in the conduct or analysis of IEs. However, IEs initiated in 2009–10 demonstrate significantly higher expectations about building staff/client capacity than IEs initiated earlier. The latter finding is consistent with the adoption of the programmatic model by many more IE programs during this period. In addition, the World Bank has also been undertaking systematic efforts to improve IE capacity (particularly SIEF and DIME), including formal training, guidance notes, and linkages with communities of practice.

There are also cases where World Bank IEs have increased the interest of counterparts in strengthening the M&E framework of the evaluated and follow-on projects. For example, for 65 percent of follow-on projects of evaluated interventions, an IE was planned for similar or complementary interventions at the appraisal stage. Country-level case studies also indicate five IEs that have contributed to encouraging governments and project teams to adopt a more evidence-based policy-making culture.

The use and influence of World Bank Group IEs is associated with their relevance, timeliness, dissemination, and engagement with local counterparts, as well as with M&E culture and political environment:

- The relevance of IE findings to potential users contributes to determining their actual use. The review of completed World Bank Group IEs found that IE questions that are not aligned with the project results framework are less likely to be cited in the Project Completion Reports. At the World Bank, following DIME's model of collaboration with operations, more use is expected from recent IEs that have been better integrated into project activities.

- The timeliness of IE findings, if not well-aligned with decision making, can undermine use. This is evident in three case studies—the Female Secondary School Education Assistance Project in Bangladesh, the Nutrition Enhancement Project in Senegal, and the Nutrition and Early Childhood Development Project in Uganda—where the long time lags in IE execution meant they missed the opportunity to influence decisions when they were being made. However, when IEs assess outcomes that manifest much later after the project closes (as in infrastructure projects), synchronization with the project cycle is not realistic.

- Many IEs are not disseminated to their potential users, which limits their use. Efforts to communicate and disseminate IEs to potential users have varied considerably. Whereas most project team leaders surveyed were aware of the IEs, IEG found that just 54 percent of World Bank IEs were shared with government.

- Limited active engagement of local counterparts in the government in the initiation, design, analysis, and review of IEs can undermine the influence of IE evidence in decision making and dialogue. For instance, 83 percent of completed IEs initiated by the client influenced policy dialogue with the government, compared with 46 percent of completed IEs not initiated by private or government client.

- The political environment and culture of evidence-based decision making also affect IE use and influence on policy making. Although these factors might be beyond the ability to influence of the evaluators and the World Bank, they highlight the importance of furthering results orientation and building capacity to use evidence in policy and program decisions.

Findings and Recommendations

The objective of this report is to provide some insights on strengthening the value, relevance, and use of IEs to enhance development outcomes. Compared with other types of evaluation, IEs are expensive, require specialized skills, and cannot be applied universally to all modalities of development assistance. Given these resource constraints, issues of strategic selection and allocation are prominent for IEs. The following recommendations focus on the IE tool, although they are often applicable to other forms of evaluations.

1. Strategic Selection of IEs. *In the World Bank,* the rapid growth in IE activity has been accompanied by efforts to improve their strategic selection and coordination, led by DIME and SIEF. Evidence is emerging that IEs initiated under these approaches over the last three to four years have better quality assurance mechanisms, greater engagement of clients and project teams, and are aligned with a broader set of sector and knowledge priorities than earlier IEs. Still, a strategic framework for IE selection from an operational and knowledge perspective is less prevalent in non-human development sectors. In the latter sectors, IEs have been more often selected opportunistically—guided by the ease of evaluation, skills availability, and funding considerations—and characterized by a lack of coordination in the identification process. The importance of strategic IE selection has been underscored during the IDA16 replenishment, in which IDA deputies requested that the World Bank increase the number of IEs and deploy a strategic approach to selecting projects for IE.

In IFC, efforts to conduct IEs, mainly to supplement Advisory Services project assessments, started in 2005 with modest resources, and 26 IEs operations have been completed to date. IE selection at IFC generally has been opportunistic, not guided by a strategic framework. IEs were initiated mostly based on staff interest, Results Measurement Team initiatives, and availability of funding. Through a recent general evaluation strategy, approved in FY12, IFC is moving toward a more strategic approach to identification and prioritization of evaluation opportunities, including IEs.

The World Bank and IFC can enhance the relevance of future IEs to knowledge priorities and operations by doing the following:

- *At the World Bank,* develop a strategic approach to guide IE selection across sectors and regions. Introduce guidelines to implement the strategic framework building on a framework developed for IDA16.

- *At IFC,* prepare and apply a strategic selection framework, in consultation with relevant stakeholders, to guide selection of IE topics of strategic relevance for results measurement, global learning, and deployment of limited IE resources.

2. Financing of IEs. *In the World Bank and IFC,* IEs increasingly depend on donor support through trust funds. Although access to multiple sources of financing eases the budget constraint, their fragmentation adds to staff transaction costs. Reliance on trust fund resources is not necessarily detrimental to IE relevance, but there is less flexibility over resource allocation and strategic planning.

These limitations can be addressed in the following ways:

- *At the World Bank,* explore options for consolidation of external funding for IEs, including pooled trust fund facilities (umbrella funds), as recommended in IEG's 2011 evaluation of trust funds, to better coordinate and mobilize trust fund resources along with internal funds to support IE production within the strategic priority areas agreed by management and clients.

- *At IFC,* explore options to coordinate IE funding from different sources (donor, business line/region budget), including possible financing window(s) under the monitoring and evaluation budget for the conduct of IEs in the Development Impact Department.

3. Utilization of IEs. *In the World Bank,* there is a modest feedback loop between IE production and project operations and learning. There are notable examples of IE influence on development practice, including project assessment, decisions to design and sustain evaluated and future projects, raising the profile of certain types of interventions, informing policy dialogue and institutional strategies, and building local M&E capabilities. Such examples indicate that, overall, IE is regarded as a valuable tool to increase development effectiveness through better evidence. But in some instances, even when IEs have been relevant and of good quality, they appear to have had limited use and influence for varying reasons: poor timeliness, failure to engage project teams and decision makers, or lack of dissemination. However, there are signs of improvement, such as dedicated SIEF support for results dissemination as well as closer collaboration with operations and clients in the design of ongoing IEs.

In IFC, the evidence indicates that IEs were often used by the project teams, while their use beyond the project has been less common. In particular, the link between IEs and learning has not been established fully. The evidence indicates that there is a limited awareness of IE applicability to operational work and policy, which constrains wider uptake and use of IEs.

The feedback loop between IE production and operations and knowledge in both the World Bank and IFC can be enhanced by:

- Stating clearly in the implementation design of the IE how it will achieve operational usefulness, serve the key decision points of the project, engage operational teams and local counterparts, and disseminate the findings to the relevant audience, in particular local counterparts.

- Strengthening the use of IE evidence in the appraisal and ex-post assessment of World Bank and IFC projects, wherever such information is available.

- Effectively communicating IE evidence to a global audience by maintaining a central repository of IEs and undertaking thematic syntheses of existing IE evidence.
- Building capacity of project teams and other local counterparts to understand and integrate IE evidence in program and policy decisions.

4. Quality of IEs. *In the World Bank,* just over half of completed IEs were of high quality and another two-fifths met medium quality standards. World Bank IEs go through varying degrees and types of quality assurance, especially IEs not initiated under IE initiatives, such as SIEF, which has formal and standardized quality review controls. In addition, there is low availability of IE data for replication, which can help to ensure quality. In addition, there is low availability of IE data for replication, which can help to ensure high quality.

In IFC, around half of 26 IFC IEs met the medium or high quality standards. The main limitations of the low-quality IEs were low sample sizes and the reliance on weak evaluation designs that affect the credibility of the IEs to claim causal results. The absence of peer review processes and standards to ensure high quality is a contributing factor. IE data for replication to ensure high quality are not publicly available.

The technical quality of IEs in the World Bank and IFC can be enhanced by adopting and consistently applying good practice standards, including peer review and availability of data for replication, in the conduct of IEs at the World Bank and IFC.

5. Operational Relevance of IEs. *In the World Bank and IFC,* there has been mixed coverage of analytical elements relevant for operational needs, such as analysis of distribution of program impacts; cost-benefit or cost effectiveness analysis of interventions; mapping of the causal chain from program inputs to outputs to outcomes; and measuring the contribution to impacts of individual components of program design. At the World Bank, IEs initiated in recent years appear to pay greater attention to some of these dimensions, and this trend should be sustained in future IE efforts. Similarly, these elements should be included in the design of future IFC IEs.

The operational relevance of IEs in both the World Bank and IFC should be enhanced by regularly incorporating, where feasible, analytical elements, such as analysis of heterogeneous program impacts and cost-benefit analysis, in the design of all World Bank and IFC IEs.

Management Response

Introduction

World Bank Group management welcomes this evaluation of its work in impact evaluation (IE). IE is an important element of the strong focus of the Bank Group on development effectiveness and results. It is a valuable tool in the continuum of approaches to measuring and evaluating the effectiveness of development interventions, notably in the context of World Bank Group operations and investments.

The first section sets out comments from World Bank management. The second section provides IFC management comments. The Management Action Record is attached.

I. World Bank Management Comments

World Bank management sees the IEG evaluation as a welcome addition to the ongoing discussion on development effectiveness. The choice of measurement tool needs to be tailored to the type of activity the Bank is supporting, knowledge gaps, and resources available. Client ownership is also key. There is no single development effectiveness measurement method that is universally applicable and, as with Independent Evaluation Group (IEG) evaluations, tools can be effectively combined to strengthen the findings. For example, IE combines well with cost-benefit analysis for some operations. Within that context, Bank management strongly agrees with IEG that IE is a fundamental implement in the evaluation tool kit and that advances in methodology have added to its strength as a development effectiveness measurement and learning mechanism.

WORLD BANK AS A LEADER IN IE

The Bank took a lead in setting out the value of IE and explaining its usefulness in providing rigorous and credible evidence of development impact. Over time, that work has helped set in motion a growing demand for IE among client countries. Internally, the Bank has also contributed to the growth of that IE culture. As a result, the Bank has the largest IE program of any development institution. The IEG evaluation graphically illustrates the growth of IE since the late 1990s, with a clear acceleration starting in 2005 after the creation of the Development Impact Evaluation Initiative (DIME). DIME was a major driver of (i) the quality of the Bank's IE work; (ii) a better strategic focus; and (iii) wider dissemination of not only the results of IE but also high-quality tools for the design and implementation of IE. Trust fund support, notably the Spanish Trust Fund for Impact Evaluation, has been important in supporting IE and IE training and dissemination. The quality of Bank-supported IE activities is evident in the number of refereed publications arising from this work.

Open Knowledge

To make the results of IE more widely available, the Bank's IE work is part of its Open Knowledge Agenda. At the April 2012 Spring Meetings, the Bank announced that the Office of the Publisher is transitioning from a traditional book publishing model to an Open Access policy—meaning immediate free access to the Bank's peer-reviewed literature and data, with no restrictions on the use and reuse of the Bank's knowledge. The Bank is also adopting the Creative Commons attribution license, lifting restrictions on the use of Bank knowledge and data and creating an Open Knowledge Repository to house all Bank books, journal articles, working papers, and relevant economic and sector work, and their associated datasets. That means that the Bank's published IE and the accompanying data sets will be available to all, just requiring appropriate citation. DIME is at the forefront with regard to open knowledge. First, DIME is working to transform the evidence-base of Bank operations. For example, the Finance and Private Development (FPD) and DIME partnership will work across all six FPD Global Practices and all regions to use operations to learn how to make policy work, systematically reviewing evidence and applying it to design of new operations. Second, DIME is opening up its programs to all other development institutions. Just one example is DIME's Agricultural Adaptation IE program that makes DIME technology and knowledge available to a coalition of a dozen external development banks and agencies working on agricultural policy as a global platform for testing innovation in agriculture, disseminating results, and exploring opportunities for scale-up along the value chain. Third, to accelerate generation and democratize the use of IE knowledge, DIME is working with other interested parties on a possible global and open IE knowledge marketplace.

The Evolution of Bank-Supported IE

That rapid expansion of Bank-supported IEs and the evolving framework in which they take place raise some issues with respect to IEG's findings. IE evaluations often take years to complete. Moreover, while the report makes an effort to distinguish between Bank and IFC IEs and some attempt is made to contrast ad hoc IEs and those undertaken or supported by DIME, the report is mostly assessing pre-2005 approaches to IEs rather than the post-2009 programmatic approach. In light of this, some of the more critical conclusions may not be entirely corroborated by the examination of a representative sample of the current IE portfolio. A large share of the IEs that IEG evaluated predates the Bank's efforts to better manage its IE support, both programmatically and with more attention to quality assurance and dissemination of results.

Counterfactual

The essence of IE is the explicit specification of a counterfactual: What would have happened in the absence of the intervention? In measuring the use and influence of IE (Chapter 5), IEG is indirectly assessing its impact. In the spirit of IE, Bank management would have expected IEG to use a counterfactual. IEG notes that measuring impact was beyond the scope of the evaluation and that there were data and time constraints that made creating a counterfactual difficult.

Management believes that there are tractable, concrete ways that IEG could use to specify a proxy counterfactual. For example, in looking at the impact of IEs on project design and policy, the report could have compared it to the incorporation of evidence-based information in general in project design. The IEG report could compare, for instance, whether use or mention of any evidence that is based on actual data increases in Project Assessment Documents or Implementation Status and Results Reports when there is an IE in the sector or the project. Evidence from such an analysis would put the report's findings about whether IEs are perceived as affecting projects in an appropriate context. A second way a counterfactual could have been established, particularly in the country case studies, is to look at policies that have been implemented and/or scaled up and assess whether IE had any role in either the implementation or the scale-up. Again, this would provide a useful counterfactual with which to assess the specific role of IEs, perhaps relative to other evidence. A third counterfactual could be established by looking at whether IEs complement or substitute for other forms of knowledge production. By looking at the overall production of knowledge (analytic and advisory activities and published papers from all sources) and seeing whether over time we are seeing an increase in the knowledge that is useful for policy would add considerably to the report. While all these ways to specify a proxy counterfactual have drawbacks, tackling the counterfactual question would appear to be more important than answering it perfectly "cleanly." As long as the samples and results were clearly explained and the evaluation did not draw unwarranted conclusions, readers could judge for themselves.

RECOMMENDATIONS

Bank management is in basic agreement with all of IEG's recommendations for the Bank. With regard to a strategic approach to IE, as part of its IDA16 commitments, management has developed a strategic selection framework to increase the learning from IE and improve institutional accountability. Financing is a concern, and Bank management is exploring options, including the consolidation of external funding. However, management notes that the bulk of the costs are in country, particularly those associated with data collection, and countries themselves will fund part of these costs, often through project financing. With regard to the integration of IE into project design, many of the elements of this recommendation are relevant to all knowledge products and are major elements of the overall knowledge agenda under implementation. With regard to quality standards and enhancing the analytical elements of IE, management agrees, while noting that responsibility for quality control rests with the Regions. Current work on quality enhancement will address these issues. More detailed responses are set out below.

II. IFC Management Comments

Management appreciates this report. While IFC is widely recognized to be in the forefront in development results measurement and reporting among private sector–oriented international financial institutions, we continue to seek opportunities for further improvement. IFC's results measurement framework has progressed over the years and now includes the Development Outcome Tracking System which covers additionality, Expanded Project Supervision Reports for Investment Services (IS), Project Completion Reports for Advisory Services, reach indicators, IEs, and most recently, the IFC Development Goals. In addition, IFC's publicly reported development results data are validated by an external assurance provider. Taken together, IFC's results framework serves as an effective tool in tracking IFC's development contribution and informing its strategic directions.

The report provides a welcome support for our continuing efforts to maximize the value of IEs for IFC, for the World Bank Group, and for our clients and partners. IEG's report rightly notes that within the World Bank Group, IFC's use of IEs is relatively much newer and smaller scale and that our evaluations' designs have grown more sophisticated as they have improved over time.

As noted in the report, IEG's recommendations reflect the intent of IFC's evaluation strategy, which was approved at the start of FY12. In particular, the strategy is designed to leverage evaluation (including IE) as a tool for learning and knowledge sharing, it articulates a conceptual framework for determining which interventions should be evaluated, and it acknowledges the importance of quality control and staff training in evaluation. The evaluation strategy covers all evaluation, of which IE is only one part, and does not anticipate rapid growth of the IE portfolio—certainly much less than the growth experienced by others within the World Bank Group. Part of the reason for this is that, as the report acknowledges, within the Bank Group, the economics of IE is very different for IFC, with much lower average absolute cost of $60,000 but significantly higher relative cost of about 7 percent of project cost. This absolute cost is no longer representative of our recent experience with larger and more sophisticated IEs, which cost upward of $100,000 and sometimes many times more. Given that high-quality IEs are growing increasingly expensive and our overall project budgets are small, IFC will continue to be highly strategic about the scope and selection of its IEs moving forward.

Thus, we broadly agree with the lessons and recommendations in IEG's report. They come at an opportune time, since IFC is now in the process of implementing and operationalizing its evaluation strategy, communicating the strategy's importance across IFC, and ensuring high-quality evaluation design and implementation.

IFC recognizes that there are standards specific to IEs (vis-à-vis statistical power, considerations of selection bias, and so forth), and therefore peer review (consistent with IEG's assessment framework in Appendix F) will now be mandatory and supervised by the Development Impact Department.

The report advocates for more IEs of IFC's IS operations, noting that all of IFC's completed IEs have been associated with its Advisory Services operations. While we agree that IEs hold value for both investment and advisory services, we think

IS is in general less amenable to IE. Among the most important reasons is that IEs require a high degree of control over the operational details of whatever it is that is being evaluated, and in IS, operational decisions about how best to put project financing to work are left to the client (within the limits of financial, environmental, and social covenants.) The rarity of IS IEs (not just at IFC, but anywhere) also means there are few if any models to emulate, making this type of IE much more difficult, and signals that such IE efforts pose a distinctive set of challenges. Even so, IFC's evaluation strategy calls for encouraging evaluation (including IE) of IS activity. In FY12, IFC launched one IS IE and will also complete its first IS IE after nearly two years of implementation.

Management Action Record

IEG Findings and Conclusions	IEG Recommendations
1. Application of a strategic approach to identify IEs **In the World Bank:** Rapid growth in IE activity in the World Bank has been accompanied by efforts to improve strategic selection and coordination of IEs, led by DIME and SIEF. There is emerging evidence that IEs initiated under more strategic and better coordinated approaches over the last three to four years have better quality assurance mechanisms, greater engagement of clients and project teams, and are aligned with a broader set of sector and knowledge priorities. However, in some sectors, particularly non-human development sectors, a strategic framework for IE selection from an operational and knowledge perspective is less prevalent. These IEs were more often selected opportunistically, often due to skills and funding availability, and ease of evaluation The importance of strategic IE selection has been further underscored during the IDA16 replenishment, in which IDA deputies requested that the World Bank increase the number of IEs and deploy a more strategic approach to selecting projects for impact evaluation.	**Apply mechanisms for strategic identification and prioritization of IEs at the World Bank and IFC to balance learning and results measurement objectives:** • At the **World Bank**, develop a strategic approach to guide IE selection across sectors and regions. Introduce guidelines to implement the strategic framework building on a framework developed in the context of IDA16.
In IFC: Efforts to conduct IEs, mainly to supplement Advisory Services project level assessments, started in 2005 with modest resources, and 26 IEs of IFC Advisory Service operations have been completed to date. IE selection at IFC has been generally opportunistic, and not guided by a strategic framework. IEs were initiated mostly based on staff interest; results measurement team's initiatives; and availability of funding. Through a recent general evaluation strategy, approved in FY12, IFC plans to move towards a more strategic approach to identification and prioritization of evaluation opportunities, including IEs.	• At **IFC**, prepare and apply a strategic selection framework, in consultation with relevant stakeholders, to guide selection of IE topics of strategic relevance for results measurement, global learning, and deployment of limited IE resources.

Acceptance by Management	Management Response
World Bank: Agree	World Bank: The IE strategic framework developed as part of the IDA16 commitments aims at increasing the coverage and learning from IDA's program of impact evaluations. With regard to the International Bank for Reconstruction and Development, the DIME steering group will continue to support Sector Boards and thematic groups in identifying priorities and in compiling middle-income country IE financed by others, notably partner countries themselves. Middle-income countries serve an important role in IE communities of practice, generating lessons applicable in both middle-income countries and IDA countries.
IFC: Agree	IFC: The strategic plan for evaluation now in place, approved in FY12, adopts best-practice guidelines for IE selection per the World Bank publication *Impact Evaluation in Practice* (2011), which establishes criteria for selecting evaluations depending upon what is at stake (resource use/cost, potential impact, and strategic relevance) as well as the extent to which evidence already exists vis-à-vis the issue to be evaluated, and the extent to which there is potential for learning something new and important.

IEG Findings and Conclusions	IEG Recommendations
2. Coordination of fragmented funding **In the World Bank and IFC:** IEs increasingly depend on donor support through trust funds. Although access to multiple sources of financing eases the budget constraint, their fragmentation adds to staff transaction costs. Reliance on trust funds is not necessarily detrimental to IE relevance, but there is less flexibility over allocation and strategic planning.	Coordinate fragmented external funding with core funds at the World Bank and IFC to strategically finance the production of IEs: • At the **World Bank**, explore options for consolidation of external funding for IEs, including pooled trust fund facilities (umbrella funds), as recommended in the 2011 evaluation of Trust Funds by IEG, to better coordinate and mobilize trust fund resources along with internal funds to support IE production within the strategic priority areas agreed by management and clients. • **At IFC**, explore options to coordinate impact evaluation funding from different sources (that is, donor, business line/region budget), including possible financing window(s) under the monitoring and evaluation budget for the conduct of IEs in the Development Impact Department.
3. Integration of IEs into project design **In the World Bank:** Overall, there is a modest feedback loop between IE production and project operations and learning. There are notable examples of IE influence on development practice, including project assessment, decisions to design and sustain evaluated and future projects, raising the profile of certain types of interventions, informing policy dialogue and institutional strategies, and building local M&E capabilities. Such examples indicate that, overall, IE is regarded as a valuable tool to increase development effectiveness through better evidence. But in some instances, even when IEs have been relevant and of good quality, they appear to have had limited use and influence due to varying reasons: poor timeliness, failure to engage project teams and decision makers, or lack of dissemination. However, there are signs of improvement, including for example dedicated SIEF support for results dissemination as well as closer collaborations with operations and clients in design of ongoing IEs.	**Improve the integration of IEs into design and review of projects at the World Bank and IFC to sharpen the focus of project operations on results by:** • Stating clearly in the implementation design of the IE how it will achieve operational usefulness, serve the key decision points of the project, engage operational teams and local counterparts, and disseminate the findings to the relevant audience, in particular local counterparts. • Strengthening the use of IE evidence in the appraisal and ex post assessment of World Bank and IFC projects, wherever such information is available.

Acceptance by Management	Management Response
World Bank: Agree	World Bank: In the overall context of trust fund reform, Bank management will explore options for consolidation of external funding for IEs and will report progress in updates to Executive Directors on the reform program.
IFC: Agree	IFC: Per the strategic plan for evaluation approved FY12, the Development Impact Department coordinates and facilitates impact evaluation funding from different sources (donor, business lines, global industry departments, regions, and so forth).
World Bank: Agree	World Bank: On the Bank side, the integration of IE into the design and review of projects is part of the IE strategic framework developed as part of the IDA16 commitments. Identified projects will explicitly acknowledge requirements for IE, describe the primary questions to be answered, and the IE plan will include baseline and endline data collection activities and an ex ante projection of the counterfactual. DIME will provide technical advice and guidance as needed. Bank management notes that the use of existing evidence in areas relevant for proposed operations is applicable to all knowledge products. As part of the overall strengthening of operational quality assurance, the role of network anchors is being strengthened; notably they will be accountable for providing the relevant sector knowledge, including on IE findings, to task teams. Progress will be monitored as part of regular reporting on modernizing knowledge services. The Bank maintains an internal and external database of impact evaluations, notably through DIME, which has an active dissemination program. The Bank is exploring options for developing an open IE knowledge market and will report progress in the context of regular reporting on modernizing knowledge services.

IEG Findings and Conclusions	IEG Recommendations
In IFC: The evidence indicates that IFC IEs were often used by the project teams, while their use beyond the project has been less common. In particular, the link between IEs and learning has not been established fully. The evidence indicates that there is a limited awareness of IE applicability to operational work and policy which constrains wider uptake and use of IEs.	• Effectively communicating IE evidence to the global audience through maintaining a central repository of IEs and undertaking thematic syntheses of existing IE evidence. • Building capacity of project teams and other local counterparts to understand and integrate IE evidence in program and policy decisions.
4. Adoption of quality standards **In the World Bank:** Over half of completed IEs were of high quality and another two-fifths of IEs met medium quality standards. World Bank IEs go through varying degrees and types of quality assurance processes, especially IEs not initiated under IE initiatives, such as SIEF, which has formal and standardized quality review controls. In addition, there is low availability of IE data for replication, which can help to ensure quality. **In IFC:** Around half of 26 IFC IEs met the medium or high quality standards. The main limitations of the low quality IEs were low sample sizes and the weak reliance on evaluation designs that affect the credibility of IEs to claim causal results. The absence of peer review standards and processes to ensure high technical quality is a contributing factor. IE data for replication to ensure high quality is not publicly available.	**Adopt and consistently apply good practice quality standards to the conduct of all IEs at the World Bank and IFC, including independent peer review protocols. Additionally, ensure data availability for replication.**
5. Incorporating analytical elements that enhance operational relevance **In the World Bank and IFC:** There has been mixed coverage of analytical elements relevant for operational needs, such as analysis of distribution of program impacts; cost-benefit or cost effectiveness analysis of interventions; mapping of the causal chain from program inputs to outputs to outcomes; and measuring the contribution to impacts of individual components of program design. At the World Bank, IEs initiated in recent years appear to pay greater attention to some of these dimensions, and this trend should be sustained in future IE efforts. Similarly, these elements should be included in the design of future IFC IEs.	**Regularly incorporating, where feasible, analytical elements, such as analysis of heterogeneous program impacts and cost-benefit analysis, in the design of all World Bank and IFC IEs.**

Acceptance by Management	Management Response
IFC: Agree	IFC: The learning agenda is at the center of the evaluation strategy approved in FY12. IFC is now using a checklist for IE design requiring articulation of how IEs will achieve operational usefulness, and so forth, and the extent to which findings may be disclosed to external audiences. IFC has also developed a database of all its evaluation documentation (including IE documentation), available to all staff and actively utilized to feed lessons from prior evaluations to address ongoing and planned (pipeline) interventions. Formal training in evaluation (including IE) began in FY12 as part of the strategy and will be consistently undertaken on an annual basis, with the goal of developing a core cadre of staff with IE expertise.
World Bank: Agree	World Bank: As part of its work on accountability and decision making, Bank management has clarified that sector units in the Regions are responsible for operational and analytic and advisory activities quality. Any movement away from that framework dilutes accountability. As noted above, networks are responsible for providing relevant sector knowledge, including on IE. Networks also have the responsibility to identify qualified and independent peer reviewers. DIME will support sectors and task teams by identifying qualified peer reviewers and consultants who can assist with IEs. Management will report on progress in the context of quality reporting. The Bank's Open Data and Open Knowledge Initiatives ensure the general availability of data for replication, with very limited exceptions as set out in the Bank's access to information and Creative Commons policies. This very openness helps enhance quality because of the (welcome) external scrutiny of Bank-supported IE.
IFC: Agree	IFC: The strategic plan for evaluation, approved in FY12, will develop good practice quality standards for IFC IEs before end FY12. These standards will include mandatory peer review protocols at design and completion. Data from prior IEs is available in the evaluation database (launched FY12), and is being consistently archived for future projects on an ongoing basis.
World Bank: Agree	World Bank: For projects, the quality of design of the results framework is a key element in the overall quality framework being developed for implementation this year. That framework gives sector anchors the responsibility for assisting task teams on results frameworks and indicators and monitoring arrangements, including these analytical elements. Their assistance and support from DIME, notably in Quality Enhancement Reviews (and at the concept stage), will be the setting to assess the importance and feasibility of these analytical elements. The new knowledge quality framework under development will be the setting for IE as a stand-alone analytic and advisory activity.
IFC: Agree	IFC: The analytical elements noted by IEG will be considered by default for every impact evaluation from FY13 onward (per inclusion in the evaluation design checklist).

Chairperson's Summary: Committee on Development Effectiveness

The Committee on Development Effectiveness (CODE) considered the Independent Evaluation Group (IEG) report entitled *World Bank Group Impact Evaluations: Relevance and Effectiveness* and the draft management response. The Approach Paper for this evaluation was endorsed by CODE on February 9, 2011.

Summary

The committee welcomed the IEG review and acknowledged its findings, namely that while the World Bank Group portfolio of impact evaluations (IEs) is relevant, there are areas for improvement. Members noted that the World Bank Group draft management response identified broad areas of agreement with the review's recommendations. The committee appreciated the Bank Group's demonstrated leadership in IE and praised the comprehensiveness of the evidence-based evaluation. Members acknowledged that increases in the Bank Group IE capacity, global learning, and identification of priority projects are largely attributable to the Development Impact Evaluation Initiative and welcomed the IDA16 deputies' request for a strategic selectivity framework.[1]

The committee suggested greater strategic selectivity to enhance IE credibility, avoid fragmentation, and make IEs more operationally relevant. Moreover, members encouraged a better feedback loop between evaluations and operations. Members also discussed the high costs of undertaking IEs, their heavy reliance on Trust Funds, as well as measurability and long-term sustainability of the impacts. They stressed the essential part that IEs play within the Bank's knowledge framework and asked how the IEs fit into the Bank Group's knowledge priorities and into the broader monitoring and evaluation system.

The committee strongly recommended the integration of IE findings into World Bank Group policies and operational work and underlined the value of optimal timing of IEs to better inform relevant projects or strategies. Members noted a concern about quality assurance and recommended the development of guidelines on quality practices and standards and their consistent application. Members noted the limited stakeholder involvement in IE design but were pleased to learn that this is on the rise.

Anna Brandt, Chairperson

---

1. During the IDA16 replenishment, IDA deputies requested greater use of IEs and requested a strategic approach, linked with associated financing and implementation plans—with measurable targets—for the IDA16 period, with the number of IEs to be included in the IDA16 Results Measurement System and the IDA Report Card.

Abbreviations

AAA	Analytical and advisory activities
AADAPT	Agricultural Adaptations Impact Evaluation Program
AIM	Africa Impact Evaluation Initiative
AIM-AIDS	Africa Impact Evaluation Program on HIV/AIDS
CCT	Conditional cash transfer
DEC	Development Economics Vice Presidency
DIME	Development Impact Evaluation Initiative
DIME-FPD	Finance and Private Sector Impact Evaluation Program
FY	Fiscal year
FPD	Finance and Private Sector Development
HDN	Human Development Network
HNP	Health, nutrition, and population
ICR	Implementation Completion and Results Report
IDA	International Development Association
IE	Impact evaluation
IEG	Independent Evaluation Group
IFC	International Finance Corporation
M&E	Monitoring and evaluation
OECD	Organisation for Economic Co-operation and Development
PAD	Project Appraisal Document
PCR	Project Completion Report
PPAR	Project Performance Assessment Report
PREM	Poverty Reduction and Economic Management Network
RMU	Results Measurement Unit
SDN	Sustainable Development Network
SIEF	Spanish Trust Fund for Impact Evaluation
SME	Small and medium enterprise

Chapter 1

Introduction

The use of impact evaluations (IEs) to assess the causal impacts of development projects has expanded rapidly. Along with major innovations in statistical methods and econometrics, the recent impetus in IE has its roots in the debate about whether development programs achieve their objectives of reducing poverty and increasing economic growth. Every year billions of dollars are spent on development programs, with the aim of improving the lives of poor people in developing countries. However, the value these interventions add is generally not measured or clearly known. Over the past decade, interest has shifted from measuring project inputs and outputs to measuring outcomes.

In parallel, the demands for using results to inform budget allocations and policy decisions have been increasing. At the 16th International Development Association (IDA) replenishment discussions,[1] donors called on World Bank management to strengthen the Bank's program of IE, including the selection framework and associated issues of financing and implementation (World Bank 2011).[2] The renewed focus on results and the increasing calls for sound evidence on effectiveness have led to expectations that IE may help build the knowledge base of what does and does not work in development and where resources may be best allocated (Thomas 2009; CGD 2006; Fiszbein 2006).

Consistent with this trend, the World Bank Group has endeavored to expand and deepen its IE work. Between 2004 and 2008, the number of Bank Group-supported evaluations increased sevenfold. This increase is partly attributable to major IE initiatives at the World Bank, including the Development Impact Evaluation Initiative (DIME), the Africa Impact Evaluation Initiative, the Spanish Trust Fund for Impact Evaluation (SIEF), and efforts by the International Finance Corporation's (IFC) Advisory Services Results Measurement Unit (RMU). In 2008, DIME was restructured and its institutional mandate expanded. Currently, DIME proposes to mainstream IE as a core instrument in the Bank's knowledge agenda and analytic toolkit as a way to "improve the quality of Bank's operations, strengthen country institutions for evidence-based policy making, and generate knowledge in 15 strategic development areas" (World Bank 2010).

At the World Bank, several regions and sectors have also expanded their IE programs: increasing the number of IEs conducted in house or in collaboration with non-World Bank researchers; supporting countries in implementing IEs of their projects; strengthening monitoring and evaluation (M&E) frameworks to provide data; and facilitating global learning activities to promote IEs and their results. In IFC, where the IE agenda is relatively new, few IEs have been conducted and focus largely on measuring performance of advisory services projects—which provide technical assistance and training to private enterprises and governments.

The contribution of IEs to improving development practices at the World Bank Group has not been systematically assessed. The Bank Group (consisting of the World Bank and IFC) is the largest producer of IEs, with 460 IEs completed or in progress during the period 2000–10. This sizable investment in IEs, together with the high expectations for them, contrasts with how little is known about whether the evaluations (i) evaluate the primary objectives of Bank Group-supported projects and help fill strategic, analytic, and policy knowledge gaps; (ii) are of high quality; and (iii) have influenced operational work (project design, implementation, and assessment), resource allocation, institutional strategy, policy making, or evaluation culture and capacity.

In this report, the Independent Evaluation Group (IEG) assesses the extent to which experimental and quasi-experimental IEs supported by the World Bank Group have contributed to its development practices along several dimensions. The study aims to evaluate the relevance of both experimental and quasi-experimental IEs supported by the Bank Group in the past decade; their technical quality; their use and influence on the Bank Group's business lines and strategies and on client countries' policies; and their contribution to building evaluation capacity. This includes assessing the relevance of IEs for operations, strategic planning, and the knowledge agenda; and their influence in the dialogue with clients and in policy making. IEG recognizes systematic differences in the level of IE adoption, motivation, and capacity between the World Bank and IFC and makes the distinction whenever appropriate in this report.

The evaluation complements the previous efforts of IEG to better understand and evaluate the contribution of analytical and advisory assistance (AAA) to the development effectiveness of the World Bank. Looking at IE as an analytical product, this report follows IEG's goal of evaluating AAA products in terms of their explicit and implicit objectives and deriving findings that can enhance their relevance and effectiveness. The objectives of the evaluation are similar to those of other recent IEG evaluations of AAA at the World Bank: the 2010 Poverty and Social Impact Analysis evaluation, the 2008 evaluation of economic and sector work and nonlending technical assistance, and other evaluations of particular AAA reports within country assistance reviews (IEG 2003, 2008, 2010).

What Is Impact Evaluation?

IE assesses the causal effects (impacts) attributable to specific interventions, where the outcomes of interest are compared with a counterfactual situation— that is, with what would have happened without the program. IEs are structured to respond to one question in particular: the causal effect of a program on short-, medium-, or long-term outcomes (box 1.1). A key challenge of any evaluation is that the actual outcome and the counterfactual outcome cannot be observed for the same units of analysis (such as a program participants), which makes it difficult to answer cause-and-effect questions. IE seeks to overcome this by creating a control group that is similar to the group that receives the treatment.

This focus on causality is at the core of IE. In contrast to other evaluation approaches (for instance, an assessment of whether targets have been achieved), IE compares what happened to treatment groups (those subjected

Box 1.1　Use of the Term "Impact" within the Impact Evaluation Community

There is a long tradition in evaluation literature defining the term "impact" as long-term effects of a development intervention. For example, the Organisation for Economic Co-operation and Development's Development Assistance Committee defines impact as "positive and negative, primary and secondary, long-term effects produced by a development intervention, directly or indirectly, intended or unintended" (OECD 2002). In this sense, any evaluation that refers to impact indicators is an IE—for example, participatory impact assessments, which rely largely or solely on qualitative approaches (3IE 2009).

However, in the IE community, including at the World Bank Group, impact is used to denote causal effects of a program on outcomes, whether immediate, intermediate, or final. For instance, Gertler and others (2011) define IEs as "a particular type of evaluation that seeks to answer cause-and-effect questions. Unlike general evaluations, which can answer many types of questions, IEs are structured around one particular type of question: What is the impact (or causal effect) of a program on an outcome of interest?" Similarly, according to the International Initiative for Impact Evaluation, "High-quality impact evaluations measure the net change in outcomes that can be attributed to a specific program." Consistent with the terminology used in the IE community and at the World Bank, this report uses the term impact to mean causal effects of an intervention, irrespective of the time dimension of the outcomes of interest.[a]

Source: IEG.

a. The definition of IE that is used in the report is consistent with how it is defined in the World Bank's operational policies and in the academic and research community and articulated in IFC's own documents. For instance, IFC defines what IFC understands from IE as "...attribution of a particular impact to a specific activity. The control group acts as the counterfactual—namely, the scenario of what would have occurred without the treatment and thereby helps to establish the causality between impact and treatment." IFC's Results Measurement effort "is moving beyond conventional 'before-versus-after' analyses to develop and implement a diverse portfolio of experimental and quasi-experimental evaluation designs, which address the issue of attribution, and are consistent with widely-accepted best-practices" (http://www.ifc.org/ifcext/rmas.nsf/Attachments-ByTitle/Innovationsmonitor/$FILE/Innovations2.pdf and http://www.ifc.org/ifcext/devresultsinvestments.nsf/AttachmentsByTitle/Challenge_of_Proving_Impact_FINAL/$FILE/Challenge_of_Proving_Impact_FINAL.pdf). At the World Bank, IE is a product line under the AAA umbrella. To qualify as an IE, an activity must meet the following criteria: "Involve empirical work to measure the effects on a set of key outcomes of a development intervention relative to a well-specified counterfactual (that is, what would have been the evolution of the outcomes without the intervention)" (World Bank 2006).

to the intervention) with what happened to the control groups (those not subjected to the intervention).

There are two approaches to constructing control groups: experimental and quasi-experimental. Control or comparison group members have to be identical to program participants (the treatment group) in all respects except for their participation in the intervention that is being evaluated. This condition is necessary for IEs to have strong internal validity—the confidence that the observed effect(s) were produced solely by the treatment and not by some other extraneous variable(s).

One methodological option to generate a counterfactual is to randomly assign units to control and treatment groups before program implementation. When randomization is not possible, a number of quasi-experimental techniques can be used to create counterfactuals that aim for statistical equivalence with the treatment group. Quasi-experimental techniques include difference-in-differences, regression discontinuity design, instrumental variables, propensity score and other matching methods, and structural equations and other modeling approaches. Each of these methods carries its own underlying assumptions regarding the nature of endogeneity bias (correlation with the error term in these regression analyses) and how to address the critical issue of selection bias—introduced by program targeting, uptake, and participation—in estimating program impacts (see appendix A for a description of these technical terms).

Although IE has clear benefits in being able to identify the causal link between intervention and outcome, it also has costs. In addition to establishing the causal link between an intervention and an outcome of interest, IE can also be used to test the effectiveness of variations in the interventions and implementation systems. Furthermore, it can provide credible information not only on what works but also on how, for whom, under which circumstances, and at what cost. This could be done if IE makes an effort to disentangle the mechanisms through which the interventions yield outcomes, differentiate the impacts across beneficiaries, contextualize the effects, and quantify the benefits to compare with the costs of interventions. IE is often perceived to have limited external validity (generalizability to other settings), but it is no more inherently limited in this regard than any other evaluation approach. External validity is a function of sampling data rather than of the particular methodology used to analyze the data. Still, because IE is data intensive and therefore costly, it may be prohibitively expensive to construct an evaluation strategy applicable to large programs or populations.

Finally, it is not necessarily true that all policies or projects have a clearly identifiable counterfactual. Even if it were possible to perfectly control for selection in a given situation, it may still ultimately be untenable to construct a sound counterfactual due to the existence of spillover effects, ethical considerations, cost, time constraints, scale, or sample size. Where the construction of a credible counterfactual is ultimately not possible, IE techniques will ultimately lack internal validity and consequently have little added value over other evaluative methods.

Evaluation Objective, Scope, and Framework

Currently, little is known about whether and how the knowledge generated by IEs has been used. Most of the available reviews are general and focus on describing the potential role of IEs in informing policy and factors that affect their influence (Weyrauch and Langou 2011; Soares 2011). Some studies examine the actual use of IEs, but they are limited in scope. The Overseas Development Institute, for example, has analyzed the patterns of IE production and use across six sectors based on information from interviews of IE producers and users.[3]

Within the World Bank, as part of the Doing Impact Evaluation Series, the Poverty Impact Evaluation Thematic Group of the Poverty Reduction and Economic Management Network (PREM) department put together 12 case studies of completed IEs to draw lessons learned from researchers' perspectives on the ways in which these evaluations had been influential—or not—and why (World Bank 2009). IEG reviewed the influence on policy and programs of 12 IEs of Bank-supported nutrition interventions in 8 countries (IEG 2011). Although both of these studies were commendable efforts to record the use of IEs, they are based on very small samples. More recently, the 2011 DIME Progress Report has attempted to document the use and influence of 100 IEs (both ongoing and completed) managed by DIME during their design and implementation stages.[4]

In this evaluation, IEG reviews the experience with experimental and quasi-experimental IEs at the World Bank Group and its contribution to development effectiveness. First, IEG takes stock of the IEs supported by the Bank Group through co-authoring, funding, analytical work, technical assistance, data collection, and capacity building. It includes evaluations that were initiated or completed between 2000 and June 2010.[5] As discussed in box 1.1, although the term "impact evaluation" is sometimes used to refer to any kind of impact assessment, the focus of this study is on those evaluations that rely on counterfactual analysis to infer program effects.

Second, IEG compiles perspectives of various relevant stakeholders, inside and outside the World Bank Group and ranging from producers to users of IEs. Third, the World Bank Group has also been involved in IEs of programs that it does not directly support. As a result, the report also covers IEs of programs it does not finance. Yet it focuses mostly on IEs that evaluate Bank Group-supported projects, because the evaluation tools available for the study cannot document the relevance and contribution of IEs to the operational aspects of projects with no Bank Group involvement.

Applying a logic model of the IE process, this report evaluates the relevance, quality, and influence of Bank Group-supported IEs. With this study, IEG aims to answer the overarching question: To what extent and why (or why not) have Bank Group-supported IEs been relevant, presented reliable causal results, and informed development practice of the World Bank Group and its clients?

The framework that guides this study divides the IE process into three sequential stages: initiation, production, and dissemination and uptake. Starting with the first stage, the framework identifies a variety of factors involved in the initiation of IEs, such as motivation (demand or supply driven) and purpose (operational or research), area of focus (sector, country, and intervention), participation of actors, timing in relation to the project cycle, and funding. These factors are themselves linked with aspects further along in the process, that is, IE production, including design of the evaluation, data collection and fieldwork, analytical outputs, and technical quality, among other factors. These, in turn, may influence the final stage of dissemination and uptake of IEs by affecting project decisions; generating knowledge for future projects; informing strategies, debate, and development policies; and promoting capacity and resources for evaluation (figure 1.1).

Three main evaluative questions concerning *relevance, quality,* and *influence* emerge from the overarching question:

- **Relevance: *To what extent and why (or why not) are IEs aligned with the priorities of the World Bank Group and its clients and relevant to closing knowledge gaps?*** This question refers to the first stage in the process chain—initiation. It requires reviewing the incentives and processes that motivate and guide the selection of IE topics, pinpointing the areas in which IEs are (or are not) done, examining existing funding mechanisms, and discussing the actual and potential coverage of IEs as well

Figure 1.1 Process Chain from Impact Evaluation Initiation to Uptake

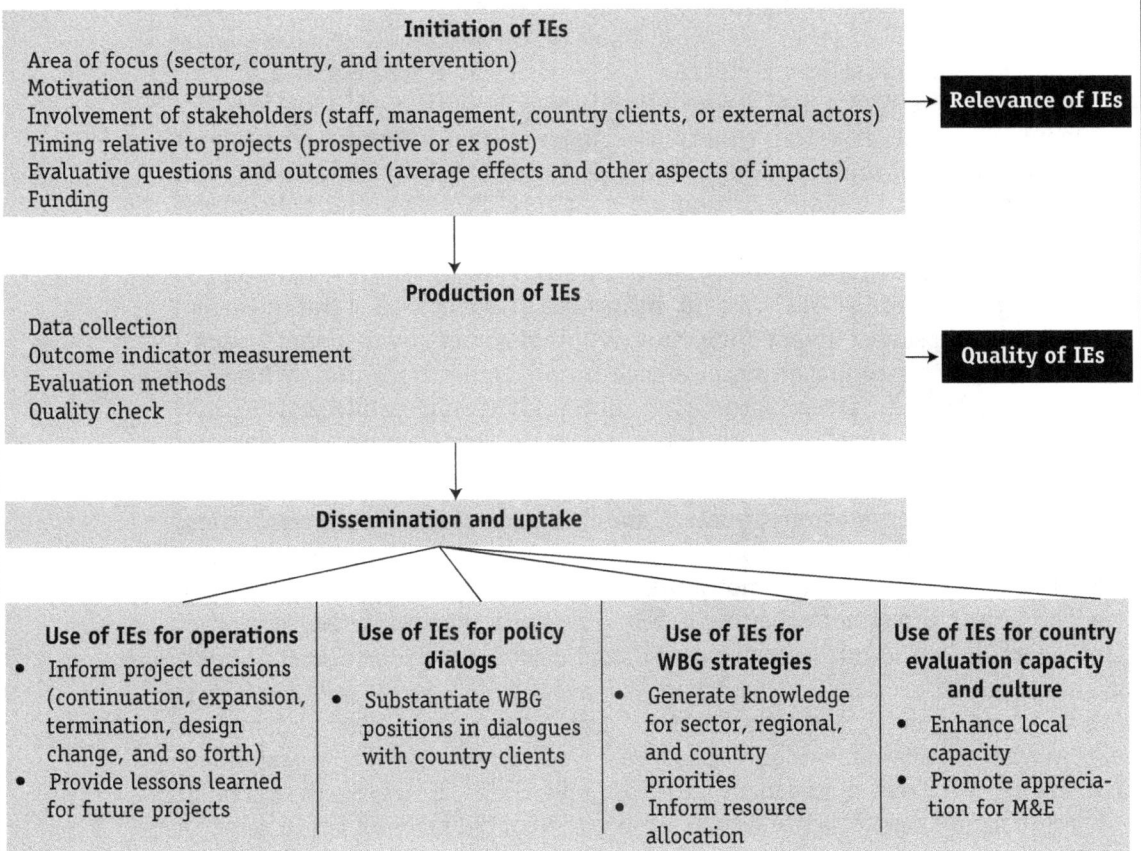

Initiation of IEs
Area of focus (sector, country, and intervention)
Motivation and purpose
Involvement of stakeholders (staff, management, country clients, or external actors)
Timing relative to projects (prospective or ex post)
Evaluative questions and outcomes (average effects and other aspects of impacts)
Funding

→ **Relevance of IEs**

Production of IEs
Data collection
Outcome indicator measurement
Evaluation methods
Quality check

→ **Quality of IEs**

Dissemination and uptake

Use of IEs for operations	**Use of IEs for policy dialogs**	**Use of IEs for WBG strategies**	**Use of IEs for country evaluation capacity and culture**
• Inform project decisions (continuation, expansion, termination, design change, and so forth) • Provide lessons learned for future projects	• Substantiate WBG positions in dialogues with country clients	• Generate knowledge for sector, regional, and country priorities • Inform resource allocation	• Enhance local capacity • Promote appreciation for M&E

Source: IEG.

Note: IE = impact evaluation; M&E = monitoring and evaluation; WBG = World Bank Group.

as their relative costs. This question also addresses the extent to which IEs examine other aspects of program impacts in addition to the "what works" question (such as treatment variations, distribution of impacts, cost-effectiveness, sustainability of impacts, and external validity) that may affect their use and influence. In addition, this question requires understanding the kinds of decisions, if any, that IEs plan to inform and, more broadly, whether these IEs are aligned with analytic, operational, and strategic priorities of the World Bank Group and its clients.

- **Quality:** *To what extent and why (or why not) do IEs meet expected quality standards?* This question refers to elements in the second stage of the process chain—production. Considering that there is no ranking of IE methods, this evaluation only rates IEs based on the extent to which they meet various quality aspects (methodologies, data, and outcome measurement). The standards used in this evaluation are determined through consulting with various IE guidelines and experts.

- **Use and influence:** *To what extent and why (or why not) are IEs used to influence development practice?* The question refers to the third step in the process chain—dissemination and uptake. Its answer will include a description of whether the World Bank Group and its clients have made a prominent and strategic uptake of IEs in decision making and, if not, what the constraints are. The applicability of Bank Group IEs for development is evaluated for four functions: (i) operational influence throughout the life cycle of projects—to evaluate performance, influence design, and inform decisions regarding program continuation, size, and subsequent phases; (ii) informing policy dialogue—to provide evidence for World Bank Group positions in engagement with clients; (iii) World Bank Group strategic planning—IEs' role in informing institutional strategies and country and sector-level policy; and (iv) promotion of evaluation capacity and culture—strengthening evidence-based decision making. Whenever possible, IEG addresses factors that underlie the applicability of IEs and the "feedback loops" in Bank Group processes that support the learning function implicit in IEs.

This study evaluates relevance, quality, and influence of IEs; it does not address other questions. First, the report cannot estimate the "impact" (or causal effect) of IEs because there is not a readily available robust counterfactual of the World Bank Group *not* engaging in IEs to measure impact. In the context of this report, it is also not feasible to *construct* a robust counterfactual because of challenges of scope, time, and budget.[6] Second, IEG recognizes that IE is just one among many tools in the AAA and M&E toolkits. Decision makers rely on the totality of evidence from various sources—not from one single instrument—to make operational and policy decisions. However, the scope of this evaluation does not extend to assessing the contribution of IEs in relation to other forms of knowledge production at the World Bank Group or elsewhere.

Third, IEG does not aim to identify the optimal scope of IE activity at the World Bank Group. Such an exercise would not only require an assessment of what is evaluable, but would also need to take into account normative factors such as external validity, knowledge gaps, institutional priorities, budget envelope, and country demand. The analysis in the report does not include this normative assessment; instead, its objective is to provide insights for strengthening the added value of IE work at the Bank Group. Finally, IEG does not formally evaluate specific IE initiatives (such as DIME and SIEF) or the models of IE selection and coordination they practice. However, the report provides descriptive information on these efforts as well as time- disaggregated information on patterns of IE scope, relevance, and use that coincides with the roll-out of said initiatives.

Building Blocks of the Evaluation

The findings are based on triangulation of information from multiple evaluation tools and sources: a desk review of IEs; a review of relevant documents of the evaluated projects; electronic surveys of IE authors and Bank Group staff who have worked on the evaluated projects; country case studies; sector case studies; and interviews with World Bank Group management.

- **Desk review of IEs:** This review covers IEs completed or initiated between 2000 and June 2010, which were supported by the World Bank Group; that is, the Bank Group was involved in funding the intervention or the IE or for authoring the IE (or several of those elements). Because IE is a decentralized effort in the Bank Group and there is no comprehensive central repository for them, it is difficult to generate a comprehensive list of all IEs undertaken by the Bank Group. To compile such a list, IEG mainly drew on the database of World Bank IEs compiled by DIME, which started in the last few years to document IEs across the World Bank. IFC does not have a common repository of IEs. Therefore, IEG contacted IFC's Development Impact Unit and regional M&E specialists and constructed the list based on the information received from the relevant staff. IEG also conducted searches in several internal World Bank and IFC databases and referred to IEG literature reviews in nutrition and social safety nets to supplement the list. To ensure that the inventory includes only evaluations that satisfy the definition of IE, IEG reviewed the list and excluded evaluations that were not deemed to be IEs. The resulting database, although not comprehensive, covers the majority of IEs with World Bank Group involvement. It includes 460 IEs, 224 of which were included in the desk review to extract information regarding the relevance and quality of IEs, including timing, actors, design, methodology, data, and findings (table 1.1).[7] Appendix B describes the sampling methodology for selection of ongoing and completed World Bank IEs not associated with a lending or nonlending project.

- **Desk review of project documents:** Project documents of 117 of 127 completed IEs[8] and a random sample of 46 of 182 ongoing IEs[9] of World Bank lending or IFC advisory service projects were reviewed (see appendix B). The documents reviewed include World Bank project appraisal documents

(PADs) and IFC project data sheets (PDSs) of the evaluated and follow-up projects (to understand if the IE's evaluated outcomes were aligned with the objectives of the projects, if the IE was planned for the project, and if the IE findings contributed to the design of the follow-up project). IEG also reviewed World Bank implementation completion reports (ICRs), IFC project completion reports (PCRs), and IEG project performance assessment reports (PPARs) of the evaluated projects (to check if the IE findings were cited in these assessments). In addition, World Bank Country Assis-tance Strategies and Bank Group sector board/business line strategies were referenced (to provide context for the priorities of stakeholders).

- **Surveys:** Surveys were sent to the people involved in the IEs in the database and the World Bank task team leaders or IFC transaction leaders of the evaluated projects (see appendix B for the method of respondent selection). The survey questions for IE authors seek information about the motivation and conduct of a specific IE and staff awareness of its use and influence. The survey questions to Bank Group project staff inquire about the usefulness and influence of the IE related to a specific project as well as factors that may explain this. The net addressable sample of evaluators was 445 and 216 for task team and transaction leaders; of these, 226 evaluators (218 from World Bank and 8 from IFC) and 92 leaders (78 from World Bank and 14 from IFC) responded, representing response rates of 51 and 43 percent, respectively. Information from the surveys was matched with the desk review to create a more comprehensive picture of the IEs and related projects. Survey responses are kept confidential and anonymous.

- **Country case studies:** IEG selected five countries (Bangladesh, Indonesia, Nicaragua, Peru, and Vietnam) for an in-depth review of the of Bank

| Table 1.1 | Desk Review of World Bank Group Impact Evaluations (2000–10) |

IE status	World Bank			IFC		Total
	Lending	**Nonlending**	**Others**	**AS**	**AS (non-IFC projects)**[a]	
Completed	105 (98)[b]	24 (21)	43 (21)	22 (22)	4 (4)	198 (166)
Ongoing	179 (44)	54 (10)	25 (0)	3 (3)	1 (1)	262 (58)

Source: IEG.

Note: Number of IEs included in desk review is in parentheses. AS = advisory services.

a. AS (non-IFC projects) includes IEs funded by IFC under Global Leadership-ideas42 initiative, which are IEs of projects funded but not implemented by IFC.

b. Seven IEs could not be reviewed because they are in a language other than English or their reports could not be found.

Group IE experience, from initiation to dissemination and uptake stages.[10] The selection is purposive and not representative of client countries of the World Bank Group; it includes those countries with a high number of completed IEs and maintains regional and sectoral balance. Subsequently, two or three projects were selected in each country as case study projects for in-depth review. Country-level reviews entailed desk reviews of the case study IEs and related project documents as well as structured interviews (including in the field) with internal and external stakeholders involved in the IEs and evaluated projects. IEG reviewed a total of 22 completed and ongoing IEs covering ten Bank projects and two IFC projects. Eighty-five stakeholders were interviewed: 34 were Bank Group staff, 29 were staff of the government or affiliations, 8 were from the private sector, and 14 were from academia or research institutions. The list of interviewees is available on request. In addition, IEG incorporated the findings (obtained from similar methods) of seven desk-based country studies done for a previous IEG review of IE evidence and use in the nutrition sector (Bolivia, Colombia, Ecuador, Madagascar, the Philippines, Senegal, and Uganda).[11] The projects in the country case studies are listed in appendix B, table B.3.

- *Sector case study:* An education sector case study investigated the World Bank education portfolio of projects closed in fiscal year 2009 to determine the scope of IE work based on technical considerations. The case study structure is outlined in appendix C.

- *Interviews with World Bank Group management:* Finally, the team conducted structured interviews with 21 World Bank sector managers, sector directors, and chief economists and with 13 IFC global and regional business line leaders and M&E officers to gain insights from Bank Group management about the motivation and influence of IEs at the institutional level. The interviewees were selected randomly to be broadly representative of the management structure with respect to sector or business line and region (appendix B).

Notes

1 The meeting of a group of World Bank member countries held every three years to replenish a major fund allocated exclusively to interest-free credits and grants for the world's poorest countries.

2 A key element of this is to increase the number of projects with appropriate evaluation frameworks, continue efforts to improve their quality, and enhance the learning stemming from the evaluation process in IDA projects to strengthen feedback loops for project design (World Bank 2011). Bank management has agreed to the request and a strategy paper is in process.

3 This review includes past and current IEs conducted by major international IE initiatives such as DIME, PREM, the Network of Networks on Impact Evaluation, and the Abdul Latif Jameel Poverty Action Lab (Jones and others 2009).

4 The progress report highlights information in terms of several relevant dimensions: design changes; quantity, quality, and use of baseline data for retargeting; reshaping of interventions; incorporation of results from variations in treatment; adoption and scale-up of IE results; and spillover to other countries. This is based on information provided by World Bank management in discussions with IEG; the report is not available to IEG.

5 The 2000–10 period covers 92 percent of all completed IEs. The report excludes IEs completed earlier because it will be difficult to track their use and influence. In addition, this study cannot track IEs that were initiated but dropped (that is, not included in the IE database).

6 In practice, an evaluator would face these questions when specifying a *robust* counterfactual: How should the control groups be defined? Are these similar interventions but without an IE (for example, health insurance in Mexico versus health insurance in Indonesia)? Or are these other non-IE interventions in the same project as the intervention with IE *and* have the same objectives (for example, demand and supply-side incentives to improve institutional deliveries in India)? Is such intervention-level coding of Bank projects available or must it be created? What are the other observable criteria on which IE and non-IE interventions/projects could be matched (for example, country characteristics, size of the intervention, evaluability, if non-IE interventions are subject to other types of assessments and if so, then what kind)? Are the data on these criteria available, or do they need to be compiled or constructed? How should selection of unobservables (for example, client's demand and ability to absorb evidence, quality of design and implementation, and so forth) be addressed? Can the same counterfactual be applied to other all questions studied in the report? Given the time frame, could this counterfactual analysis be implemented across all sectors/countries? In contrast, an analysis of "impacts" based on easily constructed but nonrobust counterfactuals (for example, comparing all projects with IEs in HNP versus all projects without IEs in the sector, or comparing any economic and sector work/technical assistance product with IE) will rely on assumptions that are imperfect and easily refuted and would make any subsequent conclusions about IE "impacts" less credible and harder to defend.

7 This number does not include some of the IEs that were dropped because of low project uptake and data issues, among other reasons.

8 Project documents of the seven IEs mentioned were not reviewed. In addition, project documents of two IEs could not be found, so they were also not reviewed. The project code for one IE was updated late in the study and the project document could not be reviewed.

9 The "universe" was restricted to IEs and projects for which the IE description was verified by the survey.

10 Country case studies for IFC IE experience were undertaken for Peru and Nicaragua.

11 Primary country case studies for countries in Africa could not be undertaken as originally intended. Instead, secondary case studies from a previous IEG evaluation on nutrition, and following the same format as the case studies in the present report, were used to make sure that IE experiences in Africa are not left out.

References

3IE (International Initiative for Impact Evaluations). 2009. "Some Reflections on Current Debates in Impact Evaluation." 3IE Working Paper 1, April 2009, New Delhi.

CGD (Center for Global Development). 2006. *When Will We Ever Learn? Improving Lives through Impact Evaluation*. Washington, DC: Center for Global Development.

Fiszbein, A. 2006. "Development Impact Evaluation: New Trends and Challenges." *Evidence and Policy* 2(3): 385–93.

Gertler P.J., S. Martinez, P. Premand, L. Rawlings, and C.M.J. Vermeersch. 2011. *Impact Evaluation in Practice*. Washington, DC: World Bank.

IEG (Independent Evaluation Group). 2011. *Assessing IFC's Poverty Focus and Results*. Washington, DC: World Bank.

———. 2010. *Analyzing the Effects of Policy Reforms on the Poor: An Evaluation of the Effectiveness of World Bank Support to Poverty and Social Impact Analysis*. Washington, DC: World Bank.

———. 2008. *Using Knowledge to Improve Development Effectiveness: An Evaluation of World Bank Economic and Sector Work and Technical Assistance, 2000–2006*. Washington, DC: World Bank.

———. 2003. *Sharing Knowledge: Innovations and Remaining Challenges*. Washington, DC: World Bank.

Jones, N., H. Jones, L. Steer, and A. Datta. 2009. "Improving Impact Evaluation Production and Use." Working Paper No. 300, Overseas Development Institute, London.

OECD (Organisation for Economic Co-operation and Development). 2002. "OECD/DAC Glossary of Key Terms in Evaluation and Results-Based Management." OECD, Paris.

Soares, Y. 2011. "The Practice and Use of Impact Evaluation in Development: Reflections for the Evaluation Cooperation Group Meeting in Manila." Mimeo.

Thomas, V. 2009. "Evaluation to Help Improve Development Results." Informal paper, Independent Evaluation Group, World Bank, Washington, DC.

Weyrauch, V., and G.D. Langou. 2011. *Sound Expectations: From Impact Evaluations to Policy Change*. 3IE, New Delhi.

World Bank. 2011. "Report from the Executive Directors of the International Development Association to the Board of Governors—Additions to IDA Resources: Sixteenth Replenishment—Delivering Development Results." World Bank, Washington, DC.

————. 2010. "Development Impact Evaluation Initiative: A World Bank-Wide Strategic Approach to Enhance Developmental Effectiveness." World Bank, Washington, DC.

————. 2009. "Making Smart Policy: Using Impact Evaluation for Policy Making—Case Studies on Evaluations that Influenced Policy." Doing Impact Evaluation No. 14, Thematic Group on Poverty Analysis, Monitoring and Impact Evaluation, World Bank, Washington, DC.

————. 2006. "Implementing Impact Evaluations at the World Bank: Guidance Note." World Bank, Washington, DC.

Chapter 2
Impact Evaluations at the
World Bank Group

The World Bank Group, particularly the World Bank, has been rapidly expanding its IE efforts in the past decade as a result of several interdependent and concurrent external and internal trends.

- **Adoption of the Results Agenda at the World Bank Group**, which is an answer to calls from donor and client countries for results and is at the core of efforts to enhance and demonstrate the Bank Group's development effectiveness. In the results-based management framework, the Bank Group identifies IE as a tool that contributes to improving decision making by generating project performance information.[1] IE is also considered an important component in the M&E system to strengthen the collection of project monitoring indicators and micro data (figure 2.1).

- **The refinement of IE techniques and the growing popularity of IE** in the past 20 years as a method for identifying the causal links between interventions and outcomes. Its increasing adoption is evident in the growing number of actors involved in IE, with academia and international research institutions as the most active players. This has also led to the establishment of global collaboration or national institutions dedicated to IE (the International Initiative for Impact Evaluation, Abdul Latif Jameel Poverty Action Lab, Innovations for Poverty Action Lab, Network of Networks for Impact Evaluation, and the Impact Evaluation Network) and IE efforts within agencies (such as the Millennium Challenge Corporation and World Bank Group initiatives), resulting in a sizable increase in the number of IEs produced.[2]

- **The focus of the World Bank Group on the knowledge agenda**, which was named among its six strategic directions in recent years. Because the

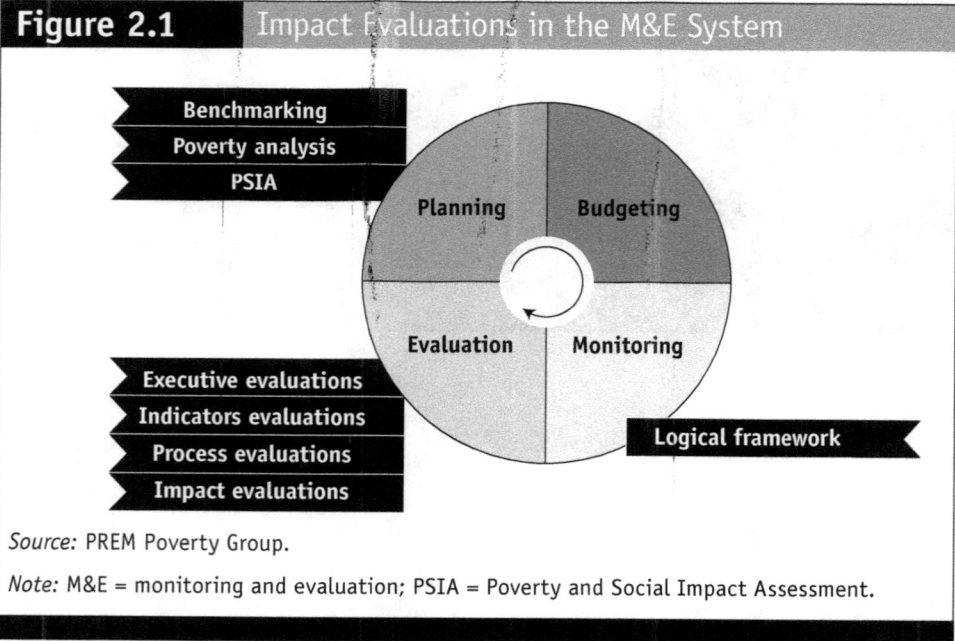

Figure 2.1   Impact Evaluations in the M&E System

Source: PREM Poverty Group.

Note: M&E = monitoring and evaluation; PSIA = Poverty and Social Impact Assessment.

Bank Group aims to become a learning organization that leverages the best global knowledge to support development, it sees the pool of evidence from IEs as adding to its knowledge base. IEs are expected to help capture knowledge from the global community and disseminate it broadly to benefit clients, motivate open dialogue on results and learning, enhance learning opportunities for staff, and craft development solutions applicable to different contexts.[3]

Institutional Efforts to Facilitate Production of Impact Evaluations

The creation of DIME in 2005 has been a key institutional effort to facilitate production of IEs at the World Bank. In the first half of the decade, there were few Bank-supported IEs and most were concentrated in a few regions and networks. In 2005, the Bank's Office of the Chief Economist (DEC) created DIME with the objective of generating knowledge on selected policies. Half a million dollars per year from the Bank's research budget was set aside to support the conduct of Bank IEs.[4] Also in 2005, IE programs were started in the Africa Region and in the Human Development Network (HDN).[5] These served as DIME's implementation backbone. In 2008, the managing director responsible for knowledge and networks transformed DIME into a Bank-wide decentralized program with its own governance structure and a coordinated approach to operational support. In addition, DIME's mandate was expanded to include institutional development for evidence-based policy and improvement in the quality of Bank operations (World Bank 2010).

DIME is coordinated by a steering group with chief economist and director-level representation from networks and regions. It sponsors 15 thematic programs, with the DIME Secretariat in DEC managing global programs in agriculture, finance and private sector, gender,[6] fragile states, local development and urban development, as well as africa programs in education, HIV, and malaria. The rollout of additional thematic programs since 2009—in addition to the eight that were already active at the time—has been informed by a Bank-wide discussion on priority sectors and themes, and validated by numerous DIME Steering Group meetings, the managing director in charge of Knowledge, Office of the Vice President, and the Committee on Development Effectiveness. Several of these thematic IE programs have adopted the programmatic model promoted by DIME (box 2.1).

DIME is not the only initiative to implement IE programs, and some regions and networks have their own history and approach to managing IE production.

- The flagship IE program in the Africa Region is the Africa Impact Evaluation Initiative (AIM). AIM is also one of the first coordinated (with full-time program coordinators and technical advisory support) IE initiatives at the World Bank (box 2.2).

- Beginning in 2005, the HDN anchor, with Bank Netherlands Partnership

From December 2008 to March 2009, DIME consulted with World Bank managers to take stock of IE activities in their networks and regions and established IE programs and clusters along thematic lines. The goal was to consolidate IE activities and facilitate identification of which topics have been covered and which are still missing, based on the network portfolio and operational agenda. Before the consultations, IE clusters were active in education, health, HIV, malaria, conditional cash transfers, active labor markets, local development, and access to infrastructure. Since the consultations, thematic IE programs have been launched in early childhood development, finance and private sector, institutional reform and agriculture in 2009–10, together with two cross-cutting themes (gender and fragile states), and three more thematic IE programs are in the pipeline (forestry, water resource management, and energy mitigation).

Several of these thematic IE programs have developed a coordinated approach—also referred to as the programmatic approach or the programmatic model—and assumed responsibility for country-specific and programmatic activities:

- *Country-specific* activities include (i) the establishment of research teams with field presence to work with the project team and government counterpart through the design and implementation of analytical products; (ii) preparation of data instruments, supervision of data collection, and analysis of data; (iii) monitoring of intervention; and (iv) training of national teams.

- *Programmatic* activities aim to harmonize learning, ensure quality, and build capacity. They are organized by full-time program coordinators, sector leads, and senior IE experts and financed by donor funds. They also include the establishment of technical advisory groups of internal and external researchers and sector experts to develop a coordinated learning agenda, assure high quality standards, develop a common measurement framework for benchmarking and comparisons, and produce knowledge products and summarize lessons.

The programmatic approach departs from the model of traditional IE conduct, where task team leaders are in charge of operations, and evaluations are led separately by researchers. In contrast, the programmatic approach promoted by DIME seeks greater integration between task team leaders and researchers-trainers in the initiation and implementation of IEs. The organizational approach followed by the programmatic model is depicted in the figure below.

Organizational Approach Under the Programmatic Model

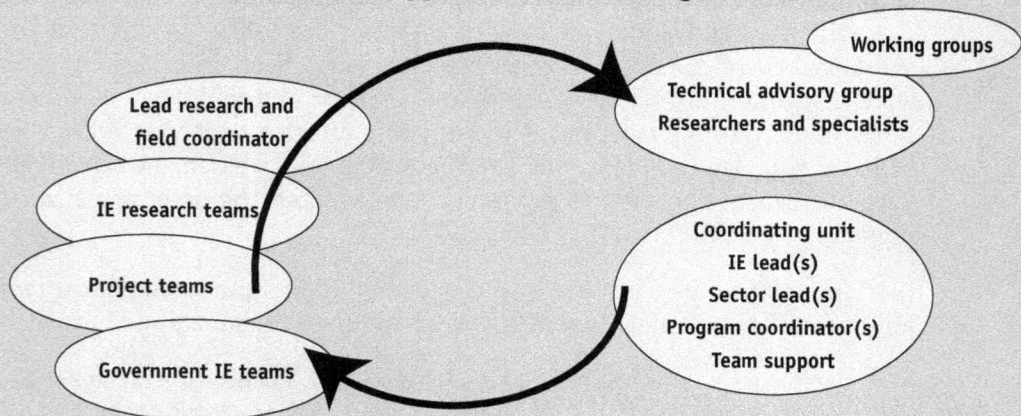

Source: DIME presentation to Results Steering Group in May 2009.

(Box continues on the following page)

The programmatic model was first tested by the Africa Program for Education Impact Evaluation. It was then adopted by the Malaria Impact Evaluation Program, the Health Results-Based Financing IE program; the Africa Impact Evaluation Program on HIV/AIDS; the Agricultural Adaptations and Rural Development IE program in Africa, Latin America, and South Asia; the Active Labor Market IE Program; the Gender Program; the IE program in Finance and Private Sector (DIME-FPD), and the Fragile States Program. The Vice-Presidential Units that manage coordinated IE programs are DEC, HDN, the Africa Region, and Sustainable Development (Water Supply and Sanitation).

Sources: World Bank 2010; discussions with World Bank management; DIME presentation to Results Steering Group in May 2009.

Program support, rolled out thematic clusters in the areas (i) accountability in basic education, (ii) conditional cash transfers, and (iii) promoting early child development and school readiness. When the SIEF was established in July 2007, the thematic areas where IEs were already active became SIEF clusters. The establishment of SIEF provided funding and a long run perspective to consolidate these and other emerging IE thematic areas—such as malaria control, HIV/AIDS prevention, pay for performance in health, and active labor market policies clusters. These clusters were not initially designed to conduct programmatic activities. Now HDN has started conducting training and dissemination activities targeted to cluster participants, and at least three HDN programs have adopted a full programmatic model (World Bank 2010).[7]

- The Sustainable Development Network (SDN) anchor provides light coordination, mainly to support financing and keep an eye on progress in the IE program regarding access to infrastructure. Going forward, the SDN anchor intends to launch three new IE programs in energy mitigation, forestry adaptations, and water resource management. In the meantime, the Social Development Department has partnered with the DIME Secretariat to implement IEs in local governance reforms and fragile states (World Bank 2010).

- The PREM anchor manages the IE program of institutional reform, which was launched in 2010. In addition, the PREM gender group adopted a gender mainstreaming approach and has provided technical and financial resources to the Agricultural Adaptations and Rural Development IE Program (AADAPT) and DIME-FPD programs to identify gender effects in Bank operations (World Bank 2010).

- The Finance and Private Sector Development Network also collaborated with DIME to launch an IE program in February 2010 (World Bank 2010). Only recently has IFC joined this program on a limited basis.

Box 2.2	Africa Impact Evaluation Initiative

The stated goals of AIM are to build government capacity to implement IEs and to provide evidence on the effectiveness of different interventions, to use the findings for making decisions, and to support learning across countries within the Region. The program also aims to promote the dissemination of the findings and lessons in an easily understood format through the AIM website, seminars, workshops, and government presentations.

AIM currently houses umbrella thematic initiatives in education, HIV/AIDS, malaria, water, and community-driven development and is closely collaborating with DIME in agriculture adaptations; it also supports country IE programs as well as single innovative evaluations. Today, AIM is supporting more than 80 IEs in Africa. The Africa Vice-Presidential Unit coordinates the AIM program in community-driven development, and coordinated AIM programs in education, water, malaria, and HIV/AIDS are managed by the DIME Secretariat in close collaboration with partners in the Africa Vice-Presidential Unit.

The financial support for IEs under AIM comes from a combination of sources, including government funds, Bank budget, donor financing (for example, Irish Aid, UK Department for International Development, and trust funds such as the Education Policy Development Fund, SIEF, the Bank Netherlands Partnership Program, Knowledge for Change Program, among others.

Sources: AIM website and discussions with World Bank management.

- IEG also produces one or two IEs per year as well as syntheses of the IE literature in selected topics.

- Other sectors and regions that do not have formal programs, or where the IE programs have just begun, seek resources from trust funds and/or clients and collaborate with World Bank researchers or external experts to incorporate IEs into projects.

In 2006, Operations Policy and Country Services established IEs as a new AAA product line at the World Bank.[8] Under this new policy, an IE initiated or supported by a specific World Bank unit—including evaluations of projects that do not receive direct Bank Group financial support—and resulting in a free-standing report is recognized as a specific type of analytical work with its own code. The establishment of IE as a formal product line aims to ensure that activities coded as IEs undergo a review process to enhance relevance and quality, both at the concept and final stages.

In practice, not all IEs supported by the World Bank Group are coded as IEs. Moreover, unlike other AAA products—such as economic and sector work, non-lending technical assistance, and fee-based services, which have associated operational policies—IE only has guidance notes that define the process for implementing and building IEs into programs. As a result, for many IEs supported by the World Bank, the initiation and implementation process remains decentralized and ad hoc, with considerable variation in application.

In 2010, the IDA16 replenishment discussions endorsed the development of a strategic framework to guide selection of IEs; it also included IEs as a monitorable indicator in the IDA Report Card. The overarching theme of the IDA16 discussions was delivering development results. As a result of the discussions, a package of policy measures and performance targets was agreed on. One important measure was the introduction of measures of IDA's operational effectiveness in the Results Measurement System. An indicator of IDA's operational effectiveness that was agreed on was IEs, which have also been included as a monitorable indicator in the IDA Report Card (performance target of 17 IEs per year from a baseline of 14 IEs per year) (World Bank 2011a).

IDA16 discussions also endorsed the development of a corporate strategic approach to the use of IEs to enhance learning from IDA-supported interventions regarding what worked well and what did not. Key elements of this will be to increase the number of projects with appropriate evaluation frameworks, continue efforts to improve their quality, and enhance the learning stemming from the evaluation process in IDA projects to strengthen feedback loops for project design. The participants at the IDA16 meeting also endorsed plans to convene a panel of experts to make recommendations on how to strengthen the Bank's IE program, including a selection framework and associated financing and implementation plans to be applied at the outset of the IDA16 period (World Bank 2011a). A panel was convened in 2011 to develop such an approach, but the final report is not yet publicly available.

IFC IE efforts are new, having begun in 2005, and respond to increasing interest in measuring the impacts of advisory services. In spite of the fact that IE is relatively new to IFC, the corporation is one of the early producers of IEs in private sector development. In 2005, in response to growing demand from stakeholders for greater evidence that the institution is delivering on its mission, IFC began using IE as one of its evaluation tools to evaluate its advisory services (box 2.3). The goal was to build a portfolio of IEs in pilot projects, enhance learning through rigorous and quantifiable approaches, and use these lessons to improve the design and implementation of advisory services.

Until recently, there has been no clear policy or strategy at IFC on what to evaluate and how to select projects for evaluations. Through its recent evaluation strategy, approved in FY12, IFC intends to move toward strategic identification and prioritization of evaluation opportunities, including IEs. Furthermore, IE efforts to date have not been accompanied by systematic IE capacity building or global learning activities.[9]

So far, the Results Measurement Unit (RMU) has provided oversight and funding for most of the IEs, working closely with regional M&E officers. In addition, regional project teams and business lines have conducted a few evaluations independently of the RMU. Irrespective of who has initiated the IEs, nearly all have been conducted by evaluators from academic institutions and consultancy firms, with some participation of by the RMU and M&E specialists. In IFC, adoption of IEs is on a small scale: there are 26 completed and 4 ongoing IEs in the organization.[10] Unlike at the World Bank, where the IE tool has been distinguished from other evaluation tools and accorded distinct corporate attention, IEs at IFC are neither considered a special product nor allocated a specific budget.

In addition to conducting IEs, the World Bank Group undertakes many activities to support countries in implementing IEs of their programs, strengthening their capacity, and facilitating global learning from IE results. Their activities include the following:

- **Workshops:** DIME and SIEF have been conducting country and regional workshops to train country staff, government officials, and local researchers in IE and to expose them to evidence that can be used for project design and policy making.

- **Clinics:** DIME, PREM, and HDN offer formal and informal sessions to support project teams with IE design. These clinics provide the space for the evaluation to be discussed and planned before or during the early stages of an intervention.

- **Brown bag lunches and seminars:** Various networks, regions, and IE initiatives organize brown bag lunches and seminars in which evaluators elaborate on their IE experiences and research. These seminars help disseminate the results of evaluations and promote communities of practice around common areas of interest.

- **Repository of IEs:** All evaluations processed under the IE code are published in the IE Working Paper Series. In addition, DIME collects infor-

Box 2.3	IFC's Advisory Services and Related Impact Evaluation: Supervisory Skills Training in the Cambodian Garment Industry

IFC's Advisory Services provide advice and capacity building to governments and private sector firms on investment climate, infrastructure, access to finance, and sustainable business practices. For example, IFC started working with the Cambodian garment industry in 2006 to help increase the sector's export performance. The components of the program included (i) improving dialogue and relationships with international buyers, (ii) improving the quality of the garment industry's human resources, (iii) supporting the building of an independent institution in Cambodia for labor standards monitoring and reporting services, (iv) helping build corporate social responsibility capacity in collaboration with other garment industry stakeholders, and (v) enhancing environmental sustainability in supply chains using a collaborative and cost-efficient method. The total cost of the program was $1.1 million.

In 2008, IFC partnered with ideas42 to conduct a randomized IE to measure the effects of the fourth component, the supervisory skills training program. The aim was to assess whether the training had been effective in improving poor working relationships between workers and supervisors and whether there were any related effects on productivity. The study covered four garment factories in Phnom Penh. The results show that the training was effective in improving workers' perceived relationships with their supervisors and resulted in moderate improvements in productivity.

Source: IEG.

mation on IEs across the Bank to include in a database available on its website.

- *Methodology notes:* As early as 2000, the Latin America and the Caribbean Region and the PREM Network spearheaded a handbook for practitioners on using IE to evaluate development projects (Baker 2000). In the past decade, the World Bank has produced a myriad of guidance notes on conducting and using IEs for a range of audiences, from evaluators to development practitioners to policy makers (some examples include Gertler and others 2011; Khandker, Koolwal, and Samad 2010).

- *Meta-analyses:* The World Bank shares lessons learned from IEs by synthesizing them in policy research reports. There has been meta-analysis work on conditional cash transfers (CCTs), local governance, educational accountability, social safety nets, and interventions to reduce malnutrition (Fiszbein and others 2009; Bruns, Filmer, and Patrinos 2011; Mansuri and Rao 2010; IEG 2010, 2011).

- *Data:* DEC's Data Group has been partnering with countries and other institutions to collect microlevel data through surveys. In addition, an increasing number of Bank Group-funded projects have incorporated an M&E framework that requires implementing agencies to collect data on monitoring indicators. World Bank projects have spent an estimated $2 billion for M&E in the past 10 years, about a quarter of this for data collection.[11] With the recently enacted Open Data Policy, many of these resources are now available and could serve as critical inputs for IEs.[12] However, their utilization rate remains low. Research teams also help project teams develop a strategy for baseline and follow-up data collection, design the questionnaires and samples, train enumerators, and supervise data collection so that data are more applicable to IEs (World Bank 2010).

Production of World Bank Group Impact Evaluations

There has been an increase in the production of IEs at the World Bank over the past decade, partly attributable to the IE initiatives described above. As seen in figure 2.2, the annual production of World Bank IEs increased markedly after 2005 when DIME was established, from an average of 16 IEs initiated per year between 1999 and 2004 to an average of 57 IEs per year from 2005 to 2010.[13] Since the creation of DIME in 2005, the advent of other IE initiatives has further accelerated IE production at the World Bank. For instance, the number of new IEs initiated rose from an annual average of 40 in 2005–06 to 53 in 2007–08 (which corresponded with the roll-out of SIEF) and further increased to 85 in 2009–10 (which coincided with the creation of additional IE thematic programs).

In parallel with the increase in IEs at the World Bank, a growing number of World Bank lending operations have been subject to an IE: 5 percent of lending operations approved between FY00 and FY04 were linked to an IE(s), compared with 8 percent between FY05 and FY10.[14] A further decomposition in recent years also reveals an increasing trend: 10 percent of projects approved in FY07–

FY10 have an associated IE compared to projects approved between FY05 and FY06 (6 percent).[15]

Compared with the World Bank, the IE agenda at IFC is at an earlier developmental stage. In the World Bank, IE has been used since the 1990s, has some dedicated resources and supporting structures, is considered as a separate AAA product, and has become a corporate priority. In contrast to the longer history, special product designation, and corporate priority status of IE at the Bank, IFC began using IEs in 2005 with small resources to supplement its Advisory Services project self-assessments. To date, 26 IEs have been completed, 10 from 2005–07 and 16 from 2008–10. Given the differences in IE experiences across the two institutions, the number of IEs produced in IFC has increased over the years but at a far slower pace than at the World Bank.

The majority of World Bank IEs assess lending operations, and their share in the IE portfolio has grown over time (61 percent of completed and 69 percent of ongoing IEs at the World Bank). In particular, a higher proportion of IEs initiated in 2009 and 2010 (75 percent) are associated with a lending project than any of the IEs initiated from 2005 to 2008 (59 percent). The rest of the IEs not associated with a lending operation usually evaluate pilots or in some cases

| **Figure 2.2** | Impact Evaluations at the World Bank by Initiation Year |

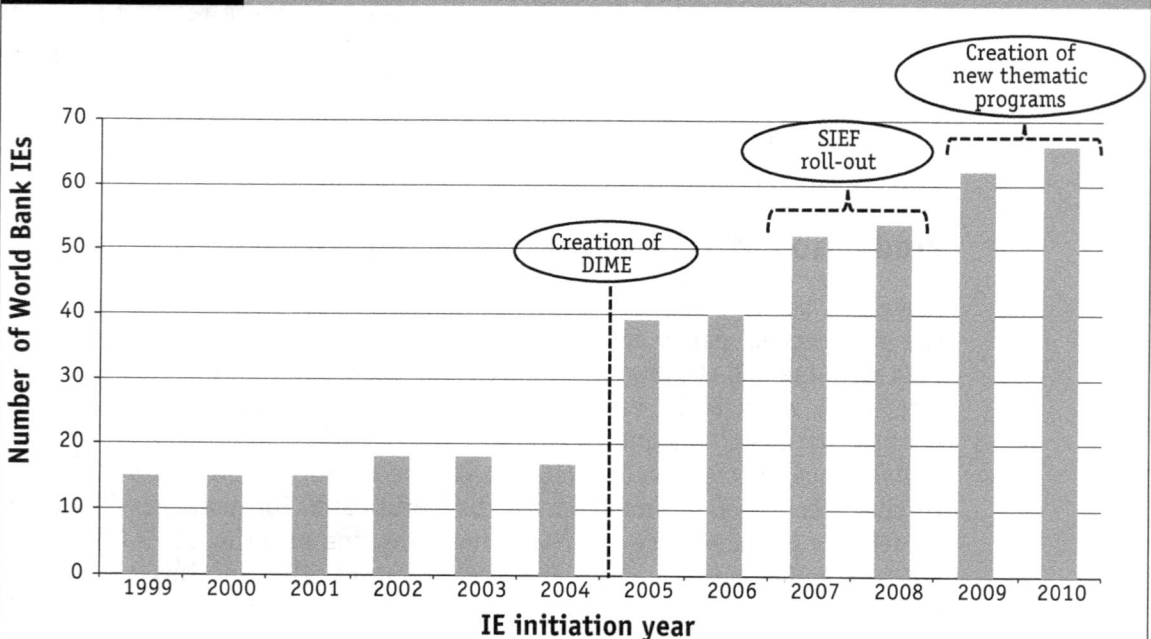

Source: IEG.

Note: Based on 411 of 430 World Bank IEs. The remaining 16 IEs were initiated before the 1999 period; for three IEs, the start year could not be identified. IE data for 2010 are partial because the IE database did not include new IEs initiated in the second half of 2010.

investigate programs that are not funded by the Bank but that may provide opportunities for engagement or learning.[16]

Among World Bank borrowers, Brazil and India account for the largest number of evaluated lending operations (17 projects in Brazil and India each, which account for 9 and 7 percent of their active lending portfolio during FY1998–2010, respectively).[17] Consistent with the growth in IEs assessing lending operations, the number of IEs linked to a lending project in Brazil and India has grown over time, particularly during the period FY08–10.[18]

In parallel, the sector board composition of lending projects with an associated IE has also broadened over time. Overall, the Agriculture and Rural Development, Education, and Social Protection sectors have the highest number of lending projects with IEs (48, 46, and 46 projects, respectively),[19] which accounts for 6, 9, and 17 percent, respectively, of the respective sector boards' active portfolio since 1998. As seen in figure 2.3, the coverage of projects with IEs in the Bank's current portfolio across most sector boards has increased over the years, most notably in the latter half of the decade. For instance, only 0.3 percent of active projects from FY1998–FY2004 that were mapped to the Finance and Private Sector Development (FPD) sector board had an IE, but that figure rose to more than 10 percent during FY08–10. In contrast, lending projects mapped to Public Sector Governance and Transport sector boards have not witnessed a rapid growth in IE coverage, and no projects in Economic Policy and Information and Communications Technology have been subject to an IE.

At IFC, all completed IEs have been associated with an IFC advisory service project; only recently, in FY11, have IEs been initiated for two IFC investment operations. IFC investment operations provide financing (loan and equity) to private sector enterprises. There is a common perception that these types of private sector operations are less amenable for IE (McKenzie 2009). Furthermore, two other additional aspects of IFC's investment operations have limited the conduct of IEs:

- Information on the ultimate beneficiaries (that is, small and medium enterprises [SME], microfinance clients, farmers, and customers, among others) is usually needed to assess the impact of an intervention. However, IFC's focus and information tracking are mainly on the client companies, not on the ultimate beneficiaries.
- IFC supports private enterprises that are mostly motivated by financial success; these financial motives create firm selection, critical to the success of the project, but which poses challenges for constructing a counterfactual in an IE. Therefore, randomly selecting what company gets the service or constructing counterfactuals to accommodate a randomized controlled trial may not align with the financial incentives of companies.

Notwithstanding these issues, it can still be possible to assess the causal effects of many IFC operations—for instance, as job creation, access to finance, and poverty—through appropriate data collection, and well-crafted experimental or quasi-experimental IE strategies.

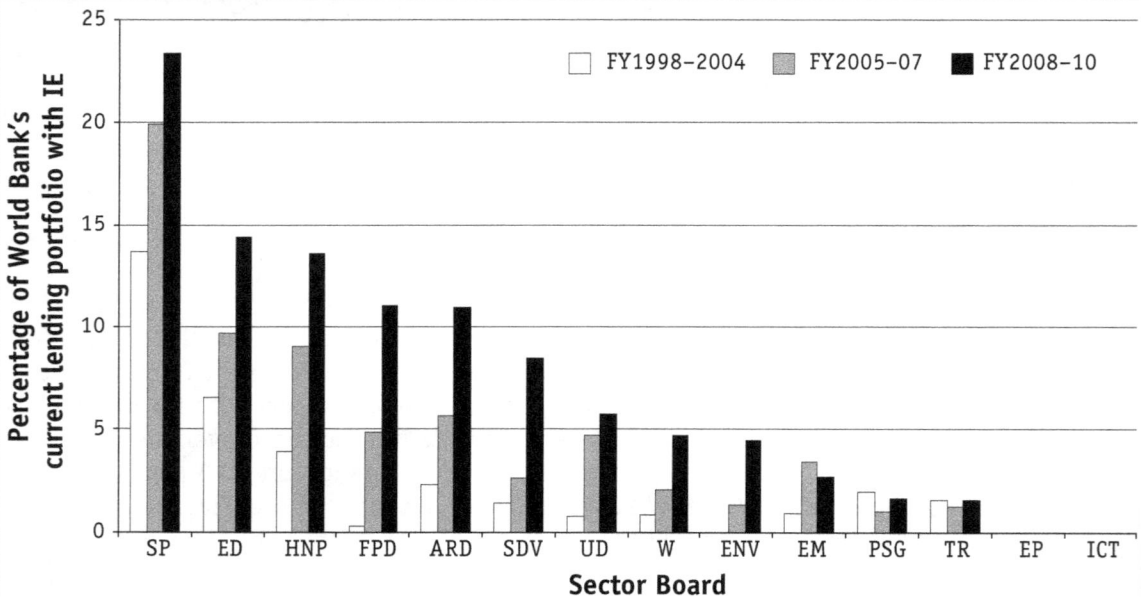

Source: IEG.

Note: Based on World Bank's current lending portfolio of IBRD/IDA projects since FY1998.and 272 World Bank IEs initiated or completed between 2000 and 2010 and linked to a an IBRD/IDA lending operation. It includes both investment and adjustment lending. Sector Boards: SP = Social Protection; ED = Education; HNP = Health, Nutrition and Population; FPD = Finance and Private Sector Development; ARD = Agriculture and Rural Development; SDV = Social Development; UD = Urban Development; W = Water; ENV = Environment; EM = Energy and Mining; PSG = Public Sector Governance; TR = Transport; EP = Economic Policy; ICT = Information and Communications Technology.

Thematic and Regional Distribution of World Bank Group Impact Evaluations

The thematic coverage of World Bank IEs has broadened over time. As seen in figure 2.4, before 2005 IEs were concentrated in local development, education, and CCT programs (16, 15, and 12 percent of total IEs initiated in this period, respectively). Since then, IEs have started to cover new themes (energy, malaria) and have rapidly grown in areas where IE work was scarce (for instance, HIV/AIDS and FPD).

Even in areas where IEs were more prevalent before 2005 and have continued to grow, these newer IEs are exploring different questions.[20] The creation of new thematic programs/clusters, in particular, appears to have spurred the increase in IEs in some areas. For instance, no new IEs were initiated in agriculture in 2007–08, but 26 IEs in agriculture were initiated in 2009–10 (which coincides with the formation of AADAPT). In the same vein, only two IEs of labor market programs were initiated in 2003–06, but with the roll-out of the cluster on

Active Labor Market, 19 new IEs have been initiated in this theme between 2007 and 2010.[21]

The range of interventions evaluated by IEs has been broad (from discrete and standardized interventions to multicomponent and dynamic ones), with varying coverage (from pilots to national programs), benefits (from cash transfers or subsidies to infrastructure investments and training), and eligible populations (from households to communities to schools to private sector entities). In addition, a few global IE initiatives have set up similarly designed experiments to understand how specific models may have impacts in varying situations. For example, the Water and Sanitation Program is evaluating hand washing and rural sanitation interventions in six countries.

In general, the types of interventions that have fewer evaluations tend to be more complicated or complex interventions (refer to appendix A for a description of these terms). For instance, projects in energy, transport, and institutional reform—examples of complicated and complex interventions—constitute 0.2, 3, and 3 percent of all World Bank IEs, respectively.[22] Nevertheless, the number of IEs evaluating complicated and complex interventions has grown over time.

Figure 2.4 Impact Evaluations at the World Bank by Type of Thematic Program and Initiation Year

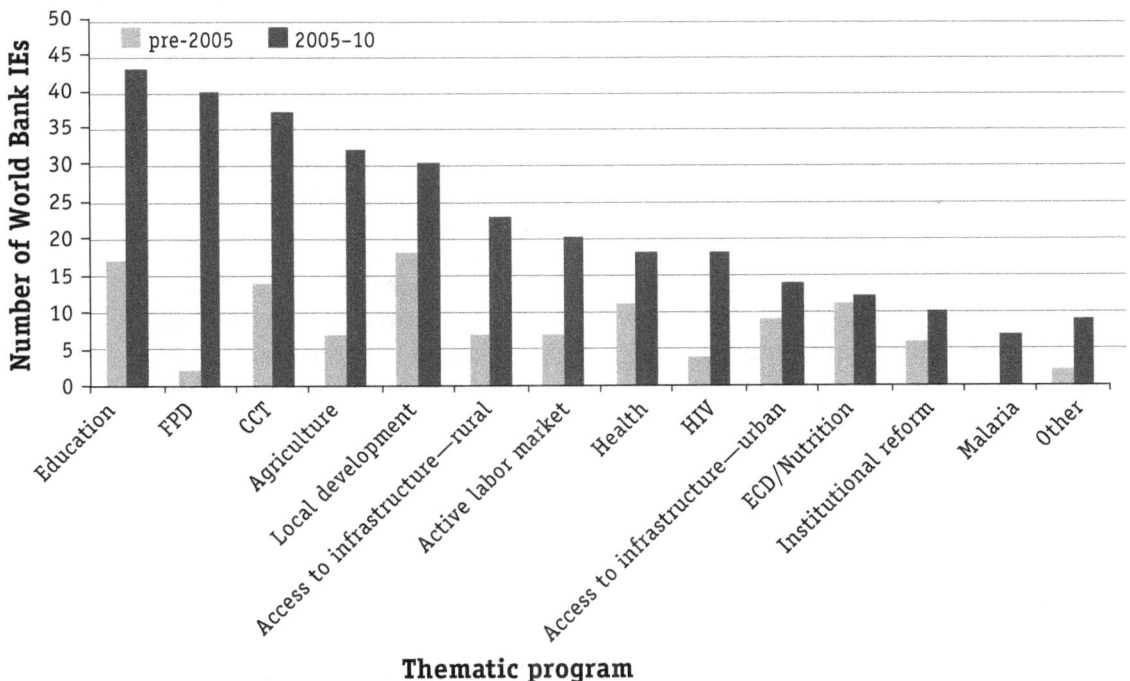

Source: IEG.

Note: Based on 427 of 430 World Bank IEs. The initiation year could not be determined for three IEs. Other includes energy efficiency and fragile states. CCT = conditional cash transfer; ECD = early childhood development; FPD = finance and private sector development.

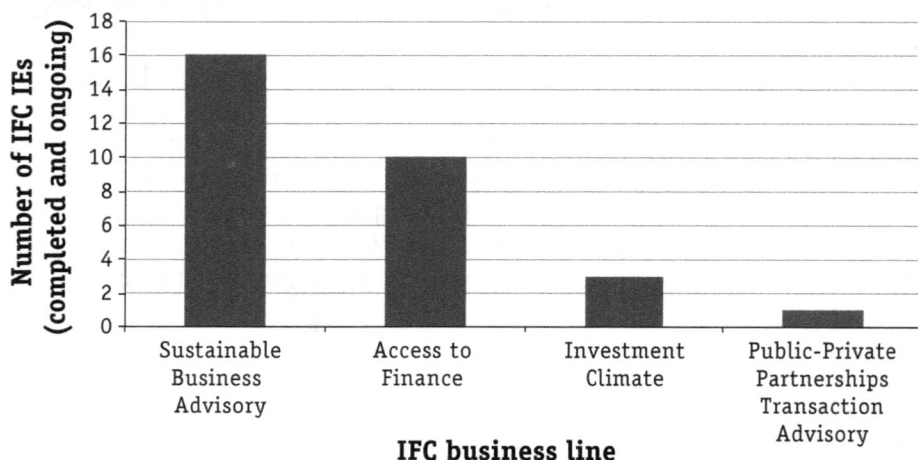

Figure 2.5   IFC Impact Evaluations of Advisory Services by Business Line

Source: IEG.

Note: Based on 30 IFC IEs completed or initiated since 2005. IE = impact evaluation; IFC = International Finance Corporation.

For example, a majority of ongoing IEs in health results-based financing aim to measure discrete results from complicated interventions involving provision of simultaneous demand and supply side incentives.[23] Similarly, a number of recent IEs in the area of community-driven development are evaluating the causal impact of complex interventions such as the process by which communities can more effectively manage their resources (not the specific activities or projects implemented) by using both quantitative and qualitative tools.[24]

Most IFC IEs are conducted in the Sustainable Business Advisory and Access to Finance business lines (figure 2.5). These evaluations mostly cover such activities as farmer and SME training and access to finance (including microfinance).[25]

At the World Bank, the share of IEs being conducted in low-income regions and countries has risen substantially over time. World Bank IEs initiated before 2005 were concentrated in Latin America and the Caribbean (45 percent), whereas IEs initiated in 2005–10 are more likely to be implemented in a low-income region like Africa (47 percent). The growth in the Africa IE portfolio over the years has been substantial, increasing from 17 percent of the IE portfolio in the years before 2005 to 40 percent in 2005–08 and 56 percent in 2009–10; this is attributable in part to dedicated IE initiatives for the Region (for instance, AIM) (figure 2.6). It is interesting to note that Africa is the region with the most IEs, while at the same time it is the region in which most countries lack the capacity to monitor poverty and other socioeconomic indicators in a timely and effective fashion. Yet, as IEs are implemented and baseline data are collected, it could lead strengthened monitoring capacity within the implementing agencies. In

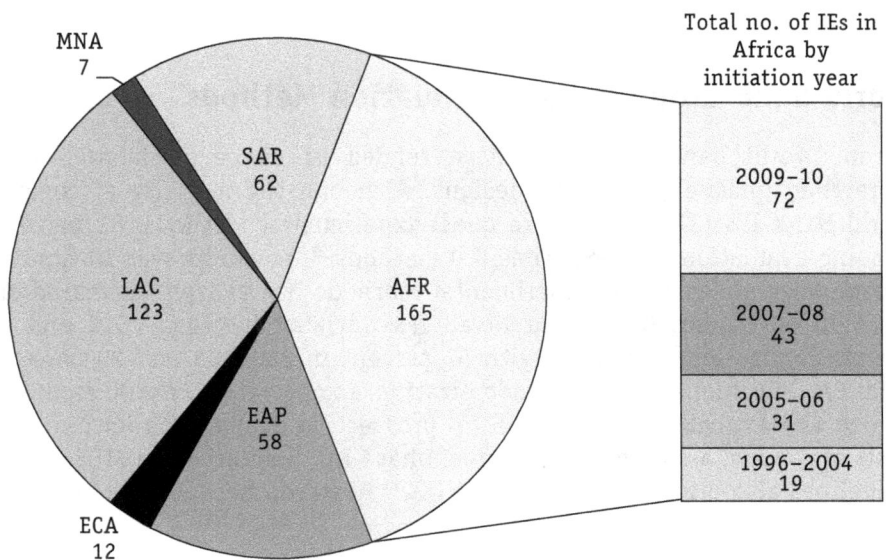

Figure 2.6   Impact Evaluations at the World Bank across Regions

MNA 7

SAR 62

LAC 123

AFR 165

EAP 58

ECA 12

Total no. of IEs in Africa by initiation year

2009–10
72

2007–08
43

2005–06
31

1996–2004
19

Source: IEG.

Note: Based on 472 of 430 World Bank IEs initiated since 2000. The year of initiation could not be identified for three IEs (two in Africa and one in Latin America and the Caribbean). AFR = Africa; EAP = East Asia and Pacific; ECA = Europe and Central Asia; LCR = Latin America and the Caribbean; MNA = Middle East and North Africa; SAR = South Asia.

contrast to Africa, in regions where resources for IE funding are more limited, the IE portfolio is quite small. [26]

There has also been an increase in IEs being implemented in low-income countries. Before 2005, IEs were initiated in 18 percent of low-income countries, compared with 44 percent from 2005 to 2010. The increase in share of low-income countries in the IE portfolio runs parallel with a more diverse country composition. IEs that have been initiated between 2005 and 2010 cover most low-income countries—the only exceptions being Comoros, Guinea-Bissau, Kyrgyz Republic, Somalia, Tajikistan, and Zimbabwe.[27] Similarly, 26 percent of IDA countries had IEs initiated in the pre-2005 period, compared with 56 percent in the years thereafter. [28]

At IFC, the majority of IEs are concentrated in the Latin America and the Caribbean and South Asia Regions. Nine IFC IEs are in Latin America and the Caribbean, four of which correspond to a regional IFC program on coffee value chain and two to a business simplification project in Peru. The South Asia Region has eight IEs (five of which are in India); six IEs have been conducted in Europe and Central Asia. Few IEs have been done for East Asia and Pacific (four), the Middle East and North Africa (one), and Africa (two) Regions.

Furthermore, although there is a balance of IEs between lower-middle and upper-middle-income countries, less than a fifth of IFC IEs correspond to low-income countries.

World Bank Group Impact Evaluation Methods

Recent World Bank Group IEs have tended to use experimental designs more than quasi-experimental designs. Although the majority of completed World Bank IEs (77 percent) use quasi-experimental methods, 81 percent of ongoing evaluations use experimental methods.[29] As can be seen in figure 2.7, the number of IEs using experimental methods has sharply increased since 2007. In particular, 83 percent of all IEs initiated between 2009 and 2010 use randomization, compared with 57 percent in 2005–06 and 20 percent in 2000-04. The higher rate of randomization among recent World Bank IEs is due to the explicit focus of DIME on prospective evaluations (either on the basis of random assignment or random phase-in). Similarly, the SIEF selection guidelines also prioritize randomized IEs.[30] However, because the IE database

| **Figure 2.7** | Impact Evaluations at the World Bank Using Experimental versus Quasi-Experimental Design by Initiation Year |

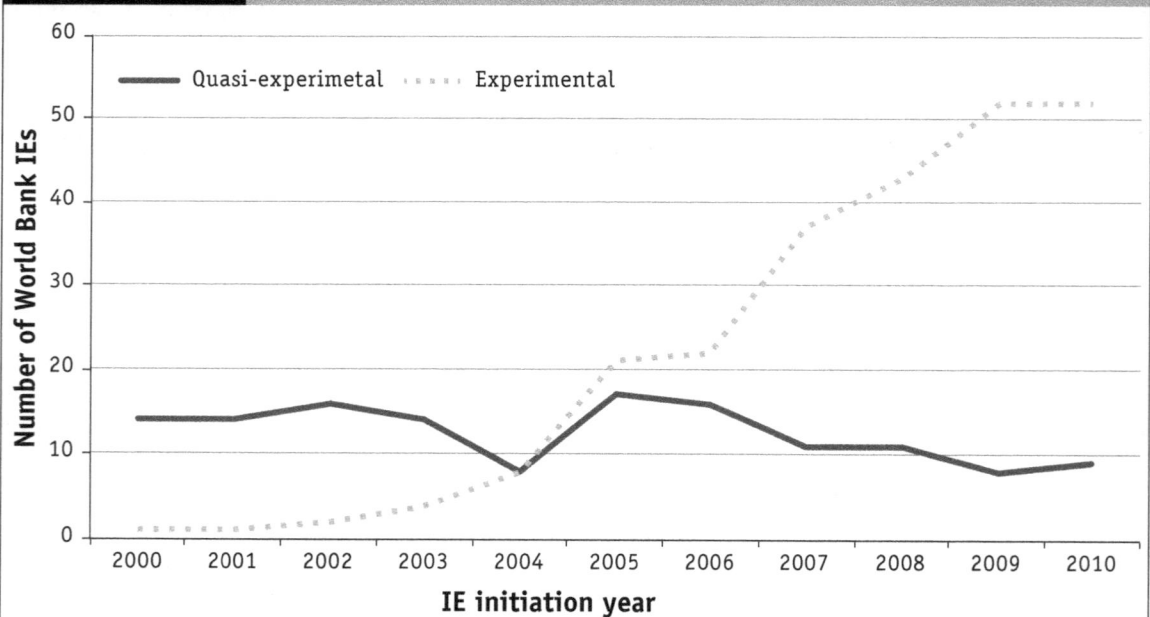

Source: IEG.

Note: Based on 381 of 396 World Bank IEs initiated between 2000 and 2010. For 15 ongoing IEs, the IE design was not specified in the DIME database. For three additional ongoing IEs, the initiation year could not be determined, so they are excluded from the count of 396 IEs referenced above. The information on IE design for completed IEs is drawn from IE reports; the source of information for design of ongoing World Bank IEs is the DIME database. IE = impact evaluation.

used for analysis was compiled principally by DIME, the high prevalence of experimental IEs reported in recent years is likely biased upward.[31] At IFC, 39 percent of completed IEs used experimental methods. Of the 10 IFC IEs using randomization, 8 were completed in 2009 or later, of which 4 were initiated under the IFC-ideas42 partnership.

Quasi-experimental methods used for completed World Bank Group IEs were primarily matching techniques (40 percent) and difference-in-differences (33 percent), followed by single differences (17 percent), instrumental variables (14 percent), and regression discontinuity design (7 percent). Quasi-experimental methods used for ongoing World Bank IEs also included matching, difference-in-differences, and regression discontinuity design, though at much lower rates (figure 2.8). Refer to appendix A for a description of each of these IE methods.

Stakeholder Involvement in World Bank Group Impact Evaluations

Client participation in different stages of the IE production process is modest at the World Bank, although it is increasing. The IE process comprises several

| Figure 2.8 | Prevalence of Methodologies Used in World Bank Group Impact Evaluations |

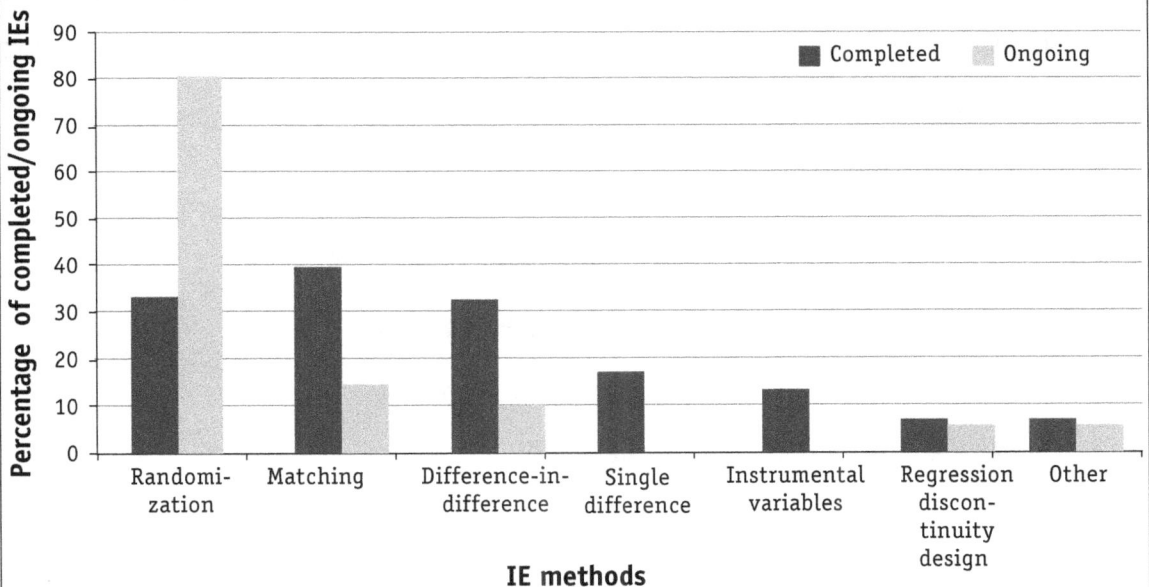

Source: IEG.

Note: Based on compiled database of completed IFC and completed/ongoing World Bank IEs initiated or completed since 2000. For completed IEs, the information is drawn from IE reports. For ongoing World Bank IEs, the source of information is the DIME database. IE = impact evaluation.

stages, including initiation, design, and fieldwork. Surveys of World Bank team leaders and evaluators indicated that a modest 23 percent of IEs started before 2005 were fully or partially initiated by the client (defined as the government or borrower) (figure 2.9). Even though the increase in later IEs being *initiated* by the government/borrower is quite small (+3 percent), there is evidence of growth in government/borrower *involvement* in the design stage among more recent IEs. For instance, 62 percent of IEs initiated in 2009–10 are reported to involve the government/borrower in the design stage, compared with 56 percent in 2007–08, 40 percent in 2005–06, and 22 percent of those initiated before 2005. The growing involvement of the government/borrower is in part reflective of improved IE coordination efforts at the World Bank.

Another stage of the process where the involvement of government/borrower has been modest is in the review and discussion of findings (39 percent of completed IEs). However, there is suggestive evidence that among completed IEs, those that were initiated in 2005 or later were more often reviewed by the government/borrower at the final stage (10 of 28) versus those that were initiated earlier (10 of 47).

Researchers from the World Bank and/or international academia or institutions are often the main authors, with less prominent participation from local researchers. More substantial involvement of local researchers is often advocated, as it can help build their capacity for IE, and the IE reports could benefit from the intimate contextual knowledge of local insights. Greater involvement of local experts could also add local legitimacy and ownership to the report, as well as to

Figure 2.9 Actors Initiating World Bank Impact Evaluations by Initiation Year

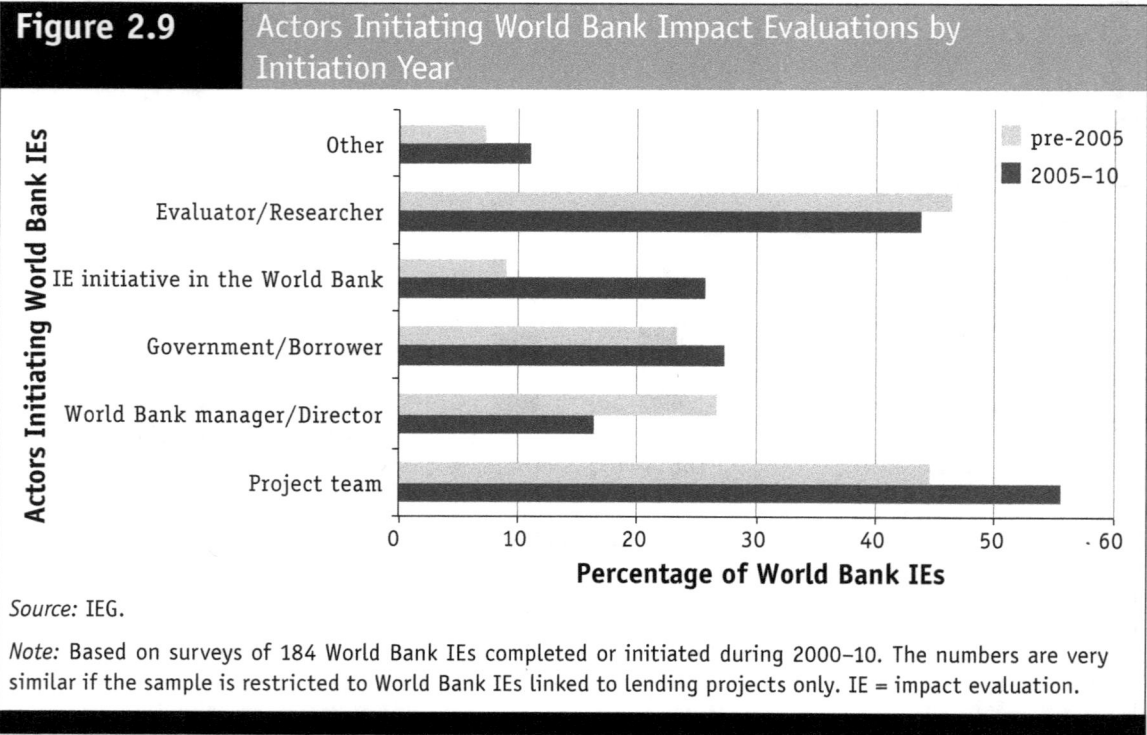

Source: IEG.

Note: Based on surveys of 184 World Bank IEs completed or initiated during 2000–10. The numbers are very similar if the sample is restricted to World Bank IEs linked to lending projects only. IE = impact evaluation.

its outreach. However, local researchers may have more limited technical skills to design evaluation strategies or analyze data.

At the World Bank, there is less engagement of local research institutions/ academics in the analysis stage. Seventy-five percent of completed evaluations have World Bank staff as co-authors and another 64 percent are co-authored by an academic, researcher, or consultant affiliated with an institution outside the country where the evaluated intervention was implemented (table 2.1).

In contrast, a local academic or research institute is listed as a core contributor in less than 20 percent of World Bank IEs. Although the authors of ongoing IEs are not always entirely known, evaluators' surveys suggest no discernible change in the *participation*[32] of local research institutions/academics in the analysis stage of completed versus ongoing World Bank evaluations (around one-fourth of IEs in both cases).[33] Instead, according to the survey, local researchers are more likely to be engaged in field work and data collection (45 percent of completed and 46 percent of ongoing World Bank IEs in the survey).[34]

Costs and Funding Mechanisms for World Bank Group Impact Evaluations

Analysis to contextualize the cost of World Bank IEs suggests that the expenditure on IE is on average 1.4 percent of the total cost of the evaluated project component. In absolute terms, IEs are often more costly than other evaluation activities in the M&E toolkit.[35] However, it is important to contextualize their cost relative to the size of the interventions whose impacts are being assessed.[36] In doing so, this analysis relies on three scenarios based on available estimates (appendix D) and compares the values against the costs of interventions evaluated by 124 World Bank IEs that are linked with 102 World Bank lending operations.[37] Results of the analysis suggest that the median cost of World Bank IEs represents 1.4 percent of the cost of the evaluated intervention—and a much smaller fraction (0.5 percent) of the costs of the entire project (table 2.2).[38]

Table 2.1	Affiliation of Authors of World Bank Group Impact Evaluations			
Author affiliation	World Bank/ IFC	Academia/research institute/consulting firm(from outside the country)	Local academia/ research	Government
World Bank (%)	75	64	18	5
IFC (%)	4	67	29	0
Total (%)	65	64	20	4

Source: IEG.

Note: Based on reports of 164 Bank Group IEs completed during 2000–10. The categories are not mutually exclusive; that is, an IE can be co-authored by a World Bank staff member and a member of an academic or research institution.

Table 2.2 Cost of World Bank Impact Evaluation as Proportion of Cost of the Intervention Being Evaluated

Scenario	Low cost (%)	Medium cost (%)	High cost (%)
Median IE cost relative to cost of intervention	0.7	1.4	2.8
Median IE cost relative to cost of lending operation	0.2	0.5	1.0

Source: IEG.

Note: This includes 102 lending programs of the World Bank that could be linked with 124 IEs, excluding 13 interventions (16 IEs) for which cost of the component being evaluated was not observed.

Compared with the World Bank, IFC IEs and evaluated project are more modest in cost and scope. The median cost of an IFC IE relative to the advisory service project budget is estimated to be 7 percent. However, comparing the ratio of IE expenditure to project cost between the two institutions is misleading because of the different cost profiles. At IFC, the median cost of an advisory

Box 2.4 Spanish Trust Fund for Impact Evaluations as a Dedicated Trust Fund for Impact Evaluations

SIEF is currently the largest source of donor financing for IEs of the Bank's programs to improve human development outcomes, combining €10.4 million from the Spanish government with $1.5 million from the United Kingdom. Launched in July 2007, SIEF is managed by the HDN Office of the Chief Economist. SIEF assigns financing to prospective, rigorous evaluations in 11 eligible human development and sustainable development sectors and 72 eligible developing countries across all regions. It also provides funding for training, publications, and dissemination of results through articles, meta-studies, and Web-based materials.

As of 2010, SIEF has funded more than 50 IEs, of which 36 are grouped in six clusters (CCT, HIV/AIDS prevention, basic education accountability, malaria control, health contracting/performance, and active labor markets/youth employment) aiming to build communities of practice to generate evidence on how programs work across different country contexts. SIEF studies not grouped into clusters mainly focus on evaluating the impact of highly innovative interventions.

SIEF guidelines limit eligibility to a specific list of countries in each region. This country restriction appears to be a binding constraint, particularly in the Europe and Central Asia Region: This region includes a number of low-income countries with low educational performance, which could make good use of SIEF financing, but only three countries in the region are included in the list of those eligible for SIEF IE support.[a]

Sources: World Bank 2010; SIEF website.

a. These are Albania, Bosnia-Herzegovina, and Turkey. See http:///siteresources.worldbank.org/INTISPMA/ Resources/383704-1184250322738/SIEF_Innovation_Fund_Final_Call.pdf.

service project that has been subject to an IE is $564,000, whereas the median expenditure on an IE is $60,000.[39]

The financing mechanism for IEs is complex, and funding sources are fragmented and difficult to trace. According to DIME, the World Bank shares IE costs with clients: the Bank provides internal funds and trust funds, and the clients use project financing. It is difficult to account for the full costs of IEs because they are often funded by different sources, with funds channeled through multiple mechanisms, and many are not coded as IE (they can be counted under other AAA codes or no specific budget code).[40] For example, IE coordination costs can be covered by the DIME Research Support Budget, the budget of IE program, or the budget of the unit under which the IE is managed. Its data collection can be financed by the government as part of the M&E framework. The funding for staff involved in its design and analysis can come from internal Bank funds or trust funds, channeled directly to the IE or through a specific IE program. And this may not account for the costs of World Bank or government staff providing support. It is, therefore, difficult to estimate the costs and funding sources of World Bank IEs.

Figure 2.10 Funding Sources for World Bank Impact Evaluations by Initiation Year

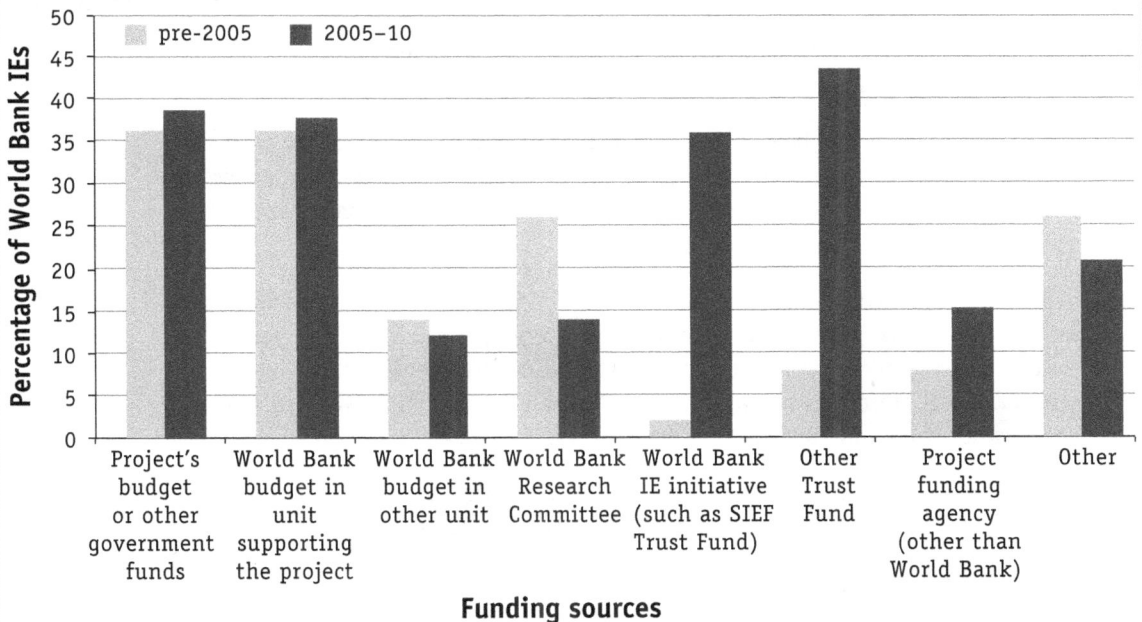

Source: IEG.

Note: Based on evaluator survey data of 156 World Bank IEs completed or initiated since 2000. The graph shows the proportion of IEs initiated in 2005–10 and IEs started in the years before, which were reported to have received funds from each of the sources listed. IE = impact evaluation; SIEF = Spanish Trust Fund for Impact Evalution.

According to the evaluator survey, 55 percent of World Bank IEs rely mainly on project budget/government funds or the budget of the World Bank unit supporting the project, probably mostly for data collection, which is a large part of the IE expenditure. This is followed by other IE initiatives within the Bank or trust funds (46 percent of IEs) (figure 2.10). In recent years, trust funds have emerged as an important source of funding, with 63 percent of IEs initiated from 2005–10 versus 10 percent IEs initiated before 2005 being financed by trust funds and/or trust funded IE initiatives in the World Bank, such as SIEF (box 2.4).

At IFC, the funding for IEs has been mainly through a general evaluation budget, although this has decreased over time. There is no dedicated funding facility in place for IEs in IFC. Generally, funding comes from a combination of several sources. The RMU has been the central source of funding for many IEs since 2005, as well as leveraging additional funds from regional and business lines. Increasingly, IEs are being conducted with more resources from regional, business line budget, and donor funding and less with RMU budget.

Notes

1 In its 2006 progress report, OPCS identified a list of possible actions to accelerate the implementation of the results agenda over the coming years and laid out next steps in its results framework. One of the proposed action items was IEs (IEG 2006).

2 For instance, there has been a fivefold increase between 2005 and 2010 in the number of papers that report results of randomized controlled trials as listed in RePEC-IDEAS, the largest database of working papers in economics and social sciences (Soares 2011).

3 The World Bank has identified nine *core knowledge products*. They include the best known Bank knowledge products and services—such as economic and sector work, technical assistance, and the World Development Report—as well as external client training and capacity development, research, *impact evaluations*, global monitoring, and new product development (World Bank 2011b).

4 The half million dollars in research support budget was established in 2005 and completed in June 2010. These funds are no longer available.

5 The Africa Impact Evaluation Initiative supports programs in education, HIV, malaria, agriculture, and finance and private sector. The management of the Initiative has been delegated to the DIME Secretariat in DEC since 2009. DEC has been at the forefront of the efforts at HDN, serving as the focal point to help regional units identify topics for evaluation and running seven IE clusters (education, early childhood development, health, HIV/AIDS, malaria, active labor market, and conditional cash transfers).

6 The Africa gender program is managed by the Public Sector Reform and Capacity Building unit in the Africa VPU.

7 Besides the Bank-Netherlands Partnership Program and SIEF, the Health Results Innovation Trust Fund has adopted a full programmatic model. In addition, the new multidonor Strategic Impact Evaluation Fund, which is being launched in March 2012 with the support of the U.K. Department for International Development, adopts the programmatic model.

8 OPCS announced the creation of IE as a new AAA product line, effective July 14, in an effort to respond to increasing demand for IE both within the country and the Bank (IEG 2006).

9 IFC dedicated the M&E network's annual meeting in 2007 to capacity building of staff to introduce key principles of IE and increase familiarity with the IE concepts.

10 In FY12, after the review period considered in this study, IEs have been approved for two IFC investment operations.

11 The figure is a lower bound estimate using a 125-keyword search across FY00–FY09 project contracts. The review of these contracts suggests they are for data collection and consultancies for M&E. A more accurate estimation requires drawing a random sample of projects, reviewing content and amount of all contracts, and expanding the estimate to the whole Bank portfolio (World Bank 2010).

12 In an effort to promote further access, DIME, in partnership with the Data Group, established the Impact Evaluation Microdata Catalogue, where data can be uploaded and made available with supporting documentation.

13 Because data for 2010 are are only available for the half year, the sum of IEs between 2005 and 2010 is divided by 5.5 years to get an annual average.

14 Excluding adjustment loans from the sample (as these are rarely subject to an IE), 5 percent of investment operations approved in FY00–FY04 were subject to an IE, compared with 9 percent of investment operations approved in FY05–FY10.

15 Focusing on investment lending only, 12 percent of investment projects approved in FY09–FY10 have an associated IE, compared with projects approved between FY07 and FY08 (10 percent) or between FY05 and FY06 (7 percent). The percentage for FY09–FY10 projects is an underestimation, as IEs conceived in the second half of 2010 are not part of the sample.

16 These IEs are mostly linked to a AAA product (for example, economic and sector work, nonlending technical assistance, or research services) or are free-standing IEs assigned an IE product code.

17 Looking at investment lending only (because among the IEs linked to lending operations in the two countries, only one adjustment loan in Brazil had a linked

IE), 10 percent and 8 percent of the investment lending portfolio in Brazil and India, respectively, is subject to an IE during FY1998–FY2010.

18 In Brazil, 7 percent of the active investment portfolio in FY2004 and earlier was subject to IE, which grew to 9 percent in FY05–FY07 and 17 percent in FY08–FY10. Similarly, in India, 4 percent of the active investment portfolio had an associated IE before 2005; this proportion increased to 10 percent in FY05–FY07 and 15 percent in FY08–FY10. If the sample is expanded to include both adjustment and investment lending operations, in Brazil, 7 percent of the projects in the active portfolio in FY04 and earlier were subject to IE, which grew to 9 percent in FY05–FY07 and 16 percent in FY08–10. Similarly, in India, 4 percent of the active portfolio had an associated IE before 2005; this proportion increased to 10 percent in FY05–FY07 and 14 percent in FY08–FY10.

19 Excluding adjustment loans, the number of IEs is 48 in Agriculture and Rural Development, 40 in Education, and 40 in Social Protection.

20 For instance, rather than examining only average impacts, new IEs of CCTs are now looking at conditionality versus income effects or how impacts vary with changes in size of the subsidy. Similarly, although 2 of 14 community-driven development IEs initiated before 2005 measured impact on empowerment or social capital or social cohesion, 12 of 15 initiated in 2007–10 (for an additional 3 IEs, outcomes could not be determined) measured impact on these governance and institutional outcomes.

21 Note that 2010 refers to the first half of 2010.

22 Rogers (2009) classifies transport infrastructure project as complicated and n anti-corruption intervention as complex. Karlan (2009) classifies community collaboration in resource management as a complex intervention. The latter two interventions are closely aligned with the institutional reform/governance theme. Also see appendix A.

23 These IEs have been initiated in 14 countries (5 funded by SIEF and 9 by the Health Results Innovation Trust Fund). The health interventions in the majority of these countries involve simultaneous interventions to improve health care utilization. More information on individual IEs is available on the SIEF website: http://web.worldbank. org/WBSITE/EXTERNAL/EXTABOUTUS/ORGANIZATION/EXTHDNETWORK/EXTHD OFFICE/0,,contentMDK:22698792~menuPK:6055199~pagePK:64168427~piPK:6416 8435~theSitePK:5485727~isCURL:Y,00.html, and http://intresources.worldbank. org/INTHDOFFICE/Resources/5485648-1290196752547/7570985-1290196814962/2_ HRITF-IE-and-Knowledge-Agenda_Martinez_ENG.pdf.

24 This is an example of a complex intervention, as it is not possible to know ex ante what inputs the particular actors will select; nor would the same process in different evaluation sites yield the same choices (Karlan 2009). Countries where Bank IEs of such interventions have been undertaken include Sierra Leone, Gambia, Guinea, and the Central African Republic.

25 Most of the Access to Finance-related IEs are conducted for non-IFC projects.

26 Europe and Central Asia and the Middle East and North Africa Regions constitute 3 percent and 2 percent of the IE portfolio, respectively. In Europe and Central Asia, the World Bank has fewer operational projects to evaluate, as these countries are moving toward more fee-for-service and other forms of engagement with the Bank. The number of IEs in both regions has shown some growth over time. For instance, before 2006, there were no IEs in the Middle East and North Africa Region, compared with 7 IEs being initiated from 2006 to 2010.

27 Myanmar, Chad, and North Korea are excluded from the list of 32 possible low-income countries because they are not Bank clients. To IEG's knowledge, IEs of health results-based financing interventions have been initiated in Tajikistan, the Kyrgyz Republic, and Zimbabwe, but these are not included in the IE database, which does not include IEs initiated in the second half of 2010 and later.

28 The large number of IEs being implemented in low-income countries is especially noteworthy, given the paucity of good quality empirical economic research in these contexts. In *The Geography of Academic Research,* Das and others (2009) find that the difference in the volume of empirical research between rich and poor countries is glaring. The 32 low-income countries that are also World Bank clients constituted less than 2 percent of all country-specific empirical articles published over the 20-year period from 1985 to 2004. There is a potential publication bias, as more prestigious journals are more likely to publish U.S.-focused articles However, papers from the United Kingdom and other OECD countries, excluding the United States, have precisely the same likelihood of publication as those from India or Vietnam (Das and others 2009).

29 Among completed IEs, 55 percent of those initiated in 2005 or later used randomization, compared with 19 percent of IEs initiated in 2004 or earlier. In terms of counting IEs using randomization or not, the reports for completed IEs were reviewed to extract the information. For all ongoing IEs, the methods described here are according to the database shared by DIME. That is, all IEs for which the variable "evaluation method" included the term "randomization" were counted as having an experimental design. The frequency count of ongoing IEs is therefore an upper bound. For instance, non-experimental IEs can use a randomized encouragement strategy to promote take-up, even though the intervention itself is not randomly assigned (for example, IE of Plan Nacer in Argentina). A detailed explanation of the design of ongoing IEs is not available, and IEG cannot make the distinction between IEs using randomized assignment and those using randomized encouragement. Also, because most ongoing IEs are still in the discussion, design, or baseline data collection stage, the type of IE design—used for this counting exercise—is intended not actual.

30 For instance, under the SIEF selection criteria on technical quality, IEs using randomization as an identification strategy can attain the maximum possible score of 10, compared with a maximum possible score of 7 that quasi-experimental IEs can obtain.

31 The increase in randomization among ongoing IEs may partly reflect a bias in the IE database compiled by DIME, as most ongoing IEs included are prospective. Second,

the count of ongoing IEs in the database is most complete for IEs initiated by DIME or for those programs that collaborate closely with DIME. Initiatives like DIME and SIEF also favor experimental methods and prospective IEs as discussed in the report. Also, because most ongoing IEs are still in the discussion, design, or baseline data collection stage, the information on IE design is based on what is planned. But it could be that when it comes to execution, it is not possible to fully implement such a design in which case non-experimental methods of evaluation are used.

32 Participation is not the same as authorship, the latter being a subset of the former category.

33 This trend is also observed to be fairly stable over time.

34 Of the six IFC IEs on which evaluator response was available, one was reported to involve local researchers/institutions in data collection. Because the sample size is small, inferences for IFC are not drawn in the report on this aspect of IEs.

35 IEs on average cost about $0.5 million each, compared with the $0.2–0.6 million generally available for project preparation or $0.1–0.15 million per year for project supervision.

36 Although focusing on the cost component alone does not present a full picture of how cost effective (or not) World Bank IEs are, it nevertheless provides useful evidence on IE resource requirements. This analysis could not be done for IFC because it was not possible to disentangle the cost of Advisory Services by component.

37 The project intervention cost is based on estimates in the ICR (or the PAD if an ICR is not available).

38 The Millennium Challenge Corporation, a U.S. government development program that carries out systematic IEs of its projects (when feasible), devotes two to three percent of the project cost to this task.

39 Based on 15 IFC projects (corresponding to 18 IEs) for which both IE and project costs were available.

40 Forty-five percent of active IEs are without an analytical budget code (World Bank 2010).

References

Baker, J. 2000. *Evaluating the Impact of Development Projects on Poverty: A Handbook for Practitioners.* Washington, DC: World Bank.

Bruns, B., D. Filmer, and H.A. Patrinos. 2011. "Making Schools Work: New Evidence on Accountability Reforms." Human Development Perspectives, World Bank, Washington, DC.

Das, J., Q.T. Do, K. Shaines, and S. Srinivasa. 2009. "U.S. and Them: The Geography of Academic Research." World Bank Policy Research Working Paper Series No. 5152, Washington, DC.

Fiszbein, A., N. Schady, F.H.G. Ferreira, M. Grosh, N. Keleher, P. Olinto, and E. Skoufias. 2009. "Conditional Cash Transfer: Reducing Present and Future Poverty." World Bank, Washington, DC.

Gertler P.J., S. Martinez, P. Premand, L. Rawlings, and C.M.J. Vermeersch. 2011. *Impact Evaluation in Practice*. Washington, DC: World Bank.

IEG (Independent Evaluation Group). 2011. *Evidence and Lessons Learned from Impact Evaluations on Social Safety Nets*. Washington, DC: World Bank.

———. 2010. *What Can We Learn from Nutrition Impact Evaluations?* Washington, DC: World Bank.

———. 2006. *2006 Annual Report on Operations Evaluation*. Washington, DC: World Bank.

Karlan, D. 2009. "Thoughts on Randomized Trials for Evaluation of Development: Presentation to the Cairo Evaluation Clinic." 3IE Working Paper No. 4, pp. 8–13. New Delhi: 3IE.

Khandker, S., G.B. Koolwal, and H.A. Samad. 2010. "Handbook on Impact Evaluation: Quantitative Methods and Practices." World Bank Training Series, Washington, DC.

Mansuri, G., and V. Rao. 2010. "Policy Research Report on Community Driven Development and Local Governance." World Bank, Washington, DC.

McKenzie, D. 2009. "Impact Assessments in Finance and Private Sector Development: What Have We Learned and What Should We Learn?" World Bank Policy Research Working Paper No. 4944, Washington, DC.

Rogers, P. 2009. "Matching Impact Evaluation Design to the Nature of the Intervention and the Purpose of the Evaluation." 3IE Working Paper No. 4, pp. 24–33. 3IE, New Delhi.

Soares, Y. 2011. "The Practice and Use of Impact Evaluation in Development: Reflections for the Evaluation Cooperation Group Meeting in Manila." Mimeo.

World Bank. 2011a. "Report from the Executive Directors of the International Development Association to the Board of Governors—Additions to IDA Resources: Sixteenth Replenishment—Delivering Development Results." World Bank, Washington, DC.

———. 2011b. "The State of World Bank Knowledge Services: Knowledge for Development 2011." World Bank, Washington, DC.

———. 2010. "Development Impact Evaluation Initiative: A World Bank-Wide Strategic Approach to Enhance Developmental Effectiveness." World Bank, Washington, DC.

Chapter 3
Relevance of World Bank Group
Impact Evaluations

To evaluate the contribution of World Bank Group IEs to enhancing development effectiveness, it is first necessary to assess how relevant they are for that purpose. Their increasing production and acceptance is largely explained by the expectation that this tool is highly relevant for identifying what in development works and what does not (as well as how, why, and for whom). IE is part of a broader agenda of evidence-based policy making: it aims to answer questions that are of interest to the development community and provide lessons that are applicable to the planning of more effective poverty reduction strategies. But IEs are more expensive than other approaches, and evaluation budgets need to be used strategically and efficiently.

A central question of this evaluation is whether Bank Group IE topics correspond to priorities of country clients, the Bank Group itself, and the development community more broadly. The focus on estimating causal effects does not guarantee that IEs address the most pressing questions in development. For instance, interventions that are easier and faster to evaluate than those of strategic importance may get subjected to an IE, or the IE agenda may be driven by preferences for certain methods (such as randomized controlled trials) or by the individual incentives faced by evaluators, project managers, and decision makers (Ravallion 2009). In addition, asymmetries in information and market failures in knowledge may also limit the scope of IE. For example, development practitioners and project staff may not be knowledgeable of the tool, the different methods, or IE benefits and limitations, therefore making it less likely that they will apply IEs.

IEG examines the relevance of IEs at three levels—project operations, institutional strategies, and knowledge generation—that correspond to multiple dimensions of IE purposes and different actors they cater to. At the *operational* level, IEs are expected to help assess program effectiveness, either for accountability or to inform decisions regarding the expansion, contraction, continuation, or cancellation of the project. IEs can also inform the design of projects. At this level, IEs can be relevant for team leaders as well as government agencies and client companies of the evaluated or similar future projects. At the *institutional* level, IE evidence could generate needed information for World Bank Group strategies or dialogue with its client countries and thus is of interest to senior management. At the *knowledge* level, IEs may draw attention to innovative ideas that are applicable to future operations and add to critical research. Their findings may be pertinent to both development practitioners and academia.[1]

In assessing these aspects of relevance, IEG reviewed the existing IE portfolio of the World Bank Group and compared it with the current operational, institutional, and knowledge areas of focus to take stock of IEs that do not fit with these priorities, the topics that IEs have covered, and the remaining gaps. IEG also examined project document reviews and conducted structured interviews with Bank Group management, evaluator and task manager surveys, and country and sector case studies (appendix B).

The main findings of the analysis indicate that Bank Group IEs are relevant for operations, institutional strategies, and knowledge purposes, but there are interventions in key areas and aspects of impacts that IEs can but have not fully addressed. In particular—

- Most Bank Group IEs are relevant to the objectives and outcomes articulated in project results frameworks and respective sector/business line strategies. In particular, at the World Bank, recent IEs are more likely to be integrated with project M&E and better aligned with global knowledge priorities than earlier ones.

- With few exceptions, completed Bank Group IEs did not examine supplementary questions of operational relevance, such as the following: Are impacts sustained over time and generalizable? What are the channels of transmission from interventions to outcomes? Which form of intervention is most beneficial? Are the interventions worth the cost? Many recent IEs at the World Bank have begun to test the impacts of alternative treatment strategies on development outcomes, and some efforts are being undertaken to encourage the use of cost-benefit analysis in IEs.

- Although there are more Bank Group IEs in some sectors than others, recent IE initiatives, especially at the World Bank, have led to more IEs being undertaken in sectors that did not have an IE or that were scarcely evaluated. Even in sectors where IE presence before 2005 was strong, World Bank IEs in recent years have been initiated in strategic priority areas with fewer IEs in the past. However, IE activities in a few sectors and sector priority areas, where IEs are not traditionally used but where IEs can have significant learning potential, remain to be further developed.

- At the World Bank, the roll-out of SIEF has led to strategic selection and financing of IEs, most widely in human development sectors. Meanwhile, other IE initiatives—such as the creation of thematic programs and the adoption of the programmatic model by a growing number of IE programs—have improved strategic prioritization of IE topics as well as coordination between DIME and project teams in the conduct of IEs. However, opportunistic IE selection remains a concern, particularly in non-human development sectors. At IFC, IE selection to date has not been guided by any strategic framework; however, the FY12 IFC evaluation strategy intends to take identification of evaluation opportunities, including IEs, in a more strategic direction.

- In both the World Bank and IFC, opportunistic IE selection, where it occurs, is characterized by weak coordination, and selection is based on evaluation methods and topics that do not respond to strategic and/or knowledge priorities or is driven by readily available funding. In recent years, strategic coordination in IE selection and the integration between IEs and the operations they evaluate has improved in the World Bank; yet issues related to staff incentives, capacity, and funding are still perceived as key constraints to the production and relevance of IEs in the World Bank as well as at IFC.

Relevance of Impact Evaluations to Operational Needs

At the project level, the majority of questions addressed by World Bank Group IEs have been aligned with development objectives and outcomes articulated in projects' results frameworks. For IEs to be useful at this level, they need to provide relevant information to the decision makers of the evaluated or similar future projects, including team leaders as well as client companies and government agencies. To assess the relevance of Bank Group IEs, IEG compared the questions addressed by *completed* IEs with the scope of the project, using the development objectives in the appraisal documents of the evaluated projects. The project objectives outline the development goals to which the project aims to contribute, but they are often broad. Consequently, almost all IEs were found to investigate outcomes that eventually led to the project objectives.[2]

Because development objective is an imperfect proxy to distinguish operationally relevant IEs from those that are not, IEG also looked at how the outcomes measured fit with the project results framework that outlines the monitoring indicators along the causal chain from the intervention to the final targets. For 70 percent of both World Bank and IFC completed IEs that were reviewed, all or some of the outcome indicators were part of the results framework of the project. Furthermore, a review of a sample of ongoing World Bank IEs showed that most of them evaluate all or some of the outcomes mentioned in the project's results framework.

Some of the IEs that did not fit outcomes articulated in the results framework explored second-order or long-term impacts (second IE of business simplification in Peru, IE of post-program [South West Poverty Reduction Program] effects in China), or spillover effects (for instance, impact of a CCT program on entrepreneurship in Brazil), among other things. These impacts are not part of the results structure that the project team needs to monitor or be accountable for. Yet it is important to understand them, because they may undermine or contribute to the objectives of the programs.

Recent IEs at the World Bank are more likely than older ones to be prospective, and also better used as an integral part of project M&E. To ascertain if the IE was prospective or not, one of the proxy measures IEG used is whether the project appraisal document referenced any plans for an IE and baseline data collection.[3] This is consistent with the definition of prospective evaluations posited by Gertler and other (2011). As described in appendix A, prospective evaluations are developed at the same time as the program is being designed and are built into program implementation. In addition, prospective IEs collect baseline data prior to program implementation for both treatment and comparison groups. Based on the measures used here, prospective evaluations can therefore be either experimental or quasi-experimental.[4]

IEG finds that, among completed IEs linked to a Bank lending or IFC advisory service operation, project documents of 25 percent of World Bank and 23 percent of IFC IEs made mention of plans for both an IE and baseline data collection. This suggests that these IEs were planned as a formal part of the project design and its M&E framework.[5] In contrast to completed IEs, for 49 percent of ongoing World Bank IEs whose project documents were reviewed, the appraisal document made some mention of plans for both an IE and baseline data collection.[6] The statistically significant difference in the proportion of completed and ongoing IEs that were referenced in the project design documents (in terms of indications to conduct an IE and collect baseline data) is robust to alternative measures and suggestive of the increase in prospective IEs at the World Bank.[7] This finding is also consistent with the reported push for such IEs by initiatives like DIME and SIEF.

At the World Bank, recent IEs are also more likely to be *used* as an integral part of project M&E, partly as a result of the increase in prospective IEs. Based on survey results, IEs initiated in 2007–10 are more often reported to be an integral part of project M&E (49 percent) than projects initiated in preceding years (29 percent). This difference is statistically significant and robust to alternative measures and sources of data.[8]

Many questions that go beyond average short-term outcomes can add value to the operational relevance of IE, but have often received less attention. Answers to questions regarding long-term effects, the distribution of impacts, the differential effects of separate program designs, the channels of transmission, the external validity of the findings, and the efficiency of programs are also of interest to project administrators and policy makers and are likely to increase the use of IEs. Not only do they contextualize the findings on average impacts, but they also reveal if these impacts contribute to long-term objectives and are generalizable, what parts of the programs matter the most, which form of treatment is more beneficial, if the treatment is worth the cost, and how to better target the beneficiaries.

- *The majority of completed World Bank IEs assessed distribution of program impacts, but it was less prevalent in completed IFC IEs.* Seventy-nine percent of completed World Bank IEs assessed the distribution of program impacts across different groups of beneficiaries based on such characteristics as age, gender, income, location, and duration of participation. In contrast, 35 percent of completed IFC IEs reported disaggregated program impacts. Understanding how program impacts vary for different beneficiary subgroups is relevant to operational decision making, as it can help policy makers decide if they need to expand or limit the treatment to certain groups in the population or pursue other alternatives to achieve intended outcomes.

- *A low number of completed World Bank Group IEs evaluated longer-term outcomes.* Eleven percent of completed World Bank and 20 percent of completed IFC IEs made an effort to evaluate any medium or long-term outcomes, which suggests that in the World Bank Group, IEs measuring outcomes that develop more quickly are favored over IEs that assess long-lasting effects, which are closer to the development objectives of programs.[9] Evaluating longer-term outcomes can also help policy makers understand if the immediate benefits of the program are sustained/eroded over time.[10] One of the reasons IEs of long-term impacts have been less prevalent is low incentives and resources to conduct evaluations that occur many years into the program, or after the program has been closed. However, recent IEs appear to evaluate interventions with longer exposure periods and so are more likely to assess longer-term outcomes.[11]

- *A limited number of completed Bank Group IEs measure the contribution to impacts of individual components of a program's design.* Around one-fourth of completed Bank Group IEs assessed the differential impacts of individual components of a program's design. Evaluations that assess the differential impacts of multiple interventions to achieve an intended outcome (for instance, demand and supply side incentives to improve health care utilization) or that assess variations within the size or scope of a single intervention (such as type and amount of benefits, conditionality, eligibility criteria, recipients, or delivery mechanism) are valuable, as they help unpack the "black box" of the program impacts. At the World Bank, there has been an increase in IEs evaluating the relative contribution of different design features.[12] In particular, IEs initiated in the last three to four years are paying more attention to the question of what works and why.[13]

- *IEs rarely made an explicit effort to embed analysis into a theory-based approach that would map out the causal chain from inputs to outputs.* This framework is critical to understand the channels of transmission from interventions to outcomes, identifying what factors matter the most in explaining the impacts (or lack thereof) and testing the assumptions underlying the causal chain.

- *Completed Bank Group IEs usually did not discuss or hypothesize the validity of their findings to scaling up and varying contexts.* The issue of external validity is rather important for evaluations of pilots with largely idiosyncratic settings, particularly randomized controlled trials. The concern is that various program features can change when the program is scaled up, for instance, the nature and composition of those who participate (that is, entry effects), unexpected migration responses, implementation models, capacity to execute the program (nongovernmental organizations relative to national-level institutions), spillovers, interactions with other policies, general equilibrium effects, and social and political economic effects. Likewise, conclusions about impacts of an intervention may not be generalizable to broader populations in other locations or contexts. In the last few years, some explicit efforts have been made to understand the external validity of IEs.[14]

- *Compared with IFC, fewer completed World Bank IEs conducted efficiency analysis.* One-fifth of completed World Bank (21 percent) and one-half of completed IFC IEs (46 percent) conducted efficiency analysis, such as economic rate of return, cost-benefit ratio, and cost-effectiveness across treatment types or with other programs, or just a basic comparison of benefits against costs.[15] Although policy makers may find information on average impacts relevant, without some kind of comparison with the costs, they may have trouble contextualizing the benefits and determining the most efficient resource allocation. But there are some modest signs of improvement. Of the completed World Bank IEs reviewed, 26 percent of those initiated in 2004 or later did some type of cost analysis, compared with 16 percent of IEs initiated earlier. In addition, some steps are now being undertaken to address this issue. For instance, HDN is currently in the process of developing tools for incorporating cost-benefit and cost-effectiveness analysis into IE.

Relevance of Impact Evaluations to Institutional Strategies

World Bank Group IEs have been well aligned with the strategies of the Bank sector boards and IFC business lines under which they are managed, but some sectors have had more IEs than others. To assess IE relevance for Bank Group strategies, IEG categorized and compared the priorities in all sector board and business line strategies *set in the last decade* against the interventions being evaluated by the IEs.[16] The strategies are generally broad, encompassing a wide range of activities that the World Bank Group deems relevant to the sector or business line. As a result, virtually all IEs are aligned with respective sector strategies.[17]

However, there is a difference in completed World Bank IE coverage under the individual priority areas identified in the sector strategy. In sectors where volume of completed IEs was small, these IEs could not have feasibly covered all priority areas. For example, all three completed energy sector IEs of projects evaluated improvements in access to rural electrification, but it would be unrealistic to expect that these three IEs could also cover sector priorities like energy efficiency and conservation or environmental health, among others. However, even in some sectors where completed IE coverage was substantial, some priority areas received more attention than others (figure 3.1). In Social Protection, for instance, the bulk of completed IEs evaluated CCTs and social funds, but very few looked at labor market programs. Similarly, at IFC, most completed IEs fall under farmer and SME training and corporate governance under the Sustainable Business Advisory business line, leaving gaps in issues such as environmental and social standards or strategic community investments.

At the World Bank, recent IEs are covering broader, especially previously underevaluated, sector priorities. As shown in chapter 2, IEs initiated since 2007 have broadened their sector coverage to include new sector priorities like energy efficiency and malaria. Meanwhile, the creation of the DIME-FPD program has spurred the growth of IEs in scarcely evaluated priorities like investment climate (including enterprise support and training); the formation of AADAPT has led to several IEs being initiated in underevaluated topics like land management and agrimarkets. Even in sectors like social protection, where IEs of CCTs and social funds predominated in earlier years, 19 IEs initiated since 2007 and coinciding with the roll-out of the thematic cluster on labor market/ youth employment have focused on labor market programs, compared with 2 in

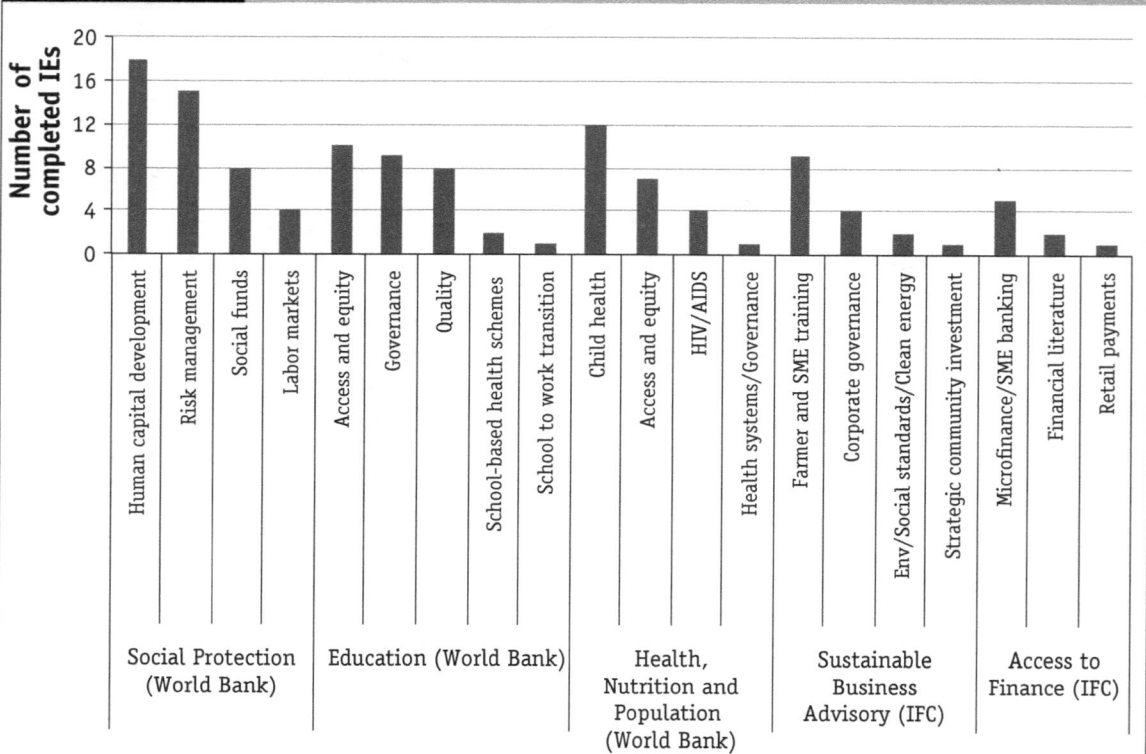

Figure 3.1 Distribution of Impact Evaluations within Sector and Business Line Strategies

Sector and business line strategic priorities 2000–10

Source: IEG.

Note: Based on the desk review of IEs completed during 2000–10. Social Protection, Education, Health, Sustainable Business Advisory, and Access to Finance are the sectors and business lines with the highest number of completed IEs. IE = impact evaluation; IFC = International Finance Corporation; SME = small and medium-size business.

the preceding 4 years. Similarly, in HNP, a number of the health results-based financing IEs have been initiated with SIEF and Health Results Innovation Trust Fund support and correspond to the previously underevaluated area of health systems/governance. However, despite this progress, there are still some sector priority areas where the IE activity to date is underdeveloped (for example, SME lending, trade finance, corporate governance, housing markets, environmental health, procurement, transport (excepting rural roads), social security, utility reform, civil service reform, and tax administration).

IEs are partially aligned with the sector composition of the World Bank's lending portfolio.[18] To the extent that the sector distribution of the World Bank's lending portfolio reflects institutional interests and investments, the sector profile of the World Bank's IE portfolio is partially aligned with these interests (figure 3.2). Sectors like environment, economic policy, information and communications technology, and public sector governance have no or few IEs (less than 3 percent of total IEs), although their share in the portfolio is 15 percent. Meanwhile, sectors like education and protection, with an active IE agenda, constitute 40 percent of all IEs linked to a lending project versus their 15 percent sector share in total lending portfolio between FY00and FY10.

Looking at lending and IE portfolio distribution across themes also confirms that IEs dominate in HDN (more than half of the IEs are in HDN, whereas it accounts for one-fourth of World Bank's lending portfolio). Meanwhile, SDN accounts for one-third of the IEs, compared with its share in the lending portfolio of more than 50 percent. Looking at the sector composition of the value of the lending portfolio yields similar results.

This alignment has improved over time. Although comparing the sector composition of the World Bank lending portfolio in relation to that of lending projects subject to an IE is an imperfect proxy for alignment with institutional interests and investments, it is evident that over time, the distribution of the IE portfolio has become better aligned with the sector profile of the World Bank's lending portfolio (figure 3.2). In the period FY00–06, the share of IEs in agriculture and rural development, HNP, and FPD was lower than their share in the current lending portfolio.

However, beginning in 2007, with the roll-out of initiatives like SIEF, the Health Results Innovation Trust Fund, AADAPT, Gender Action Plan, DIME-FPD, AIM-AIDS, and the Malaria Impact Evaluation Program, among others, the share of IEs in these sectors is now commensurate with (or greater than) their share in the lending portfolio. Even in some sectors like urban development, water, and energy, where the share of IEs remains lower than the share of these sectors in the lending portfolio, the proportion of IEs has grown over time. For instance, 2 percent of projects in water had an IE in FY00–06, compared with 8 percent in FY07–10. However, there have not been any discernible improvements in the share of projects with IEs in transport, environment, economic policy, and information and communications technology—the latter two not having any projects being subject to an IE.

Low coverage of IEs in some strategic priority areas, and the uneven alignment between the IE portfolio and World Bank's investments, is partly because interventions in sectors like environment, economic policy, and public sector governance are more complicated and/or complex (refer to appendix A for the definition of these terms) and have not traditionally been subject to IEs. However, a few recent IEs (for example, in local governance) demonstrate that *sometimes* what is needed to evaluate complex programs is innovative thinking about design of the IE (Karlan 2009).[19] Additionally, in *some* cases, conventional IEs may not be suitable for the project, but the principles of IE remain valid, and there are tools (such as spatial General Equilibrium models) that could be employed to simulate counterfactual outcomes. The same also applies to various economy-wide sectoral reform programs. Of course, many more assumptions are required, and the work is closer to the structural

Figure 3.2 — Sector Distribution of All World Bank Lending Operations versus Those Operations with Impact Evaluations (FY2000–10)

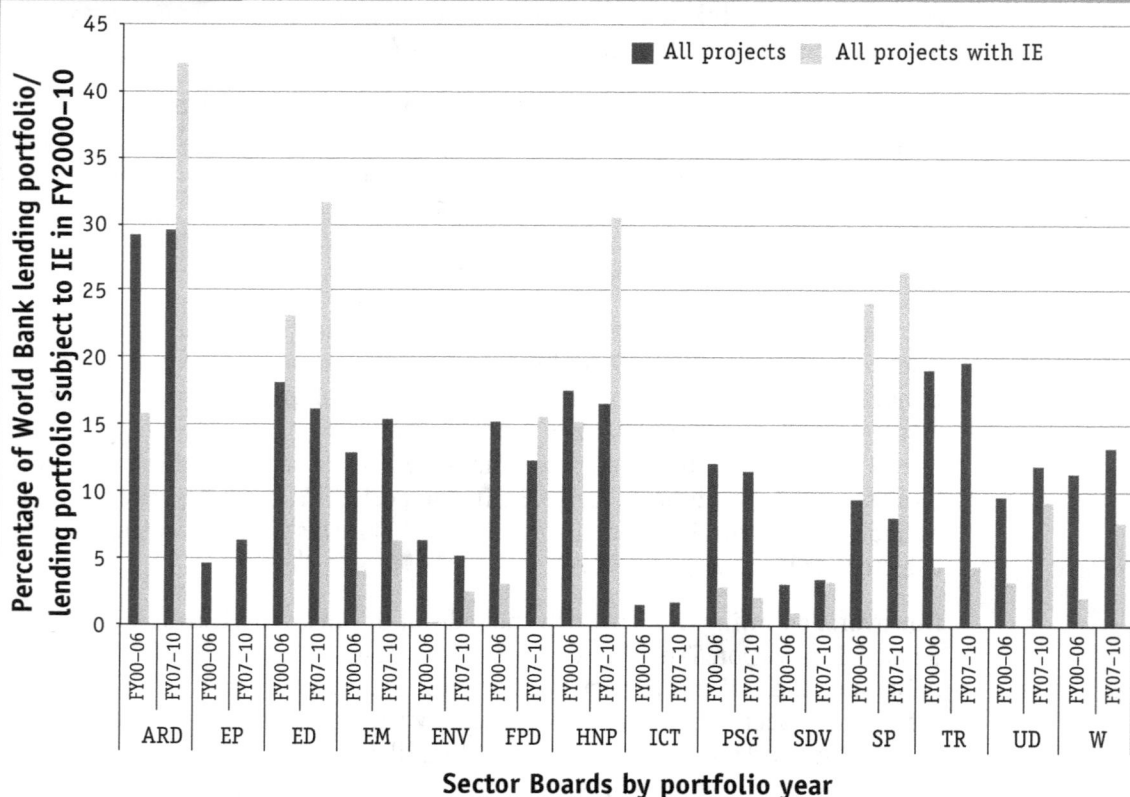

Legend: ■ All projects   ▨ All projects with IE

Y-axis: Percentage of World Bank lending portfolio/lending portfolio subject to IE in FY2000–10

X-axis: Sector Boards by portfolio year (FY00–06, FY07–10 for each): ARD, EP, ED, EM, ENV, FPD, HNP, ICT, PSG, SDV, SP, TR, UD, W

Source: IEG.

Note: Based on projects in the World Bank's current lending portfolio betweenFY2000-10 and compiled database of IEs completed or initiated since 2000 that are linked to projects active in Bank's lending portfolio between FY2000-10. Sector Boards: ARD = Agriculture and Rural Development; ED = Education; EM = Energy and Mining; ENV = Environment; EP = Economic Policy; FPD = Finance and Private Sector Development; HNP = Health, Nutrition, and Population; ICT = Information and Communications Technology; PSG = Public Sector Governance; SDV = Social Development; SP=Social Protection; TR = Transport; UD = Urban Development; W = Water.

economic modeling tradition than to the reduced form IE approach. Spillover effects[20] may also be managed by exogenously varying the intensity of assignment ex ante. These are the sort of tools that would be needed to cover the full range of development projects and policies.

There is more potential for applying IE as a strategic learning and assessment tool than is perceived. Not all sectors and operations are equally easy to evaluate, nor would all evaluations add value. It may be more difficult to construct credible counterfactuals for some interventions (such as broad economic policy and governance reforms), and the mismatches outlined above partly reflect the difference in the nature of the operations (appendix A). Nevertheless, IEG finds evidence that suggests that there is still significant potential to apply IE as a tool. In fact, an analysis of a very active IE sector such as education shows that there is a considerable difference between the percentage of operations for which IEs are feasible and where evaluations were actually done, based on *technical* considerations IEG assessed what *could* have been done by identifying that an IE was technically possible for around 40 percent of Bank-supported education projects closed in FY09.

In reality, IEs were conducted for around 5 percent of all projects amenable to such a tool (refer to appendix C for details). This finding suggests that there is potential to broaden strategic use of IEs within the World Bank beyond what is commonly perceived. However, the proportion of projects that *could* have been subject to IE does not mean that these projects *should* have been subject to IE, based on multiple considerations such as the duplication of intervention types; the methods that are available for evaluation; existing knowledge gaps; external validity; availability of skills and resources; and the clients' demands for knowledge and ability to absorb the message. [21]

Relevance of Impact Evaluations for Knowledge Generation

Beyond their evaluative purposes, IEs are a knowledge product and as such are expected to be relevant for knowledge generation, in particular for the priorities of the research community. IEs can contribute in many ways. First, by estimating program impacts in a causal manner, they can fill knowledge gaps about what works in development. Some IEs may add more value in informing public policy than others if they evaluate important programs (involving a lot of resources and beneficiaries and making large impacts) or are the first of their kind (testing new types of treatment or new settings). Another important role of IEs, especially randomized controlled trials, is experimenting on a small scale to facilitate scaling up or spreading an intervention to other contexts. More recently, IEs have also contributed to testing fundamental hypotheses in economics and other social sciences by estimating the parameters of economic models and mechanisms that underlie the behavior of households and firms. Finally, IEs of the same treatment in a variety of settings and on different scales will help understand what works in different settings, hence adding to knowledge about the intervention's external validity.

An assessment of the contribution of World Bank Group IEs to knowledge generation is beyond the scope of this report; however, there is agreement that the knowledge gained through World Bank IEs has been valuable for the development community. Overall, World Bank IEs have helped advance the state of knowledge about the impacts of a large variety of interventions and encouraged global learning in development. IEs that the World Bank supported have estimated the impacts of numerous programs, ranging from standard CCTs to infrastructure rehabilitation to land titling to various incentive mechanisms for increasing microcredit repayment and health care performance. Indeed, three-quarters of survey responses of evaluators and task team leaders perceived that the World Bank IEs have contributed (or are anticipated to contribute) to the global knowledge of "what works."

World Bank management interviewed for this evaluation also recognized the role of IEs in facilitating knowledge generation and exchange. Many IEs have also been published in prestigious journals and enriched discussions in different academic settings and media outlets. The contribution to knowledge is expected to be sustained through a large number of IEs that are currently under way and that, in addition to exploring average impacts of standard and innovative interventions, are also studying the factors that explain the impacts of (or lack thereof) and the conditions under which they can be achieved in other contexts.

More recent IEs at the World Bank are more likely to correspond to global knowledge priorities in development than older ones. In an effort to partly assess the relevance of IE to global learning priorities in development, the subject of World Bank IEs was compared against a list of 59 priority knowledge questions gathered from researchers and development practitioners.[22] The analysis indicates that about 39 percent of completed World Bank IEs were relevant to global knowledge needs; the proportion is much higher among ongoing IEs (72 percent). In particular, there was a statistically significant difference in the proportion of IEs initiated in 2007–10 that were aligned with knowledge priorities compared with IEs initiated in earlier years.[23]

However, knowledge priorities evolve over time, and this finding does not explain if older IEs appear to be less responsive because they correspond to an older, and not still pertinent, set of knowledge priorities or because newer IEs are deliberately geared toward filling knowledge gaps. Although it is difficult for this evaluation to fully capture these dynamics, there is some evidence to suggest that the higher degree of alignment with knowledge priorities among newer IEs is purposeful. Based on surveys of evaluators and team leaders, the proportion of IEs started in 2007–10 were more likely to be reported as being useful for filling a global knowledge gap (at the time when IE was active) compared with IEs that began in earlier years—the difference being statistically significant.[24]

At IFC, with a few exceptions, IEs have not been selected based on systematic identification of *global* knowledge gaps and learning needs. Compared with other sectors, fewer IEs have been done in the private sector context. These evaluations have been mostly conducted in microfinance, microenterprise, regulatory reform, and privatization-related areas (McKenzie 2009). This leaves many private sector development knowledge gaps, such as financial literacy, consumer protection, business training, SME-related issues, and trade credit policies (McKenzie 2009). IEs of IFC Advisory Services projects are for the most part conducted primarily to supplement self-assessment of projects by project teams and are not selected deliberately to close *global knowledge gaps*. At the same time, this does not mean that these IEs have not contributed at all to global learning, as the two are not mutually exclusive. Indeed, M&E staff and transaction leaders who responded to the IEG survey perceive that IFC IEs contributed to the global knowledge of what works.[25]

In a recent effort to play a bigger role in contributing to the private sector knowledge base and IFC's business, IFC partnered with the academia and provided grants for conducting IEs of non-IFC projects. However, these studies have been conducted in isolation from IFC staff, their direct relevance to IFC's operational needs is ambiguous, and there is no evidence of use of these evaluations in IFC (box 3.1).

Factors Affecting Scope and Relevance of World Bank Group Impact Evaluations

STRATEGIC SELECTION AND COORDINATION OF IMPACT EVALUATION ACTIVITIES

In recent years, there have been efforts to improve strategic IE selection at the World Bank, most visibly in HDN. A key IE initiative of the World Bank to deploy a strategic approach to IE selection and financing, via a competitive process, is SIEF. IE proposals under SIEF have been generated through two channels: cluster funds and innovation funds. IE cluster selection under SIEF in 2007–08 followed a two-stage process: The *first stage* was the identification of priority clusters of work. To this end, a call for cluster proposals was made, and a technical committee was convened in to review and vet suggestions. The committee produced a ranked list of topics/areas agreed to be of highest priority—areas where country demand for policy guidance is high, the evidence base for policy is currently inadequate, and good opportunities for rigorous evaluation exist. In addition, the committee commissioned cluster managers to prepare "cluster briefs"[26] to be approved by the relevant country directors before final submission.

Box 3.1	Relevance to Operational Needs versus Knowledge Generation

In 2008, IFC provided a $1.5 million grant to Harvard University for high-quality research (including experimental evaluations) in behavioral economics, investment climate, and access to finance areas. The insights from IEs were expected to add to the knowledge base on private sector development, as well as improve the quality and design of existing advisory projects, and suggest innovative delivery methods for future projects.

To date, five IEs have been conducted under this initiative; however, the findings have not been shared with IFC staff in an understandable and relevant format. Although IFC's contribution to the global knowledge base is commendable, this experience raises questions about whether and how these findings can be easily channeled directly back to staff in IFC.

Source: IEG.

In the *second stage,* the technical committee scored cluster briefs selected in stage one, based on policy relevance, cluster depth, technical quality, capacity for delivery, and timeline for results (refer to appendix E for a description of the scoring criteria and their weights). Subsequently, six clusters were selected[27]— all corresponding to human development sectors. Once the SIEF clusters were selected, all individual IEs were subject to an independent review by two qualified peer reviewers. Proposals for free-standing IEs submitted through the innovation funds window are subject to the same technical review by qualified internal and external reviewers.[28] At present, SIEF is funding 50+ IEs, which constitute almost one-fifth percent of ongoing IEs (and almost one-third of IEs in HDN).

Another notable effort to identify strategic IE priorities was the series of consultations organized by DIME and held in late 2008 to early 2009, which led to the establishment of IE programs along thematic lines. From December 2008 to March 2009, DIME consulted with managers to take stock of IE activities in their networks and regions and established IE programs along thematic lines. The goal was to consolidate IE activities and facilitate identification of which topics have been covered and which are still missing, based on the network portfolio and operational agenda. Before the consultations, eight IE clusters were active. Since the consultations, six additional thematic IE programs, including two cross-cutting themes, were introduced in 2009–10, and three more IE programs are in the pipeline.

In some thematic areas, IE programs have adopted a programmatic model,[29] whereby each program develops a research agenda and the data instruments and indicators that will be used (also see box 2.1). For instance, a brainstorming session with a large gathering of political scientists and economists was used to understand what critical policy questions should frame the fragile states program. DEC's Agricultural Living Standards Measurement Surveys are being used for the AADAPT program to ensure data comparability within and across countries and the ability to benchmark results (World Bank 2010).

IE selection *within* the IE programs that have adopted a programmatic model is characterized by collaboration between the project teams and DIME. When it comes to selection of IEs *within* thematic programs that follow the programmatic model, the final decision to conduct an IE rests with the government, but the process is characterized by close collaboration between project teams and DIME. In fact, many IEs that have been initiated under these programs were first designed in IE workshops and clinics coordinated by DIME. Before organizing these workshops and clinics, DIME communicates with sector managers,[30] who then ask task team leaders to work with their local counterparts and agree on the activities for which to have an IE. The project teams that agree to participate are invited to the workshops, which are combined with clinics.[31] The clinic, facilitated by IE experts, is where delegations initially design their IEs and present these designs for plenary discussion. Afterward, these delegations share the IE design with their ministries, and once the delegations confirm their intention to do the IE, technical assistance needed for the implementation is provided (World Bank 2010). Evidence from survey also suggests a notable increase in IEs initiated jointly by project teams and IE initiatives (such as DIME) in more recent years.[32]

The institutional efforts in the World Bank described here have led to improved strategic IE selection and coordination, but there is still room for improvement. Although several IE programs (a mix of human development and non-human development) now follow a programmatic model and a subset of IEs in some thematic programs (mostly human development) benefit from SIEF support (funding, training, and dissemination), some programs and clusters still lack coordination and remain informal.

Interviews with managers and directors also suggest that in general, IE selection at the World Bank is perceived as partially opportunistic. Of the 19 managers and directors who were interviewed, 3 characterized IE selection in their sectors or regions as strategic, 5 as wholly opportunistic, and 11 as a mix of strategy and opportunity.

Human development sectors were perceived to have deployed a more strategic approach to IE selection (9 of the 19 interviewees cited HDN as an example of a sector where IE selection is better organized), but non-human development sectors are still perceived as not having a well-developed systematic selection approach (for example, all 5 interviewees who characterized IE selection as wholly opportunistic were not based in these sectors). Opportunistic selection, where it occurs, is chiefly perceived to be characterized by (i) lack of coordination in decision making about choice of IE questions (9 of 16 interviewees), (ii) IE selection decisions being based on methods and topics that do not respond to strategic and/or knowledge priorities (8 of 16), and (iii) IE prioritization being driven by where the funding is readily available (4 of 16 interviewees).[33]

At IFC, there has been no strategic framework to guide IE selection efforts, and IEs have been initiated mostly based on staff interest, results measurement team initiatives, and availability of funding. The uneven coverage of IE topics and questions suggests that future IEs need to be selected more efficiently (for instance, by focusing more systemically on pressing knowledge gaps and making them more strategically relevant) so they increase the marginal benefits of evaluation. As indicated in IEG's recent report on IEs in social safety nets (IEG 2011), with the establishment of the new Development Impact Department there is a great opportunity to conduct IEs to demonstrate IFC's actual impact on poverty. Going forward, IFC intends to improve strategic IE selection, as stated in the IFC evaluation strategy, which was approved in FY12 (box 3.2).

OPERATIONAL LINKAGES

A contributing factor to relevance is the engagement of clients and project teams in IE design, which has increased over time at the World Bank. According to surveys, 25 percent of World Bank IEs have been fully or partially initiated by the client (defined as the government or the borrower)—the changes over time being small. Interviews with Bank management also suggest that in general client demand is a constraint to production of IEs at the World Bank (13 of 21 interviewees). This is unfortunate, because IEs initiated by clients can also rely on their ownership and are more likely to be incorporated into policy making (box 3.3). However, even though the increase in IEs being *initiated* by the government/borrower has been small, there is evidence of growth in government/borrower *involvement* in the design stage among more recent World Bank IEs, as described in chapter 2.

There is an increasing trend toward IEs being motivated by project teams. This aligns with the initiation of the programmatic model, beginning in 2007 with the Africa Program for Education Impact Evaluation and expanding to several other programs in later years, to support project teams in the initial design of IEs. In particular, 59 percent of IEs that started in 2007–10 were initiated by project teams, compared with 45 percent in earlier years.[34]

In principle, the advantage of an IE conceived by the project team is that the evaluation then often has access to project information and is more relevant to project management. Fifty percent of IEs initiated by project teams are used as an integral part of the project M&E, compared with 25 percent of IEs not initiated by project teams.[35] The time trends are especially interesting and suggest that strengthening the engagement with project teams at the Bank has had some success. For instance, 63 percent of IEs initiated by project teams in 2007–10 have been used to inform project M&E, compared with 32 percent of IEs in the preceding years.

An increasing number of World Bank IEs are being conceived as a formal part of the project plan. Only a small proportion of completed World Bank IEs were cited in the appraisal documents or conceived as part of project and/or its M&E. Yet this is changing, as discussed earlier. Having IEs that are integrated in formal project planning and M&E frameworks helps ensure that the evaluation

---

Box 3.2   IFC's Evaluation Strategy

IFC's senior management endorsed an evaluation strategy in FY12. With this strategy, IFC intends to establish evaluation guidelines, policies, and a database, as well as link evaluations with pipeline projects. IFC plans to conduct more thematic and programmatic evaluations, including IEs; establish and adhere to quality standards; streamline evaluation into product development; and strengthen the impact of advisory and investment operations on economic growth, jobs, and poverty.

In addition, IFC has developed evaluation selection criteria. The criteria are based on three factors: (i) cost (that is, whether an evaluation yields operationally useful information for programs with significant budget); (ii) impact (whether an evaluation yields lessons for programs affecting a large number of people, or a large percentage of people in an important country or sector); and (iii) strategic relevance. The criteria also take into account the amount of evidence that exists and may be relevant to answer specific evaluation questions.

Source: IFC.

Box 3.3	Impact Evaluations Demanded by Government: The Case of *Familias en Accion* in Colombia

Familias en Accion is a CCT program run by the Colombian government to foster the accumulation of human capital in rural areas. The program provides cash to poor families conditional on their investments in the education, health, and nutrition of their children (vaccination; growth and development checks for infants; courses on nutrition, hygiene, and contraception for the mothers; and school attendance for children).

The program started in 2001, one year before a new political administration came to power. The Colombian National Planning Department commissioned multiple series of IEs of the program. There was reportedly great concern about the severe fiscal situation that affected all government programs. However, the results of the first wave of the evaluation were soon available and showed impacts on schooling, health, labor supply, and consumption.

These early results helped persuade the new administration not to cancel the program, and they define the larger social protection in the country. The IEs have also contributed to a culture of M&E not only in the presidency and National Planning Department, but throughout the Colombian government. The government committed to broader agenda of IEs of social sector programs (between 2002 and 2009, the number of evaluations launched by the government rose from 3 to 46). Based on the proven results and success of this program, many countries have been adopting similar mechanisms to improve human capital development of the poorest segments of their populations.

Source: IEG country case study.

questions are relevant to the project[36] and that the M&E data requirements are aligned with the evaluation needs, and it could complement other evaluation products.

For instance, around one-half of IEs linked to lending projects that mention the IE and/or reference any baseline data collection plans are perceived by team leaders and evaluators to have been *used* as an integral part of project M&E, compared with less than one-fourth of IEs not cited.[37] Restricting the sample to IEs that were planned before the intervention but not necessarily articulated in the formal project and M&E design, those that have been part of the project plan are more often reported to be *used* as an integral part of project M&E than those that were not.[38]

However, even if IEs are planned early and articulated in the project planning documents, the long and complex procurement process to select survey firms could prevent the collection of baseline data before the start of the program (box 3.4). Securing sufficient funding may also take a long time, hence delaying the IE implementation—and thereby reducing its relevance and scope. Finally, the World Bank's accounting rules, which allocate funds to be spent in a particular fiscal year, are not well suited for evaluating projects that are fast-tracked or have a quick roll-out timeline.

At the World Bank, strategic IE selection, coordination, and operational linkages have improved in recent years; however, issues of incentives, capacity, and funding *still* constrain the scope and relevance of IEs in the World Bank as well as at IFC. As described earlier, strategic IE selection, financing, and coordination have improved in recent years, led by SIEF and DIME. Partly as a result of this, recent IEs at the World Bank are better linked with project design and M&E framework, and project teams and clients (namely, governments/borrowers) are more involved in the IE initiation and design process.

Meanwhile at IFC, where the IE agenda is relatively new, there has been no systematic selection strategy to identify IEs, although the recently approved IFC Evaluation Strategy plans to roll out a strategic selection framework. However, in both institutions, issues related to staff incentives, capacity, and funding persist and continue to constrain the scope and relevance of Bank Group IEs. Indeed, in IEG surveys, the three main factors identified by evaluators and team leaders as currently constraining the conduct of IEs in the World Bank Group relate to funding, staff incentives, and staff capacity (figure 3.3).[39] Interviews with Bank Group management are consistent with these survey findings.

STAFF INCENTIVES AND CAPACITY

Lack of staff incentives is perceived as one constraint to the conduct of IEs at the World Bank Group. In both the World Bank and IFC, almost half of evaluators and team leaders of evaluated projects who were surveyed cited lack of staff incentives as constraining the conduct of IEs. Similarly, the majority of World Bank managers and directors interviewed (13 of 21) considered staff incentives as a constraining factor to the preparation of IEs in their regions or sectors.[40] Based on surveys and/or interviews with senior management and Bank Group staff, the incentive issues that emerge are the following:

Box 3.4	Complexities of the Procurement Process: Cases of Indonesia, Nicaragua, and Vietnam

The IEs of the Kecamatan Development Program in Indonesia, the Coffee Value Chain Project in Central America, and the Scaling Up Hand Washing Project in Vietnam illustrate how cumbersome and complex procurement processes can affect the conduct of IEs. In Indonesia and Vietnam, the local capacity for conducting high-quality surveys is limited to very few institutions, which are pre-identified. Yet in both countries, the institutions had to go through a lengthy selection process even though competition was almost nonexistent. This contributed to delays in the start of data collection.

In the Coffee Value Chain Project, the selection of a survey firm was delayed because of two prior unsuccessful bid openings, wherein none of the bidders fulfilled the requirements of the contract. Consequently, baseline data collection was delayed until after the project started. Some stakeholders indicated that the lengthy IFC process and delayed collection of the baseline information affected the quality of the IE.

Sources: IEG country case studies.

Figure 3.3 Main Institutional Factors That Constrain the Conduct of World Bank Group Impact Evaluations

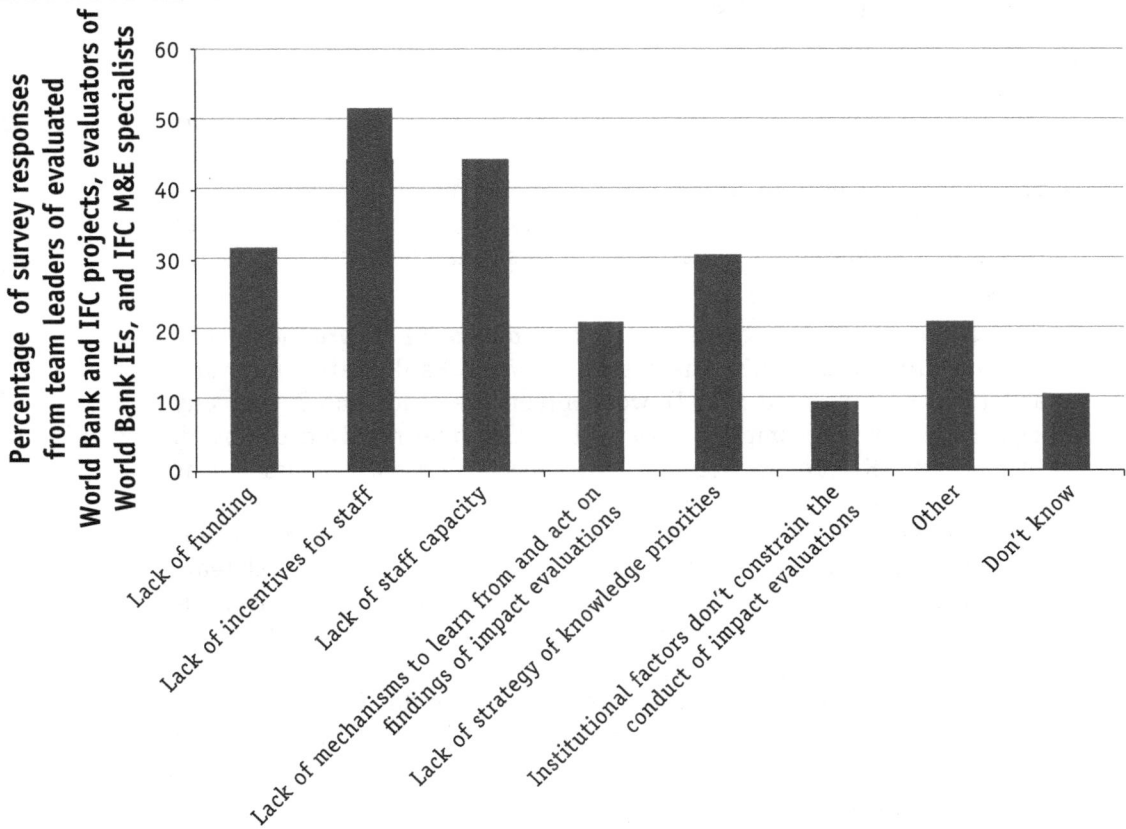

Source: IEG.

Note: Based on survey of 627 evaluators and project leaders of evaluated interventions. IE = impact evaluation; M&E = monitoring and evaluation.

- *Incentives to evaluate less strategic interventions:* Fifty percent of World Bank managers and directors interviewed were concerned that IEs converge on interventions that are "easier" to evaluate (for example, based on timing and nature of the intervention) or where the funding is more readily available, rather than being strategically directed toward knowledge priorities and gaps. This issue was perceived to be more prominent in non-HDN sectors.

- *Lack of awareness about the IE tool:* There is not adequate awareness among operational staff of the value of the IE tool. More than 50 percent of surveyed team leaders in both the World Bank and IFC said that training should be organized for team leaders so they can better understand the benefits and limitations of IEs. Consistent with this, one-third of survey respondents cited lack of capacity as a constraint to conducting IEs. At IFC in particular, limited understanding of the use of the IE tool in operational and policy purposes is perceived by the majority of product leaders interviewed as a constraint to the production of IEs.[41]

- *Incentives to avoid evaluating and reporting on failures:* In open-ended interviews with World Bank senior management, one-third of the managers expressed the need for more tolerance for IEs that evaluate and report on failing interventions. It is unclear if this represents a bias toward selecting well-performing projects for IE or a tendency to not publish negative findings. There is as much learning potential from failure as from success, suggesting an institutional push may be needed to facilitate such learning.

- *Project timing and staff transitions as a constraint to producing relevant and high-quality IEs:* The system of World Bank staff tenure and rotation can pose problems for IE work, given the long time it typically takes for an IE to be completed, as well as the time required to absorb learning from IE.[42] In open-ended interviews, this specific issue was raised by 4 of 21 World Bank managers and directors. Similarly, a PREM note (World Bank 2008) points out that most IEs outlast the average tenure of a task team leader, and there is no guarantee that the next team leader will be committed to, or capable of, undertaking this activity. Additionally, in areas where program impacts are realized after a long lag (for example, infrastructure) and after project closure, the interest of operational teams and clients as well as resources to do IEs are more difficult to obtain, contributing to fewer evaluations in these topics despite their learning potential.[43]

- *Weak incentives to produce IEs if they are not used:* If learning from IEs is not absorbed or used, there is also less incentive to conduct them. One-third of surveyed evaluators and team leaders in the World Bank Group cited lack of mechanisms to learn from and act on IE findings as a constraint to the production of IEs. At IFC in particular, this is a challenge, as the M&E system (that is, reach indicators) focuses on measuring access to end users (funding or number reached), whereas measurement of outcomes further down the results chain is not required as long as there is demand from stakeholders.

At the World Bank, the technical capacity of staff to conduct IE is not sufficient in certain units; in IFC, capacity is more sharply constrained. In the World Bank, according to a 2010 DIME estimate, there are 79 people (including both full-time and part-time staff) who are doing IE and who have IE skills, and they are unevenly distributed across 12 departments. Almost one-third of the people with IE skills are in DEC (25), followed by the Africa Region (12) and HDN (World Bank 2010). These departments are also coordinating the majority of IE work at the World Bank (for example, IE initiatives such as DIME, SIEF, and AIM are housed in DEC, HDN, and the Africa Region, respectively, and account for more than half of ongoing IEs).

In contrast, the growing portfolio of IEs in other departments with fewer IE skills (such as SDN and FPD) relies greatly on DEC/DIME support (for example, AADAPT and DIME-FPD). A few managers who were interviewed (3 of 22) were of the opinion that many teams have people with skills that can be retooled to work on IE and that there are many IE experts at the World Bank who can provide technical assistance to other teams.

Capacity poses a greater constraint to IE production at IFC.[44] In IFC, the conduct of IEs started with the efforts of a few technically skilled staff, but overall staff capacity to conduct an IE has not developed significantly. In interviews, some transaction leaders and business lines staff indicated that operational staff in IFC does not have the capacity to decide whether or what to evaluate or to supervise IEs. Even M&E specialists who are responsible for the selection of the most appropriate evaluation approaches for the project have varying knowledge and skills on this type of evaluation.

FUNDING

As mentioned in chapter 2, the reliance on external sources of funding for IEs has increased over time. At the World Bank, IEs initiated in 2007 and later (70 percent) are more likely to be paid for by various trust funds than IEs started in 2005–06 (47 percent) or earlier (10 percent).[45] The growing dependence on trust funds to finance IEs is reflective of the trend toward increasing reliance on trust funds to finance analytical work at the World Bank (IEG 2011b). At IFC, funding for IEs has been mostly from the RMU's M&E budget. Increasingly, IFC IEs are being conducted with more resources drawn from regional, business line budgets, and donor funding and less from the RMU budget.

At the World Bank, the fragmentation in available external resources for IE adds to staff transaction costs.[46] The increasing reliance of World Bank IEs on trust fund resources has been accompanied by several of these IEs receiving support from multiple external sources, which leads to high transaction costs for staff (IEG 2011b).[47] For instance, a single IE of a malaria intervention in Nigeria is receiving funding from six different sources, including four separate trust funds (the Bank-Netherlands Partnership Program, SIEF, the UK Department for International Development, and the Japan Social Development Fund).[48]

The growing reliance on trust funds at the World Bank is not necessarily detrimental to IE relevance, but it is less flexible. Donor support for IEs through trust funds is motivated by several factors. In some cases, donors are interested in learning about and funding topics of significance to their mission (for example, Gates Foundation support for IEs in hand washing and sanitation). In other instances, donors earmarks specific funds for topics that have been previously under-researched (such as results based financing in health) and/ or they might prioritize funding to low-income countries or regions such as Sub-Saharan Africa (for instance, the Education Policy Development Fund and the Bank-Netherlands Partnership Program), where financial support and/or capacity for IEs is otherwise scarce.[49]

Although some of the conditions on prioritization of topics and countries have facilitated IE production in previously underresearched regions and questions, the conditions on and where and how[50] to allocate resources can also limit flexibility in allocating money *across* diverse priority areas.[51] In open-ended interviews with Bank management, one-fifth of interviewees mentioned lack of predictability and flexibility in funding as a problem.

Notes

1 The relevance of IEs assessed in this chapter does not appraise the relevance of the evaluated project components—or the entire project—to addressing major development challenges.

2 There are only four IEs not aligned with the development objective, mainly because the IEs look at indirect (CCT objectives versus entrepreneurship) or second-order effects (reduction in transaction cost from business simplification versus firm profitability). There are four other cases where the objectives are not available.

3 An alternative measure used was if the appraisal document made *any* reference to a planned IE, irrespective of any plans for baseline data collection. A third measure was based on the assessment of the team member, after having reviewed project documentation and IE reports. This exercise was done for completed and ongoing IE linked to a World Bank lending operation, which were also included in the desk review. Because the objective of this exercise is to check alignment between IE and operational needs, the measures of "prospective" IEs are intended to capture the extent to which IEs are mainstreamed in the design of World Bank Group operations, not based on the choice of IE design (experimental or quasi-experimental).

4 Among prospective World Bank IEs (that have been *completed* and *linked to a lending project)*, around a third used experimental methods. The incidence of experimental designs in nonprospective IEs was smaller but by a small (and not statistically significant) margin. The findings are robust to using two alternative measures of prospective IEs mentioned in the preceding endnote. IEs not linked to a lending operation are far more likely to use experimental methods, but these have been *excluded* from the results presented. These IEs not linked to a Bank lending operation are usually of two types. The first type evaluates impacts of nongovernmental organization, other donor, or government programs not supported by the Bank. Because the documentation on these programs is not available to the team, it cannot be verified whether the IEs are prospective (from an operational standpoint). The other, far more prevalent, type evaluates small-scale *stand-alone* interventions that have been set up *for the purpose* of testing causal impacts. Such IEs are therefore by default built into the design of the intervention.

5 Using an alternative measure, IEG finds that appraisal documents linked to 31 percent of completed World Bank and 50 percent IFC IEs made any reference to a planned IE, irrespective of any plans for data collection. There was no statistically significant

difference between projects of randomized and nonrandomized completed Bank IEs in the referencing plan for an IE in the appraisal documents. IEG also finds that lending and advisory service projects linked to 35 percent of World Bank IEs and 30 percent of IFC IEs, respectively, mentioned any plan for baseline data at the design stage, irrespective of any mention of a planned IE, which could be useful for conducting nonprospective IE. Planning the baseline with the IE in mind could ensure that data are collected in a way that makes postproject comparison useful. This raises the importance of planning and budgeting data collection early, ideally before the project starts.

6 Alternatively, project documents for 70 percent of a random sample of ongoing World Bank IEs made any mention of the IE being planned IE for the project (31 of 44), and projects linked with 52 percent of ongoing IEs reviewed made reference to a plan for baseline data collection (23 of 44). Similarly, among IEs subject to desk review, projects of IEs initiated in 2005–10 are more likely to reference plans for an evaluation in the appraisal document (42 of 72)than those initiated earlier (26 of 70).

7 Alternatively, the difference in the proportion of projects linked to ongoing versus completed IEs that made any reference to a planned IE is also statistically significant. The results are still statistically significant if IE design is controlled for (whether the IE is experimental or non-experimental).

8 Disaggregating survey results by active and completed IEs yields similar numbers as those based on the desk review of projects linked to active and completed IEs. The finding holds if the sample is restricted to IEs initiated during 2005–10 and/or if IE design is controlled for (whether the IE is experimental or non-experimental).

9 Among completed IEs, there is no statistically significant difference between experimental versus non-experimental IEs in their propensity to measure longer-term outcomes. The difference is still statistically not significant when controlling for time trends.

10 Evidence of this has been found, for instance, for some early childhood development programs, which led to learning gains in early primary school that disappeared in later years of schooling. The IE of the Southwest China Poverty Reduction in China, ten years after program started and four years after disbursement ended, shows sizeable short-term income gains that were mostly saved. However, only small and statistically insignificant gains to mean consumption emerged in the longer-term.

11 For instance, around 40 percent of IEs initiated in 2009–10 will be spanned over 4–6 years, compared with around 30 percent of IEs initiated in preceding years. The difference is much more pronounced if IEs spanning 3–6 years are compared across these two time periods (74 percent versus 52 percent). These numbers are based on IE start and end dates, as given in the DIME database, and have not been cleaned. Comparing this proxy measure of exposure with the actual exposure period recorded for 75 completed IEs led to the belief that the finding is not completely misleading.

12 Among completed IEs, those initiated in 2005 or later are more likely than those initiated in the pre-2005 period to evaluate treatment variations—the difference being statistically significant. Similar results are obtained when the IE method (experimental and non-experimental) is controlled for. The results also suggest a positive association between experimental IE design and the propensity of completed IEs to evaluate treatment variations. This is robust to including time fixed effects. If we introduce an interaction effect between the dummy for experimental IEs and the dummy for IEs initiated in 2005 or later, the marginal effect is positive and statistically significant—that is, experimental IEs initiated in the later time period are more likely to assess differential impacts of treatment variations. This is partly because it is sometimes more feasible for randomized controlled trials to test alternative treatment strategies and the interaction between them in affecting outcomes. For instance, it might be politically infeasible for a government to roll out a national CCT program where beneficiaries with similar characteristics get different levels of cash subsidies. But a small-scale pilot in two villages that are geographically separate enough to avoid information spillovers can feasibly test the impacts of varying levels of cash subsidies. Consistent with this, among completed IEs, those linked to lending projects were less likely to evaluate treatment interventions.

13 For instance, an AADAPT IE in Ethiopia, initiated in 2009, is testing alternative information interventions to measure their effect on smallholders' livelihoods. In Malawi, another AADAPT IE, also initiated in 2009, is testing a variety of communication strategies to promote both "conservation agriculture" practices and fertilizer management among smallholder maize producers. In contrast, no completed IEs in agriculture evaluated treatment variations. Health results-based financing IEs are another notable example; as mentioned before, IEs in at least 10 of 14 countries implementing such interventions are testing simultaneous interventions. In another example, CCTs initiated in the past few years are assessing complicated aspects, for instance, by combining CCTs with other interventions (for example, IEs in Indonesia, Morocco, South Arica, and Nicaragua) or varying the CCT structure across different groups (for example, IEs in Pakistan, Burkina Faso, and Malawi).

14 For instance, the Water and Sanitation Program has set up similarly designed experiments in hand washing and rural sanitation interventions in six countries to understand how certain models may have impacts in varying situations.

15 Completed IEs using experimental methods were more likely to do an efficiency analysis (the difference being statistically significant). However, if the sample is restricted to IEs of lending operations, the difference—though positive—is not statistically significant.

16 An IE was mapped to the relevant sector strategy based on the sector board of the project that includes the evaluated intervention. IEG assigned the evaluated intervention to a different sector strategy only if the sector board of the project did not correspond to the particular intervention being evaluated. For each sector strategy, the team grouped the priorities into three to five key focus areas (or

substrategies) and matched the evaluated intervention to one relevant focus area in the strategy to which it was mapped. For example, an evaluated education access intervention in a project managed by the Education Sector Board would be assigned the substrategy Access and Equity under the Education Sector Strategy, whereas an evaluated CCT intervention with education objectives under a Social Protection project would be mapped to the Human Capital Development focus area under the Social Protection Sector Strategy. Based on this approach, there was no double counting. This coding exercise was also carried out for the random sample of 54 World Bank IEs selected for desk review, but the sample size is considered too small to capture intrasectoral variations, as shown in figure 3.1 for completed World Bank IEs.

17 Five IEs are not aligned with the priorities of the sector board under which the evaluated projects were managed because they assessed components that are more relevant for other sector boards.

18 There are only 30 IFC IEs, and they cover only a small part of the IFC portfolio, so comparison with the portfolio is not suitable.

19 Some recent IEs in local governance are using behavioral group activities or "games" (such as risk games, altruism games, trust games, public goods games) to capture institutional outcomes, relationships, attitudes, and values that govern interactions among people and contribute to economic and social development. For instance, in the IE of the GoBifo project in Sierra Leone, one of the IE questions was to assess the impact on inclusion, participation, and collective action. However, it is difficult to gauge these dynamics through survey responses alone. To this end, the IE team conducted three participatory exercises. During these activities, the research teams introduced a standardized, real-world decision, asset and opportunity, and observed how the communities responded. One of these exercises examined whether GoBifo had lingering effects on the capacity for collective action and if it served as a catalyst for group activity beyond the life of the project itself. The communities received six vouchers they could redeem at a nearby building materials store if they raised matching funds. Specifically, each card was worth 50,000 Leones only if accompanied by 100,000 Leones from the community. Topping up all six cards generated 900,000 Leones or approximately $300 for use in the store. During the final survey five months later, the research team explored the relative take-up of the program, how inclusive and transparent the management of the resulting project was, and the quality of final construction. This exercise captures the degree to which the experience of project management under GoBifo enhanced the capacity of villagers to act collectively and take up a development opportunity outside the direct sphere of the project. If community-driven development has long-term impacts on communal ability to come together and "help themselves," greater take-up and better management of the building materials program in treatment communities would be expected. In another exercise, the research team left each village with a large plastic tarpaulin, frequently used as a makeshift shelter or roof and in agriculture to dry grains or protect them from rain. This activity examines elite capture, a common concern and risk inherent in community-driven development's emphasis on devolving

control to local power structures. During the follow-up visit, enumerators explored the distribution of access to the tarp across households, as well as who received any salt/batteries and who contributed funds to and received benefits from the building materials. This exercise also has a collective action component, as teams gauged whether the village had come up with a use for the tarp and whether they put it toward public or private ends.

20 One of the most famous products of an IE within the Bank and in the academic community specifically measures the externality that deworming drugs in Kenya may have on populations that did not receive it. The World Bank collaborated with the Harvard-MIT team and used the results of this work in the Bank's program. If the researcher and/or the implementing institution identifies spillover effects as a priority, then the sample design can be used to accommodate these concerns. A recent methodological paper focusing specifically on IEs and spill-over effect has been featured in the Inter-American Development Bank working paper series (Angelucci and Di Maro 2010). This information is based on discussions with World Bank management.

21 When IEG applied some of these normative assumptions (namely, whether bias is expected to be a major issue and existing knowledge gaps) to projects that could have been assessed based on technical grounds, the exercise identified around 20–25 percent of education interventions where IEs, if done, would have been valuable.

22 A list of 59 priority knowledge questions was gathered from researchers and development practitioners at the Australian Agency for International Development, the U.K. Department for International Development, and the International Initiative for Impact Evaluations (3IE). These questions now guide the joint call for proposals by the three institutions for systematic reviews. Although some of the questions may be influenced by the strategic objectives of these three institutions, the topics reflect emerging issues that are of interest to three major players—and probably many other institutions engaged in development.

23 Although a greater proportion of completed IEs using randomization was aligned with knowledge priorities (44 percent versus 37 percent), the difference is not statistically significant. If ongoing IEs reviewed in the sample are included, randomized IEs are more likely to be aligned—the difference being statistically significant, even when time fixed effects are controlled for. According to surveys, which include responses for both completed and ongoing IEs, randomized IEs are on average more often reported to be filling a global knowledge gap; the difference is statistically significant. However, if time fixed effects are included, the statistical significance is diluted.

24 When the IEs that were reviewed for knowledge relevance as defined by 3IE, the U.K. Department for International Development, and Australian Agency for International Development are included, again a statistically significant difference in the proportion of IEs initiated in 2007–10 and that were aligned with knowledge priorities compared to IEs initiated in earlier years is seen.

25 Survey respondents for eight of eight IFC IEs believed that these IEs have contributed to filling the knowledge gap.

26 Cluster briefs set out the nature of the intervention, the rationale for the work, the outcomes to be measured, a set of possible countries where interventions of this type may be able to be implemented, and estimated costs and time-table for the work over the following three years.

27 The six clusters were CCT, HIV/AIDS prevention, basic education accountability, malaria control, health contracting/performance, and active labor markets/youth employment.

28 The process is as follows: Proposals are submitted to the program manager and then sent for initial vetting by the technical committee. If the committee recommends the proposal for further development, it will be sent for anonymous technical peer review. Up to the overall allocation ceiling specified by the Steering Committee, for all proposals that pass review and that are endorsed by the technical committee, the program manager will have the authority to fund the evaluation (up to a ceiling of $600,000 per evaluation).

29 The Africa Program for Education Impact Evaluation, Malaria Impact Evaluation, the Health Results-Based Financing IE program, the Africa Impact Evaluation Program on HIV/AIDS, AADAPT in Africa, Latin America, and South Asia, the Active Labor Market IE Program, the Gender Program, the IE program in Finance and Private Sector, and the Fragile States Program.

30 DIME tries to implement programs in partnership with sector management (World Bank 2010). Good examples are the management of the Africa Region's education, health, agriculture, and private sectors; the Latin America agriculture and private sectors; Brazil Country Management Unit; PREM in the Middle East and North Africa Region; and South Asia's rural livelihood team.

31 The core delegation usually includes a director-level official from the relevant ministry (policy making); a program manager (knowledge of the intervention); and an economist/statistician (follow-up). The delegations are trained in IE methods and exposed to international IE results relevant to their sector. In the clinics, the delegations design the IE, facilitated by an IE expert. On the last day, each delegation presents its designs for plenary discussion. The clinics are facilitated by IE experts, who stimulate discussion around the evidence and foster a process of critical thinking aimed at defining a learning agenda (World Bank 2010).

32 Consistent with the expansion of the programmatic model in 2009—first piloted in the Africa Program for Education Impact Evaluation in 2007—under which project teams are supported with the design of IEs through workshops and clinics described here, there is evidence of an increase in IEs being jointly developed by project teams and IE initiatives at the World Bank. According to surveys, in 2009–10, 26 percent of IEs were initiated by project teams *and* IE initiatives at the World Bank (for example, DIME), compared with 4 percent in the preceding years.

33 This information is based on open-ended questions. The responses must be interpreted with care, as absence of any mention of a particular issue by a sector manager, for instance, does not mean that the issue is not extant in that sector. The response rates should therefore be interpreted as a lower bound.

34 The programmatic model was first tested for the Africa Program for Education Impact Evaluation. In Abuja in 2007, the country delegates and the team task leaders received training on IE and international evidence on education policies. Each team applied its new knowledge to the development of the IE for its education program. Ghana was interested in evaluating school management committees, and Senegal was interested in school grants.

35 Based on a desk review of completed IEs for alignment with the results framework and the survey question on who IE initiated the IE, 88 percent of IEs initiated by project teams are aligned with the project results framework, compared with 65 percent of IEs not initiated by project teams.

36 For instance, among completed IEs that were linked to a lending project, IEs that are a formal part of the project design are more likely to measure outcomes articulated in project results, even after controlling for type of IE design and time fixed effects.

37 The *use* of IE as an integral part of project M&E was compared against (i) reference to IE *and* baseline data collection plans in the appraisal document, (ii) reference to IE *or* baseline data collection and plans in the appraisal document, and (iii) a survey question on if IE was conceived alongside the project and M&E plan. The three comparisons yielded similar results. Projects that had IE as part of the formal project design and M&E were considered more useful (50–58 percent) than projects that did not integrate the IE in the project and M&E design (16–23 percent). In addition, a simple double difference analysis, using survey data, suggests that this relationship is fairly stable over time. Although both IEs that are a formal part of the project plan as well as IEs initiated in 2007–10 are on average more like to be considered useful, the interaction term between the two is not statistically significant. The results hold if the sample is restricted to randomized IEs or if this is added as a control. Additional specifications using triple differencing with HDN as the third variable does not yield any different patterns either. Robust standard errors were clustered at the country level in all specifications.

38 These questions were looked at using data from surveys (where responses for ongoing IEs dominate) as well as data based on the desk review (where the sample is mostly completed IEs). In the subsample analysis, whether the IE was planned in advance (irrespective of whether the IE is mentioned in the PAD) was also measured using different definitions: those that were coded prospective based on desk review of project documentation (including PADs, aide-memoires, other mission documents, or IE reports) or those that used randomization. Similarly, whether the IE is part of the formal project plan was measured in two ways: based on a desk review of PADs as well as survey questions to the effect. Regardless of the data source or measure used, the results were fairly similar. For instance, the results consistently showed that even among IEs planned prior to the intervention,

around half (48–56 percent) of IEs mentioned in project plans were used as an integral part of project M&E, compared with less than one-fourth (13–25 percent) of IEs not part of project plans but planned in advance.

39 The three main constraining factors identified in the interview are same for both World Bank and IFC.

40 Reference to an interview question on factors affecting the production of IEs in their sectors or regions, 13 of 21 World Bank managers and directors scored staff incentives as 3 or lower on a scale of 1–6 (1 being not available and 6 being wholly available).

41 Four of six product leaders.

42 The exception is DEC, where researchers have longer tenures (World Bank 2008).

43 This issue was raised by two interviewees and in the comments from World Bank management.

44 Forty-three percent of IFC versus 30 percent of World Bank survey respondents considered lack of staff capacity as a constraint on the IE production.

45 Interviews with Bank management also confirm that trust funds have become a more prominent source of IE financing over time.

46 Interviews with trust funds recipient officials conducted for the IEG evaluation of trust funds (IEG 2011b) reveals that when trust funds *pool* piecemeal bilateral aid, it reduces transaction cost.

47 The trust fund evaluation (IEG 2011b) finds—based on country reviews and staff interviews—that although staff look to trust funds to supplement Bank budget, they perceive at the same time that it costs more to manage trust-funded activities than trust funds typically provide for this purpose. In other words, it costs the Bank more to manage trust funds than is captured in available data. Furthermore, in IEG's trust fund evaluation, one of the specific problems cited by Bank staff and managers interviewed was the need to "reinvent the wheel" with each new trust fund. The IEG evaluation of trust funds also cites that, in general, heavy reliance on trust funds at the World Bank has had implications for management oversight. However, there is no evidence to suggest that heavy reliance on trust funds has had implications on quality assurance of IEs—quality assurance being one of the oversight functions. In fact, IEs initiated in recent years—most of which are trust fund supported—are more likely to be subject to expert review; they also have higher participation of operational teams in the review process, especially for the SIEF, the largest trust fund to support IEs at the World Bank.

48 This is by no means a unique example, and several other IEs receive funding from multiple external sources. For instance, in both Senegal and Burundi, the HIV/AIDS IE is receiving funding from four external sources: In Burundi, the HIV/AIDS IE is funded by UNAIDS Unified Budget and Work Plan; the Global Fund to Fight AIDS, Tuberculosis and Malaria; the Bank-Netherlands Partnership Program; and the

Belgian Poverty Reduction Partnership. In Senegal, the HIV/AIDS IE is funded by UNAIDS Unified Budget and Work Plan; the Global Fund to Fight AIDS, Tuberculosis and Malaria; ILO Youth Employment Network; and SIEF.

49 Partly as a result of these resources, IEs in Africa have increased substantially in recent years. By contrast, the increase in IE activity in middle-income countries has not been as large. Although the number of IEs grew from 54 to 98 from 2000 to 2006 versus 2007–10 in low-income countries, it increased from 108 to 136 from middle-income countries. Excluding Brazil, Nigeria, and South Africa—the three middle-income countries with the largest increase in IEs between the two periods—the number of IEs in middle-income countries initiated in 2007–10 is lower than the number of IEs initiated in 2000–06. In parallel, surveys suggest that the proportion of IEs in upper-middle-income countries funded by government/projects has somewhat declined, the decline being more pronounced after excluding Brazil and South Africa, which had the largest increase in IEs among upper-middle-income countries between the two reference periods.

50 For instance, IEG's evaluation of trust funds (IEG 2011b) notes that in the Japan Social Development Fund and the Trust Fund for Environmentally and Socially Sustainable Development (and in the Bank-Netherlands Partnership Program until FY10), officials in the donor's capital retain final say over proposals selected by the Bank screening process. This practice attenuates the Bank's accountability for selections that have been made according to agreed processes.

51 In the same vein, the Trust Fund Quality Assurance and Compliance Group in 2010 posed the question: Is it appropriate to have donors approving what has already been delineated in trust fund agreements, especially where such proposals have already been vetted by the Bank's quality assurance and management framework (IEG 2011b)?

References

Angelucci, Manuela, and Vincenzo Di Maro. 2010. "Program Evaluation and Spillover Effects." SPD Working Paper 1003, Inter-American Development Bank, Office of Strategic Planning and Development Effectiveness, Washington, DC.

Gertler P.J., S. Martinez, P. Premand, L. Rawlings, and C.M.J. Vermeersch. 2011. *Impact Evaluation in Practice*. Washington, DC: World Bank.

IEG (Independent Evaluation Group). 2011a. *Evidence and Lessons Learned from Impact Evaluations on Social Safety Nets*. Washington, DC: World Bank.

———. 2011b. *Trust Fund Support for Development: An Evaluation of the World Bank's Trust Fund Portfolio*. Washington, DC: World Bank.

Karlan, D. 2009. "Thoughts on Randomized Trials for Evaluation of Development: Presentation to the Cairo Evaluation Clinic." 3IE Working Paper No. 4, pp. 8–13. 3IE, New Delhi.

McKenzie, D. 2009. "Impact Assessments in Finance and Private Sector Development: What Have We Learned and What Should We Learn?" World Bank Policy Research Working Paper No. 4944, Washington, DC.

Ravallion, M. 2009. "Evaluation in the Practice of Development." *World Bank Research Observer* 24(1): 29–53.

World Bank. 2010. "Development Impact Evaluation Initiative: A World Bank-Wide Strategic Approach to Enhance Developmental Effectiveness." World Bank, Washington, DC.

———. 2008. "Assessing Our Work on Impact Evaluation." PREM Notes No. 126. World Bank, Washington, DC.

Chapter 4

Quality of World Bank Group
Impact Evaluations

The quality of IEs is critical for their credibility, use, and influence. The credibility of IE findings affects their potential influence on development practice. Even if an IE has the appropriate motivation and asks questions that are important to development policy, constraints in data, evaluation design, and technical capacity may undermine its ability to credibly assess the effectiveness of an intervention. Inaccurate findings can contradict what is observed on the ground or lead to incorrect recommendations, which could undermine the reliability of the IE and its usefulness. In addition, the possibility of "inferential risk" arises from asymmetric information about the quality of these evaluations. Some users—program administrators and decision makers—may not differentiate between reliable and flawed evidence and would use both to guide decision making.

This chapter appraises the technical quality of World Bank Group IEs to shed light on the extent to which they meet expected standards. Multiple factors determine the quality of an IE, including how thoroughly it manages to accurately capture and measure outcomes, isolate and estimate the contribution of a particular intervention, and interpret the findings in a meaningful way. In this report IEG recognizes a broad range of approaches, ranging from randomized controlled trials to different quasi-experimental techniques, used to address the central issue of attribution of impacts to interventions.

To assess the quality of IEs is not to indicate which methods are superior. Rather, the main IE principle focuses on establishing causal effects. Irrespective of the method used, the evaluation needs to demonstrate that the assumptions of the methods are acknowledged and tested and that the findings are robust to methodological issues. Similarly, IEG assesses the choice of indicators (depending on what is available or can be measured) and whether this affects how well the outcomes are predicted. Following this logic, the chapter first lays out the methodology for assessing IE quality, then examines quality through three lenses—data, outcome indicators, and establishment of causal effects—and discusses the factors that affect quality. The analysis is based on evidence from 166 completed IEs (140 from the World Bank and 26 from IFC).[1]

The analysis of quality for completed IEs to which the World Bank Group contributed reveals that:

- World Bank IEs are of medium or high quality, but some quality aspects could be improved, especially among those that rely on quasi-experimental methods.

  - Ninety-four percent of completed World Bank IEs meet medium (40 percent) or high (54 percent) standards of quality based on their frequent reliance on baseline data, use of well-defined and appropriate outcome indicators, and ability to credibly establish the causal effects of the intervention and deal with potential selection biases. This is aligned with the perception of senior management about the technical quality of World Bank IEs (12 of 13 respondents rated them 4 or higher, on a scale of 6).

- Even though most of the IEs tested the validity of their methods and conducted some form of robustness check, their scope and technical quality vary widely, particular among those employing quasi-experimental methods.

- There has been an improvement in the technical quality of completed World Bank IEs over time. For instance, 51 percent of completed IEs that were initiated from 2000–04 met high quality standards (90 percent met at least medium quality standards). Comparatively, 71 percent of completed World Bank IEs initiated in 2005 or later met high quality standards (98 percent met at least medium quality standards).

- With some exceptions, there are presently no *formal and standardized* mechanisms at the World Bank to ensure that all evaluations go through similar quality controls. Recent IE initiatives like SIEF have established formal quality review procedures that apply uniformly to all SIEF IEs. It is too early to assess these IEs for their quality, but IEs initiated under this approach are more likely to be subject to specialist review at concept stage. A more formal process could guarantee that, with the large number of new IEs being initiated each year, individual evaluations continue to receive the scrutiny and feedback needed to ensure high quality.

- Around half of IFC IEs are of medium (27 percent) or high (19 percent) quality—their weak evaluation design being the main cause of low quality. Problems include weak construction of counterfactuals, little analysis of potential biases and other methodological issues that can affect the validity of the evaluation to estimate causal effects, and inference analyses that rely on very small samples.

  - Forty-six percent of completed IFC IEs (12 of 26) meet medium or high standards of quality. IEs that did not meet medium or high quality standards were less careful in constructing a robust counterfactual to assess what would have happened to beneficiaries in the absence of the program, which can result in misleading conclusions. They were also less likely to adequately address selection bias and other methodological issues that can affect the validity of the evaluation. Finally, the quantitative analyses of some of these IEs relied on samples that were too small to infer outcomes in a statistically meaningful sense.

  - Thirty-five percent of completed IFC IEs (9 of 26) were subject to some form of review by specialists not part of the project team, usually M&E specialists at IFC.

- The weakness in the technical quality of IEs is explained in part by weak quality review controls. In IFC, in particular, the lower technical quality of IEs reflects that the IFC IE agenda is still in its formative stage—the conduct of IEs started in 2005 as a pilot and with limited resources, and there have been no policies or strategies—with limited staff capacity to understand and supervise IEs, and no quality assurance mechanisms.

Quality Review Methodology

The framework used to review the technical quality of World Bank Group IEs originates from a well-developed literature. The IEG team referred to theoretical and practical guidelines that mandate how IEs should be conducted to fulfill its scope and adapt to the available resources (Gertler and others 2011; Khandker, Koolwal, and Samad 2010; NONIE 2009; Duflo, Glennerster, and Kremer 2006; Imbens and Wooldridge 2009; Imbens and Lemieux 2008; and Blundell and Costa Dias 2008). The assessment framework follows objective standards that cover the bulk of the aspects that make up the quality of IEs (detailed description in appendix F). It was developed and validated with guidance from an IE expert. The following criteria were applied to identify IEs that provide reliable and well-measured evidence on effects in a causal manner, regardless of the intended audience of the report:

- **Data:** IEG characterized the type of data used by the evaluation (longitudinal, pooled cross-section, or single cross-section), the source of data (survey, administrative, or census), and the availability of real-time (as opposed to retrospective) and baseline data. This information would help determine the reliability of the data.

- **Outcome indicators:** IEG examined whether the indicators chosen are good proxies for the outcomes and questions of interest and whether they logically result from the program results chain. In particular, IEG explored whether the outcome variables are well defined; are presented with proper measurement units; can be affected within the timeframe of the evaluation; are distinct from the program inputs, outputs, or conditions; and reflect effects on short- or long-term outcomes of the program.[2]

- **Evaluation design:** IEG documented the different strategies and methods used by each IE to attribute the impacts to the intervention (for example, randomization, double differences, matching, instrumental variable, and regression discontinuity design). Depending on the method, the review verified whether the IE tested or discussed the validity of the assumptions that would make the method credible. It also checked whether the IE assessed the comparability in observable characteristics between the control and treatment groups at baseline and explicitly addressed any differences between the two groups that can threaten the validity of the evaluation to attribute impacts to programs.

- **Robustness of the analysis:** IEG reviewed the various ways that the evaluation tested the robustness of the findings. The credibility of the results is enhanced if they are not sensitive to different model specifications, estimation methods, and other issues that can threaten the internal validity of the analysis. Special attention was given to evaluations that use quasi-experimental approaches because of their reliance on stronger assumptions, compared with those that rely on randomized evaluation designs.

- **Review process:** Finally, IEG gathered information on whether the evaluation went through an internal/external peer review process, either at the concept or completion stage, to validate its methodological quality.[3]

The assessment included 140 completed World Bank IEs (all 119 completed evaluations of World Bank lending or nonlending projects[4] and a random sample of 21 [of 43 total IEs] completed evaluations of projects or interventions not financed by the World Bank) and 26 completed IEs of IFC advisory service projects.[5] A separate team member then reviewed all the assessments to ensure consistency.

Each IE was coded for how thoroughly it adhered to different quality criteria. It was then assigned a value of *high, medium,* or *low* quality based on its overall ability to demonstrate the credibility of its findings across several aspects related to the validity of the evaluation design, type of data and outcome indicators, and robustness to potential methodological issues (appendix F). In other words, the objective of the analysis was to distinguish IEs that produce reliable findings (that is, *medium* and *high* quality) from those that have findings that require significant additional analytical work and discussion to be credible (that is, findings of *low* quality).

Data Quality and Outcome Indicators

The majority of IEs, particularly those supported by the World Bank, used baseline data, many of them to strengthen the quality and scope of the analysis. IE is a data-intensive exercise and, at a minimum, requires data on the allocation of the benefits, the outcomes of interest, and the relevant characteristics of the treatment and comparison groups. Ideally, however, IEs should also include baseline data to illustrate the preprogram situation and enhance the quality of the evaluation design and the ability to make statistical inferences. Three-quarters (74 percent) of World Bank IEs used at least some baseline data and so did more than half (58 percent) of IFC evaluations. Baseline data allow comparison of the characteristics and outcomes of the treatment and control groups (the core aspect of IE). Two-thirds (66 percent) of World Bank and more than half (58 percent) of IFC IEs conducted this check.

Most IEs conducted their own surveys, including collecting longitudinal information, and relied on real-time data so they had more control over the quality and suitability of the data for analytical purposes. Because information on potential data problems (missing data, measurement errors, and sampling errors) is not consistently presented in the IE reports, the IEG team could only collect information on some factors that could call into question the quality of data. First, data collected through recall may not be accurate, especially if they involve events that are difficult to remember or happened a long time before. IEG found that a number of evaluations relied on recall data (50 percent of IFC and 29 percent of World Bank IEs). Fortunately, the ones that did rely on recall data mostly used retrospective data for only some of the outcomes.

Second, existing survey data could be useful and save costs, but they can have many limitations in size, scope, sampling, and frequency. The researchers have no control over what is collected. Although no IFC IEs used solely existing data, 38 World Bank IEs (27 percent) used only data from such sources as national household surveys or program administration (table 4.1). Three-quarters of World Bank and all IFC IEs collected some additional data, whereas 41 percent of World Bank IEs and 85 percent of IFC IEs used data exclusively from surveys especially conducted for evaluation purposes, likely allowing for stronger evaluation designs and a broader scope for the analysis. Although more costly and difficult to obtain, longitudinal data could also be very beneficial to account for other factors (for example, individual characteristics) that could bias the findings. Two-thirds of the IEs (64 percent) used some of this type of data.

The data sources used in the IEs are likely not widely available for replication or further work. One way of checking the credibility of an analysis is through replications of the findings by other researchers using the same data sets. In addition, considering that data collected for IE purposes are often rich and cover a variety of socioeconomic variables, they can also be used to initiate follow-up evaluations using the same cohort through further waves of the panel data, undertake additional analysis, and, more broadly, generate other knowledge products and advance the research agenda on other development subjects. Although the availability of data was not directly measured, existing evidence regarding the larger M&E databases of projects shows that data tend not to be widely accessible. For the FY00–09 period, the World Bank lending and technical assistance projects spent $419 million on data collection; only an estimated 5 percent of those data sets are available in any Bank data repository.

In addition, the general view among people interviewed for this study is that the access to IE data is highly restricted both externally and within the World Bank, partly because the data are a valuable source of information to generate journal publications for researchers. All of the data documentation efforts in SIEF and DIME are coordinated with the DEC Data Group's micro data initiative

Table 4.1	Sources of Data Used in Completed Impact Evaluations (percent)		
Sources	Surveys conducted for the evaluation	Pre-existing surveys	Administrative data
World Bank	73	35	36
IFC	100	0	15

Source: IEG.

Note: Based on reports of 140 World Bank IEs and 26 IFC IEs completed during 2000–10.

and researchers are strongly encouraged to register their data and make them publicly available, but this is a recent initiative.

Eighty-nine percent of Bank Group IEs used well-defined and appropriate indicators. Many indicators chosen reflect what needs to be measured, for example, school enrollment and attendance as a proxy for educational use, tests scores for learning, height and weight for children's nutritional status, and income and consumption for the welfare of households. Most indicators were directly measurable using specific units that are comparable across evaluations. Even outcomes that are more likely to be defined subjectively (such as corruption and social capital) were converted into measurable and comparable indicators, as established by the relevant literature.[6]

Most of the outcomes evaluated are distinguishable from the inputs or outputs of the projects and can be plausibly affected within the evaluated time frame of the project. Only a few IEs investigated indicators that measure the outputs of the interventions and compliance with their conditions (kilometers of roads built in a road rehabilitation program). This might not be the best use of IE, because these are immediate outputs and could be measured more easily and cheaply (although with a more limited ability to infer attribution) through monitoring or process evaluations.

Another characteristic of Bank Group IEs is that most (85 percent of IFC IEs and 92 percent of World Bank IEs) investigated changes in outcomes that could possibly be achieved during the time elapsed since the intervention.[7] However, the majority of IEs (81 percent of IFC and 89 percent of World Bank IEs) have focused only on measuring short-term outcomes; as a result, they have not contributed much to the understanding of medium- and long-term impacts of development interventions (19 percent of IFC IEs and 11 percent of World Bank IEs) (figure 4.1).

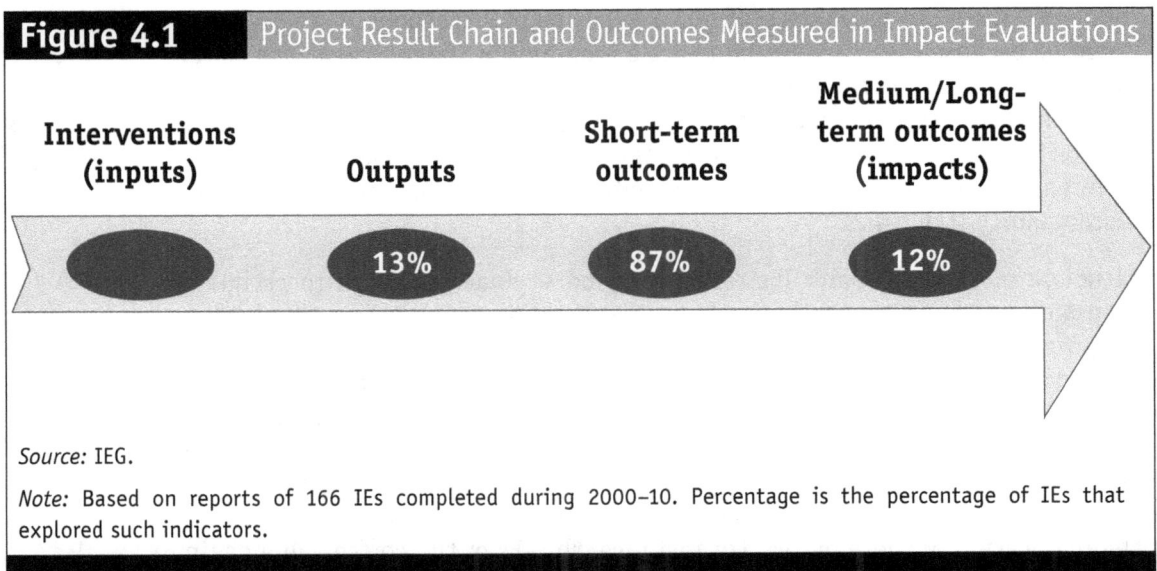

Figure 4.1   Project Result Chain and Outcomes Measured in Impact Evaluations

Interventions (inputs)   Outputs   Short-term outcomes   Medium/Long-term outcomes (impacts)

13%   87%   12%

Source: IEG.

Note: Based on reports of 166 IEs completed during 2000–10. Percentage is the percentage of IEs that explored such indicators.

Ability to Infer Causal Effects

Attribution of impacts to the intervention is the core principle of IE. Irrespective of the method used, the quality of an IE largely depends on its ability to construct a counterfactual population that parallels the beneficiaries in all respects except for their participation in the intervention. Ideally, this could be achieved by randomizing units to control and treatment groups before, or during, program implementation. When randomization is not possible, a number of quasi-experimental techniques can be used to create counterfactuals that are statistically equivalent to the treatment group, including matching methods (propensity score matching), difference-in-differences, regression discontinuity, instrumental variable, and structural and other modeling approaches.

Each of these methods carries its own underlying assumptions regarding the way to enhance the credibility of the counterfactual in estimating program impacts (see appendix A for details). Although the majority of completed evaluations reviewed used quasi-experimental techniques, the choice of methods varies across sectors and throughout the years. Seventy percent of completed World Bank IEs and 62 percent of IFC IEs used quasi-experimental methods. However, as described in chapter 2, more recent IEs are using experimental designs. Among the completed World Bank IEs reviewed for quality, 55 percent of IEs initiated since 2005 used randomization compared with 20 percent initiated between 2000 and 2004.

The choice of methods is also different across sectors. For instance, at the World Bank, almost 50 percent of IEs evaluating CCTs or FPD interventions used experimental methods. Completed World Bank IEs of local development and infrastructure programs were more likely to use quasi-experimental methods (85 percent). At IFC, IEs of access to finance interventions used randomization (four of five) more often than IEs in the investment climate business line (none of four). The prevalence of quasi-experimental methods in these areas might be because these involve large-scale programs or the interventions being evaluated are not of the dose-response variety, thus making randomization more difficult. Among quasi-experimental IEs, the strategies to construct a counterfactual are diverse, with matching being the most used, followed by difference-in-differences, then instrumental variables, and finally regression discontinuity (table 4.2).[8]

Although most World Bank IEs relied on good evaluation design to estimate program impacts in a causal way, fewer IFC IEs did so. Regardless of whether they were experimental or quasi-experimental, a large number of World Bank evaluations (87 percent) discussed and checked *all or some* of the potential biases that could create problems to conclude attribution. However, fewer IFC IEs (59 percent) adequately discussed or checked *at least some* of the selection issues and other biases. Of these IFC IEs, a few discussed the selection problems in some detail, but the estimation of program impacts did not take into account the implication of these biases. For instance, the IEs of the coffee value chain

Table 4.2	Strategies Used by Completed Impact Evaluations to Identify Causal Impacts (percent)								
World Bank/IFC	**Characteristic of the IE**	**Experimental**	**Quasi-experimental**						
		Total	Total	SD	DD	IV	PSM	RD
World Bank	Main method	32	68	6	15	11	30	6
	Checked, addressed or discussed at least **some** of the assumptions underlying corresponding methods	100	80	44	74	82	92	67
	Checked, addressed or discussed **all** of the assumptions underlying corresponding methods	87	31	11	30	47	31	22
IFC	Main method	38	62	37	15	4	7	0
	Checked, addressed or discussed at least **some** of the assumptions underlying the corresponding methods	80	47	60	0	100	50	n/a

Source: IEG.

Note: Based on reports of 140 World Bank and 26 IFC IEs completed during 2000–10. Main method refers to the IE method used to estimate program impacts that are reported in the abstract and/or conclusions sections of the IE report as the main findings of the study. DD = difference-in-differences; IV = instrumental variable; PSM = matching; RD = regression discontinuity; SD = single difference.

in South America are transparent about observable differences between treatment and control groups, yet the estimation of program impacts is based on bivariate analysis, without taking further steps to improve the balance (at the very least on observable characteristics on which data was available) between the two groups.

Furthermore, the statistical inference of some completed IFC IEs has been compromised by the questionable statistical power of analyses that often rely on very small samples, in part because of the small scale of many of IFC's advisory services subject to IE. However, there are signs that IFC IEs in the future are taking steps to deal with the small sample size problem. Three ongoing IFC IEs (of four) whose baseline report was available had adequate sample sizes.[9] In addition, the two IEs of investment operations approved in FY11 (after the study review period) also have large sample sizes—one with about 3,000 respondents, the other with about 500.

The extent to which IEs test the validity of their methods is particularly high among randomized experiments; among quasi-experimental methods, such tests are more prevalent in World Bank evaluations than IFC ones. The extent to which World Bank Group IEs formally tested or adequately discussed whether the assumptions underlying the method were fulfilled was assessed based on the evaluation strategy used in each paper (see appendix F for the list of assumptions). Among the randomized evaluations in both the World Bank and IFC, most checked whether the relevant characteristics of the treatment and control groups were balanced at baseline, discussed the possibility of cross-over between the two groups, or identified the factors that explained why some units of analysis left the sample (attrition) and the possible consequences of attrition on the validity of the randomized design. Among IEs using quasi-experimental methods, the majority of World Bank evaluations (80 percent) checked or discussed *at least some* of the most fundamental assumptions underlying the preferred estimation method, compared with 47 percent of IFC IEs (table 4.2).[10]

Over time, the discussion of internal validity in both World Bank and IFC IEs has shown some signs of improvement. In the World Bank, 93 percent of IEs initiated in 2005 and later adequately discussed *all or some* of the assumptions to establish robustness of evaluation design. Similarly, in IFC, 11 of 14 IEs completed since 2009 provided an adequate discussion of *some or all* of the identification assumptions underlying the corresponding IE method used to estimate program impacts. Moreover, of these 11 IEs, 6 discussed or checked *all* the identification assumptions.

Most World Bank IEs conducted some form of robustness check, but fewer IFC IEs did so. To the extent possible, it is important that IEs check whether their results are stable across different statistical model specifications, estimation methods, evaluation designs, alternative control groups, samples, and placebo or falsification tests (that is, analysis of other groups or outcome variables that are not supposed to be affected by the intervention).[11] Ninety-one percent of the World Bank and 48 percent of the IFC IEs conducted some form of robustness check. Among the completed IEs, only 17 percent did no type of robustness test (52 percent at IFC and 9 percent at the World Bank); of these IEs, one-third are randomized controlled trials for which the authors may have more confidence in the credibility of their method and hence did not feel the need to check the robustness of their findings.

However, randomized designs can also be compromised; it is equally important to examine the extent to which randomization was successful and the results not affected by spillover effects between the treatment and control groups. In addition, only a few papers explicitly discussed the possibility of spillover effects of programs on the local market or spillovers originating from changes in the behaviors of participants, nonparticipants, the government, and other intervening agents.

There is a wide range in the technical quality of robustness analysis. In general, even among the papers that did some type of robustness check, there is a wide range in the technical quality of the analysis. A few tried to exhaust different possibilities, yet many only performed or discussed one or two tests that were easily done. For instance, 26 percent of Bank Group IEs using quasi-experimental methods (30 percent for World Bank and 6 percent for IFC) did robustness checks using different specifications, different estimation methods, and some other type of robustness or sensitivity analysis. In the same vein, 34 percent of World Bank and 13 percent of IFC quasi-experimental IEs checked the robustness of findings using multiple specifications and some other type of analysis to test the credibility of impacts.

Factors Associated with the Quality of World Bank Group Impact Evaluations

Evaluations that do not go through some type of external review are more likely to be of lower quality. Because of their high technical content, the quality of IEs is better assured if they include feedback of experts outside the evaluation team, including whether the data, outcome indicators, and evaluation approach are credible and well adapted to the actual program implementation. Indeed, IEs that were reviewed by experts and people with specialist knowledge of the IE tool are of higher quality than the rest (78 percent of *medium-* or *high*-quality IEs were reviewed, compared with 17 percent of low-quality IEs). Most World Bank IEs (76 percent) were reviewed or discussed by external researchers; fewer (35 percent) of the IFC evaluations were subject to such assessment.

Review procedures vary across IEs in the World Bank. A survey of evaluators reveals that, at the concept stage, review was mostly done by the project team (56 percent), followed by World Bank specialists who were not part of the team (48 percent) and funding agencies (44 percent). At the completion stage, some IEs were reviewed by anonymous referees as part of the publication process in academic journals (49 percent of completed IEs in the survey). Many evaluators also took the initiative to publish their drafts in working paper series, circulate them to researchers inside (65 percent) and outside (29 percent) the World Bank, and present the methodologies and findings in academic and policy conferences.

Some departments at the World Bank have their own review processes, where IEs were reviewed by experts within the unit/the anchor teams/research staff in DEC/the Chief Economist's Office/academia. This wide range of mechanisms and degrees of peer review and their formality suggests that the process to ensure the quality of World Bank IEs is variable.

As the IE agenda at both the World Bank and IFC has deepened, the proportion of IEs that receive specialist feedback has also improved. For instance, 50 percent of IFC IEs that were completed since 2009 have received some sort of specialist feedback. Similarly, survey results suggest that second to the project team,

IFC IEs have been most frequently reviewed by IFC specialists who were not part of the project team (usually M&E specialists) at both the design stage and completion stages.[12] Going forward, the evaluation strategy of IFC, approved in FY12, has recommended that evaluations, including IEs, undergo independent peer review to ensure high quality.[13]

At the World Bank, the evaluators' survey suggests that the *final evaluation report* of 63 percent of IEs that were initiated before 2005 (and have since been completed) were reviewed by specialists who were not part of the project team, compared with 76 percent of IEs initiated after 2005 that are now complete. Broadening the sample to include ongoing IEs, survey results suggest that the *concept note* of 49 percent of the IEs initiated before 2005 was reviewed by specialists who were not part of the project team (this includes both World Bank and non-World Bank specialists), compared with 70 percent of IEs initiated between 2005 and 2010.[14]

With some exceptions, formal and standardized mechanisms to ensure that all IEs go through similar quality control are lacking. In interviews with managers and directors at the World Bank, 5 of 13 interviewees who talked about IE quality controls in their sector or region *explicitly* mentioned that there is no *standardized* review mechanism that is applied to *all* IEs. However, recent IE initiatives like SIEF have established built-in quality review procedures. By design, IE proposals submitted to SIEF for funding are subject to anonymous technical peer review by qualified internal and external reviewers. In fact, one of the criteria for SIEF proposals is technical quality, which carries a weight of 25 percent.[15]

Analysis of survey data also suggests that IEs initiated in 2007–08 in human development sectors (which corresponds with the SIEF cluster fund roll-out period) are more likely to be subject to specialist review at the concept stage than IEs in non-human development sectors during the same period, as well as same sector IEs initiated in any other year between 2005 and 2010.[16] IEs that are managed by DIME or developed in close cooperation with DIME and IE experts (via workshops and clinics) also provide better quality control.[17] For instance, among non-human development IEs initiated in 2009–10, 67 percent were reviewed by a World Bank specialist at concept note stage, compared with 50 percent of IEs initiated in 2005–08.

Staff skills in IE are concentrated, with some units lacking adequate capacity to undertake and supervise IEs. World Bank staff engage in IE in two main ways: doing the evaluation (especially the analysis) themselves and supervising the execution of the evaluation (and using the results). This suggests a human resource issue: making sure that there is a sufficient skill base across regions and sectors to perform these IE tasks (World Bank 2008). As mentioned in chapter 3, 79 people in the Bank are doing IE and have IE skills; one-third are in the Chief Economist's Office, another one-third are in the Africa Region and HDN combined, and the remaining one-third are distributed among nine departments (figure 4.2).

Interviews with World Bank senior management suggest that knowledge of IEs among operational staff is not very deep. The survey of World Bank task team leaders also showed that more than 50 percent cited the need for more training on IE—its fundamentals, benefits and limitations.

Limitations in staff capacity are a greater constraint at IFC. Compared with the World Bank, the capacity constraint is more serious at IFC, where very few staff have IE skills.[18] Because not all staff understand what techniques and rigor IE entails, they can be satisfied calling any assessment of impacts an "impact evaluation," whether or not it meets acceptable IE quality standards. Nearly all IE work at IFC is outsourced, but staff are still needed to supervise and coordinate the conduct of IEs, select the appropriate people to carry out the work, and discern the credibility—or lack thereof—of the IE findings they consume.

The capacity constraint is especially notable at the local level, where project teams usually coordinate IEs. For instance, the quality of IFC IEs that were managed by local teams was lower than those supervised by the headquarters results measurement team at IFC.[19]

Figure 4.2 Number of World Bank Staff with Impact Evaluation Skills by Department

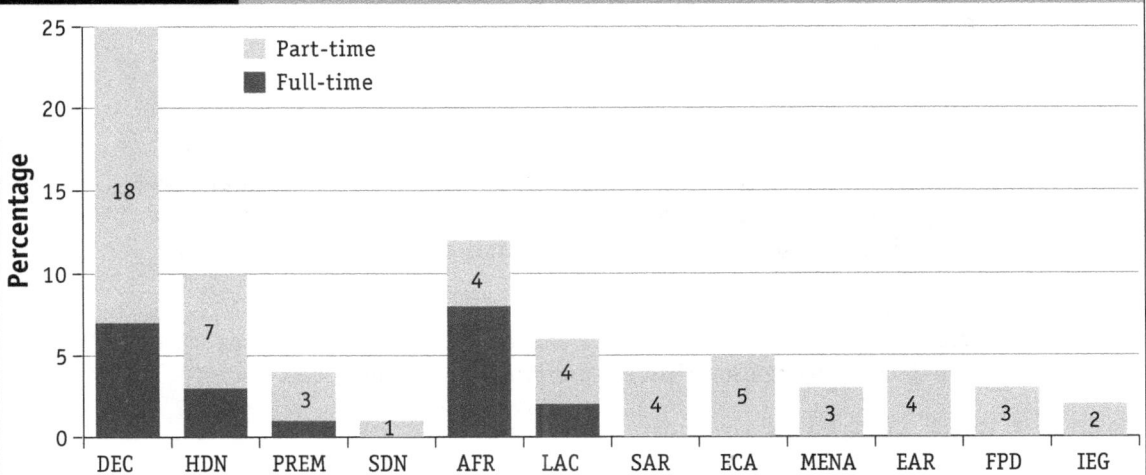

Source: World Bank 2010.

Note: DEC = Development Economics Vice Presidency; IEG = Independent Evaluation Group. **Networks:** FPD = Financial and Private Sector Development Network; HDN = Human Development Network; PREM = Poverty Reduction and Economic Management; SDN = Sustainable Development Network. **Regions:** AFR = Africa; EAP = East Asia and Pacific; ECA = Europe and Central Asia; LAC = Latin America and the Caribbean; MENA = Middle East and North Africa; SAR = South Asia.

Notes

1 In one of the IEs, IEG and IFC jointly developed the survey instrument and questionnaire.

2 The distinction between short-, medium-, and long-term outcomes is not used to assess the quality of the IEs but to characterize their scope.

3 This information is extracted from the IE reports and therefore is not fully accurate.

4 Out of a total of 129 IEs.

5 More details on the sampling method are in appendix B. This review excludes evaluations that do not fit the IE definition (although they are called IEs by the authors) and those written in languages other than English.

6 Examples of this among the evaluations reviewed include a paper on the effects of social investment funds on social capital in St. Lucia, where the authors defined social capital as structural (participation in activities pertaining to the life of the community, emergence of community-driven projects or requests for projects) and cognitive (the extent to which people trust others, confidence in getting support from neighbors and friends when they face problems, time and money spent on activities that benefit the community, and so forth) (ESA Consultores International 2004). Another paper on Indonesia measures the impact of community-driven development on corruption by defining corruption levels as the difference between independent estimates of the amount each project actually cost to build and villages' actual reports on what they spent (Voss 2008).

7 Interventions take time to take effect and achieve outcomes that are further along the results chain. For example, an intervention that provides nutritional supplements to infants would only see increases in their height and weight after an extended period of time; for a social infrastructure project, the behavioral change of beneficiaries would only be observed after the facilities have been completed and put in function.

8 Single differences were used in some of the quasi-experimental evaluations, but often as a robustness check rather than the preferred evaluation design.

9 DSCL: 504; CTI: 4,801; Incentives for better repayment: 1,466.

10 In both institutions, however, fewer quasi-experimental IEs (31 percent in World Bank and 6 percent in IFC) managed to adequately test or convincingly discuss *all* the assumptions required for each method to ensure that the counterfactual was credible.

11 The rigor of an IE is also determined by its ability to ensure that results are not highly sensitive to potential methodological issues and aspects of the project context that can threaten the validity of the method chosen.

12 Of the six completed IEs to which a survey response to this question was given by IFC staff, five were reviewed by the project team at the concept stage and three were reviewed by IFC specialists who were not part of the team. At the completion stage, three of the six IEs were reviewed by the project team and three of six IEs were reviewed by IFC specialists who were not part of the project team. Documentary evidence from evaluation reports also suggests that nonproject persons that usually provided feedback or review were M&E specialists at IFC.

13 This information was captured by IEG from the IE reports. Therefore, this assessment cannot capture the rigor of review that the IE underwent or information on peer review if the IE report does not acknowledge it. For IFC, mention of review/feedback/guidance from IFC M&E specialists was coded yes for review.

14 Further disaggregation points to greater specialist involvement, particularly of external non-Bank specialists, in the review of IE design at conception. For instance, 54 percent of IEs initiated in 2005–06 were reviewed by external non-Bank specialists, compared with 68 percent of IEs initiated in both 2007–08 and 2009–10.

15 The criteria are defined as: What is the overall technical rigor of the evaluation? How rigorous is the identification strategy given the constraints of the intervention? How robust is the sample frame?

16 This is a simple difference-in-difference estimate with robust standard errors clustered at the country level. The interaction term on HDN and cohort dummy for 2007–08 was statistically significant. The sample of IEs was restricted to those that were initiated in 2005–10 for which a survey response to the question was given (n = 103).

17 According to a PREM note (World Bank 2008), the feedback processes for IEs assigned a AAA code are usually informal.

18 For instance, 43 percent of IFC staff surveyed mentioned lack of staff capacity as a constraint to conduct of IEs, versus 31 percent in the World Bank.

19 One IE of 12 supervised by field teams and 7 IEs of 11 supervised by the headquarters RMU team had a medium or high level of quality.

References

Blundell, R., and M. Costa Dias. 2008. "Alternative Approaches to Evaluation in Empirical Microeconomics." CEF.UP Working Papers 0805, Universidade do Porto, Faculdade de Economia do Porto.

Duflo, E., R. Glennerster, and M. Kremer. 2006. "Using Randomization in Development Economics Research: A Toolkit." MIT Department of Economics Working Paper No. 06-36, Cambridge, MA.

ESA Consultores International. 2004. "Poverty Reduction Fund, Saint Lucia—2003 Impact Evaluation Survey: Final Report." http://www.stats.gov.loc/PRF2003%20 Impact%20Evaluation.pdf.

Gertler P.J., S. Martinez, P. Premand, L. Rawlings, and C.M.J. Vermeersch. 2011. *Impact Evaluation in Practice.* Washington, DC: World Bank.

Imbens, G., and T. Lemieux. 2008. "Regression Discontinuity Designs: A Guide to Practice." *Journal of Econometrics* 142(2): 615–35.

Imbens, G., and J. Wooldridge. 2009. "Recent Developments in the Econometrics of Program Evaluation." *Journal of Economic Literature* 47: 1, 5–86.

Khandker, S., G.B. Koolwal, and H.A. Samad. 2010. "Handbook on Impact Evaluation: Quantitative Methods and Practices." World Bank Training Series, Washington, DC.

NONIE (Network of Networks for Impact Evaluation). 2009. *Impact Evaluations and Development: NONIE Guidance on Impact Evaluation.* Washington, DC: NONIE.

Voss, J. 2008. *Impact Evaluation of the Second Phase of the Kecamatan Development Project in Indonesia.* Washington, DC: World Bank.

World Bank. 2010. "Development Impact Evaluation Initiative: A World Bank-Wide Strategic Approach to Enhance Developmental Effectiveness." World Bank, Washington, DC.

———. 2008. "Assessing Our Work on Impact Evaluation." PREM Notes No. 126, World Bank, Washington, DC.

Chapter 5

Use and Influence of World Bank Group
Impact Evaluations

This chapter examines to what extent, how, and why Bank Group IEs are used. IEs have assumed benefits (appendix G). Whether or not they have stated objectives of influencing decision making, rigorous IEs provide evidence for what does and does not work. This knowledge can potentially influence program design and broader strategies to enhance development effectiveness. The evidence can also affect how people think about development issues.

Moreover, IEs can contribute to developing evaluation capacity and institutionalizing evidence-based evaluations. This expectation about the use and influence of IEs is heightened by their high cost relative to other evaluation tools. It should not be assumed that IEs are used: poor quality, inaccurate results, long delays, or poor familiarity among policy makers all risk undermining IE use and influence. This chapter explores how World Bank Group IEs are used and why some are more influential than others.

Establishing the value of IEs for project operations and policy making is not straightforward. First, there is no mechanism in place and no comprehensive evidence base to systematically document whether and how IE findings are being taken up. Second, IEs can influence multiple levels and different stakeholders. Policy influence may range from improving the knowledge of certain stakeholders (and therefore expanding policy capacities) to fundamentally redesigning policies (Lindquist 2001). Finally, IEs are not the only source of information that fits into policy making; they could affirm or reject an existing belief or complement other evidence considered by policy makers. As a result, IEG does not claim to fully capture the extent to which IEs are used, because there could be many incidents of influential IEs that are not revealed.

This chapter aims to portray IE use and its prevalence (past or potential), analyze a selection of cases where IEs are (or are not) influential, and suggest patterns that determine whether an IE is likely to be useful. It focuses mostly on uses related to the World Bank Group at both project and institutional levels. A few cases of IE uptake at the client country level are presented, but it is beyond the scope of the report to discuss the usefulness and influence of IEs among other international organizations or the broader research community. The analysis is based on triangulated information from structured interviews with Bank Group management, surveys of evaluators and team leaders, country and sector case studies, and reviews of project documents (appendix B).

Two interconnected questions are addressed: Do IEs affect development practice, and if so, how? What are the factors that may be associated with such influence? The answer to the first question is structured along four different types of influence that IEs tend to pursue on development policy making (although they may not be the objectives explicitly stated): *project operations, policy dialogue, institutional strategies,* and *evaluation culture and capacity.*[1]

As a project assessment tool, IEs generate knowledge that may be useful for operational decisions to continue, modify, expand, or terminate the evaluated projects or motivate and improve the design of subsequent phases or other projects. At the institutional level, the evidence from IEs could contribute to building the stock of knowledge on development challenges, best practices, and what is effective in a particular setting. This could help motivate policy dialogue between the World Bank Group and its clients as well as influence institutional strategies and resource allocation. Finally, if effective, IEs could showcase how evaluations may be useful and thus promote a culture of evidence-based policy making in both the Bank Group and countries.

The production of IEs may facilitate future evaluation efforts by enhancing the technical capacity of and collaboration between different stakeholders. Regarding the second question about factors, this report examines attributes of effective (and ineffective) IEs. The factors investigated span the entire cycle of an IE, from motivation and initiation to production to dissemination to uptake.

The main findings of this chapter are as follows:

- Although there is no comprehensive evidence to quantify the benefits of IEs, many sources point to how IEs have influenced aspects of development practice and had real benefits, and many people believe in their potential to yield much greater benefit (see appendix G regarding assumed benefits of IEs). Yet overall, the use of IEs is much less frequent than generally thought within the World Bank Group.
  - When influential, Bank Group (mostly World Bank) IEs chiefly contributed to project assessment and decisions to design and sustain evaluated and future projects. They also raised the profile of certain types of interventions, substantiated the Bank Group's knowledge and position in policy dialogue, and promoted the appreciation for M&E. In addition, in areas with a critical mass of IEs, they have contributed to the formulation of strategic priorities.
  - In earlier years, stand-alone IEs had limited influence on increasing local capacity, which requires a concerted and sustained engagement. Recent IEs initiated under the programmatic approach, which emphasizes a coordinated learning agenda and capacity building, are more likely to contribute to capacity building of staff and clients. In addition, the World Bank has been undertaking systematic efforts to improve IE capacity, including formal training, guidance notes, periodic workshops, and linkages with communities of practice.
- Factors that strengthen the usefulness of IEs for enhancing development effectiveness include their relevance, timeliness, quality, dissemination, engagement with potential decision makers, political environment, and a culture of using M&E evidence in decision making.

Influence of Impact Evaluations on Project Operations

IEs are primarily used as a project assessment tool at the World Bank Group, but this use is not as prevalent as perceived in the World Bank. IEs are perceived to be useful by Bank Group staff and management.[2] Particularly because IEs provide credible information on the impacts of projects, their evidence could be expected to be included in documents that report the project results. A review of ICRs and PCRs indicates that the findings of 47 percent of completed World Bank and 53 percent of completed IFC IEs were mentioned in the project completion documents to demonstrate project effectiveness. World Bank team leader and evaluator surveys suggest that 37 percent of IEs linked to a lending project were used as an input to the ICR or midterm review.[3] For IFC, all eight IEs for which survey responses were available and both country case study IEs (equivalent to six IEs) reportedly were used in completion or midterm review documents.

IEG itself makes little systematic use of IE results in reviewing or evaluating World Bank-supported projects, including in the more in-depth project evaluations (PPARs) that IEG conducts. Among the 10 projects (linked to 12 IEs) that were evaluated by PPARs, only two of the PPARs reference the IE findings.

It is too early to assess how the use of IEs is changing under new IE initiatives and coordination in the World Bank, although some indicators point toward improvement. Recent efforts to improve coordination and prioritization (led by DIME) are difficult to gauge because most IEs are ongoing. The survey of evaluators and project team leaders engaged in ongoing IEs reveals that *expectations* about their greater use in midterm reviews and project ICRs (54 percent) exceed the actual incidence of IE use reported for completed evaluations (37 percent). However, no discernible time trend in these expectations is observed for ongoing IEs initiated in 2009–10 versus those initiated in 2005–08 (55 percent versus 54 percent).[4]

IEs are at times used for decisions to continue, expand, scale down, or cancel a project or to influence the design of the subsequent phase, although not regularly. According to the team leader and evaluator surveys, 36 percent of completed World Bank IEs and half of completed IFC IEs were used to make decisions about continuing, stopping, reducing, expanding, or changing the design of the evaluated project. Forty-five percent of World Bank IEs and half of IFC IEs helped inform the design of follow-on or new projects. Reported World Bank use of IEs in design of follow-on or new projects has improved: 54 percent of completed IEs initiated since 2005 versus 40 percent of completed IEs initiated in the years before. However, the difference in IE use on operational decisions related to the evaluated project between these two IE initiation periods is less discernible.[5]

The documentation of the use of IEs is sparse. In particular:

- ***One-fifth of the reviewed completed IEs were reported in the ICRs/PCRs to have contributed to strategic decisions.*** The ICRs linked to 19 of 87 World Bank completed IEs explicitly mentioned the use of IEs in making operational decisions or providing lessons for future endeavors. Among the 12 projects linked to these 19 IEs, ICRs of 10 projects cited the contribution of the IEs in decisions to scale up or continue or to inform policy and/or project design.[6] The Philippines' Integrated Early Childhood

Development Project, for example, was reportedly used to justify expanding program innovations. The implementers of the *Familias en Accion* program, armed with positive results from the IEs, gained support for the continuation and expansion of the program. In IFC, PCRs linked to 3 of 17 IEs explicitly mentioned the demonstration effect of IEs for future investments.[7] In particular, the IE of the Life Enrichment Project in India provided estimates of worker welfare in the construction industry and information to support replication.[8]

- **Completed IEs of projects were mentioned in around half of the follow-on lending operations.**[9] Around one-third of these citations are marginal, another one-third summarize the effects of the preceding phases, and in the remaining one-third of cases the IE was cited as having some influence on project design. For example, the Mexican Compensatory Education Project was built on the demonstrated success of the Basic Education Development Project; the results of the IE on the El Salvador Basic

Box 5.1	Use of Impact Evaluations to Continue and Expand Programs: Two Cases in Peru

Interviews with local stakeholders revealed that the findings of the IEs (i) contributed to discussions with the Ministry of Finance and informed decisions to continue the project, formulate the third phase—Peru Decentralized Rural Transport Project—and expand it to a national scale; (ii) gave more prominence to the issue of rural roads in the policy agenda and helped legitimize the policy-making process around the project; (iii) helped identify and introduce complementary activities to reinforce the positive impacts of the project (such as electrification, irrigation, communications, promotion of small firms, business plans); (iv) provided evidence of impacts that go beyond the improvement of roads and reduction in travel times (for example, impacts on education, employment patterns, income sources), which facilitated the engagement of other relevant institutions; and (v) helped leverage funding for subsequent IE program activities.

The Business Simplification Project was a pilot supported by IFC in Lima and six other municipalities to reduce the time, requirements, and costs related to obtaining a business license in Peru. IFC commissioned the Poverty Action Lab to conduct an IE and contracted a local think tank to do an IE three years after the reform.

The first IE found that the intervention had a large and positive effect on formalization rates and access to the formal sector, but the second IE showed that, in the long term, sales, profits, number of employees, access to credit, and investment in infrastructure were not affected by the firm operating with a municipal license. IFC used the findings of the first evaluation[a] internally and externally to build interest for the intervention. In particular, the program was expanded to other municipalities in Peru and replicated in Brazil, Colombia, Ecuador, Honduras, and Mexico.

Sources: IEG country case studies.

a. This evaluation relied on a before-after approach and was argued to be an IE under the untested assumption that there were no additional factors (such as differential preprogram trends) that could confound the effects of the license simplification process. This methodological limitation, however, did not seem to have affected the use of the report.

Education Modernization Project were incorporated into the design of the proposed Education Reform Project. The Senegal Nutrition Enhancement Project was scaled up with the IE findings helping direct the subsequent phase. It is unclear whether the IEs were a key source of information or supported decisions that had already been made.

- *Case studies show that IEs have helped shape decisions on scaling projects up or down, and the design of follow-on cases.* Of the 19 projects with completed IEs reviewed in the case studies, IEs helped shape (sometimes marginally) (i) the decision to scale up or down and continue the projects in eight cases and (ii) the design of follow-on in five cases. This includes examples in Indonesia, Bangladesh, Colombia, Madagascar, the Philippines, Senegal, and Peru[10] (box 5.1). In addition, an IE of an IFC's agribusiness project in Indonesia that did not find significant evidence of success in improving farmers' knowledge, practices, and incomes was partly responsible for the decision to phase out the program. The latter use includes examples where the findings of previous IEs helped improve the program's targeting and in others helped refine the benefit structure.

The use of IE evidence pertaining to pilot interventions has also been modest. When IEs test pilots, not only do the small scale and specific treatment of pilots pose fewer technical constraints to IEs, but their innovative features justify the need to evaluate and learn. According to the desk review of completed World Bank IEs, 40 of 140 (29 percent) IEs tested pilots, of which 20 (50 percent) were attached to 13 lending operations. The other pilots are associated with the technical services that the World Bank provided in setting up or assessing the effectiveness of some innovative approaches. Nevertheless, even though the majority of these pilots showed positive impacts, only two were scaled up with funding from the World Bank; a third was used to inform the decision to discontinue the intervention.

A second dimension of feasible usefulness of IEs is when they test different design features to compare their effectiveness (box 5.2). Yet only 5 of the 18 World Bank interventions (whose IEs are complete) that were linked to a lending project testing treatment variations had a follow-on operation that was informed by IE findings.[11]

Some World Bank IEs contributed to the motivation and design of other projects, but infrequently. IEs can have substantial knowledge spillovers to future projects and policies, especially ones that are similar to the ones evaluated. However, identifying objective evidence that captures such benefits is complex. According to surveyed task leaders of projects with IEs, 24 World Bank programs (40 percent of IE level responses) were to some extent influenced by IEs of *other* projects. IEG was unable to review the PADs/Project Data Sheets of all projects to identify whether they have been influenced by IEs of *other* projects. IEG sought evidence of successful cases where evaluated projects influenced others. The review of PADs of 117 World Bank evaluated programs (corresponding to 142 World Bank IEs) reveals that just below

The Reaching Out-of-School Children Project tests alternative approaches of providing access to quality primary education in remote areas. The project assists in the establishment of learning centers in communities by providing grants; it also provides education allowances. Of the 60 pilot *upazilas* (subdistricts), 23 receive school grants only and 37 receive both school grants and student allowances. The IE aims to evaluate the relative effectiveness of the two types of interventions (school grants relative to student allowances) in terms of improving enrollment, dropout rate, reduction in out-of-school children, and learning.

The preliminary results provided evidence to support the government's confidence in its implementation of the combined treatment (both school grants and student allowances) and the continuation of the program. This project has now been expanded so that 30 more *upazilas* receive the combination treatment; it has the potential of being incorporated in the national primary education program. The government also built on the design of the IE to conduct its own quantitative evaluation.

Source: IEG country case study.

one-fourth (23 percent) had their design or implementation influenced by previous IEs of *other* projects.[12]

The country case studies and World Bank senior staff interviews also reveal a few cases where the IE findings of some programs may have raised the awareness of development practitioners about the success of particular interventions and contributed to the motivation and conceptualization of similar programs. Survey and project document evidence shows that few IFC projects mention being informed by other IEs.

CCTs provide the clearest evidence of IE influence across projects. There is a large and rigorous evidence base on CCTs to which the World Bank has contributed substantially. The positive IE findings and lessons of a pioneer CCT program in Mexico *(Progresa/Oportunidades)*[13] were an important factor in influencing other countries in the region (Colombia, Ecuador, El Salvador, Jamaica, Nicaragua, and Peru) to adopt similar instruments (Rawlings and Rubio 2003). The inspiration for the Punjab girls' scholarship program in Pakistan was partly the success of the girls' scholarship program in Bangladesh. CCTs now have been implemented in more than 30 countries, in almost all regions of the world (figure 5.1).[14]

In addition to having an influence across borders, CCT projects learned from evaluations of earlier experiences in their own country. For example, the interest in and design of Nicaragua's CCT pilot *Atención a Crisis* was modeled after a previous successful CCT program.[15] Similarly, the project preparation team of the Cambodia Education Sector Support Project, in designing the CCT component, benefited from IEs of two similar interventions.[16] The

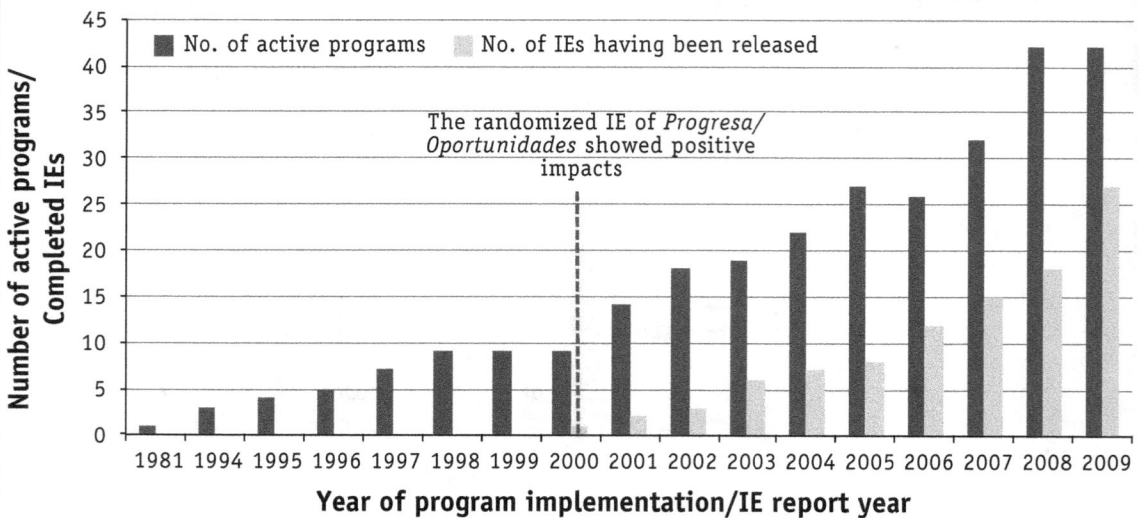

Sources: Compiled from Grosh and others 2008; Fizsbein and others 2009; and the IE database.

Note: The number of active programs is the cumulative number of programs in implementation in each year (excluding closed programs). The number of IEs having been released is also the cumulative number of IEs by their report years. CCT = conditional cash transfer.

expectation is that this cross-fertilization of knowledge within and across countries will be consolidated as the IE evidence base for other types of interventions grows.

IEs have also raised the profile of other interventions. Interviews with World Bank Group management, together with other anecdotal evidence, indicate that the existing IE literature on the effectiveness of some instruments (such as social funds, school-based management, scholarships, and teacher incentives at the World Bank and business simplification at IFC) has been important in raising the profile of these interventions and leveraging more Bank Group resources to projects that include them.

Influence of Impact Evaluations on Policy Dialogue

IEs appear to be useful for Bank Group staff in policy dialogue with government counterparts, clients, and donors. As discussed in chapter 3, many senior management staff view one of the motivations of IEs to be advocacy or policy influence. Most of them also find IEs very influential in informing policy dialogue. Because IEs often provide credible and quantifiable information on the value added of the project and of the World Bank Group, they could empower Bank Group staff in client discussions.

Credible and relevant IE findings do not automatically translate into policy changes because of a variety of factors that range from political interests to fiscal conditions to priorities within the policy agenda. However, where the right conditions exist, IE findings could be critical to foster the legitimacy of existing policies or introduce substantial changes. This could range from informing policy debates to advocating for a certain instrument or policy to substantiating the role of the Bank Group to emphasizing development priorities and reformulating the direction of policies. Indeed, 10 of 16 World Bank management responders rated this role of IEs to be above average—a score of 4 or higher on a 6-point scale.

This is consistent with survey results that show that 55 percent of completed World Bank IEs helped influence policy dialogue with clients, according to surveyed team leaders and evaluators. There is suggestive evidence that IE use in policy dialogue has improved over time, especially at World Bank: 75 percent of completed World Bank IEs initiated since 2005 were reported to have informed policy dialogue, compared with 42 percent initiated before 2005.[17] At IFC, although it is rare, there are a few cases where IEs have been used to inform dialogue between client and donors, such as in the case of an Indian agribusiness project—IE methodology and early evaluation findings were critical for company's decision to roll out and replicate the pilot intervention.

There are some notable examples where World Bank IEs have been instrumental in raising political support for effective programs and influencing policy decisions. For instance, the positive effects of the *Familias en Accion* CCT in Colombia on consumption, schooling, and health that a set of IEs demonstrated helped convince new governments not only to continue and to expand the programs, but also to broaden the eligibility to additional children (Soares 2011). Similarly, positive results from IEs of the Kecamatan Development Program in Indonesia, also validated by a wide array of qualitative studies, gave credibility to the program and paved the way for decisions by the government to expand the program nationwide, increase the size of the grants, and adopt a financial auditing system (box 5.3).

The rigorous IE of the *Plan Jefes y Jefas* workfare in Argentina provided evidence in the policy debate about the program and helped guide the development of the transition strategy. IEs of nutrition interventions in Madagascar and Senegal were found to have contributed to maintaining political support for the programs; moreover, IE results are thought to be a contributing factor to the multiple expansions of the program in Madagascar. Former directors of the Rural Roads Rehabilitation Program in Peru stated that the results from a series of IEs empowered them with a credible source of evidence to make a stronger argument to the Ministry of Finance for ensuring financial sustainability for the program. Finally, expansion of an early childhood development program in the Philippines was justified in part by the positive results of rigorous and independent IEs.

The Kecamatan Development Program is a government program in Indonesia aimed at alleviating poverty, strengthening local government and community institutions, and improving local governance. The IE of the program's second phase found that the program increased real per capita consumption and helped households move out of poverty.

This second phase was most effective at reaching poor households and subdistricts. Disadvantaged groups, other than the poor, were less likely to benefit from the program. The program also reduced unemployment but had no impact on school enrollment rates.

The positive findings of the IE, complemented by encouraging results from various qualitative analyses and cost-effectiveness calculations, which the project team presented to the government, helped seal the government's decision to scale up the program nationwide and increase the size of the block grants. The early engagement with the government has contributed to a gradual increase in government interest in evaluation efforts. This support was initiated by champions within the government, which helped enhance the government's interest and trust in the IEs. The IE team engaged relevant government agencies from the beginning, not just informing them of the approach and findings but also engaging them in discussion of the design and preliminary results.

Source: IEG country case study.

Influence of Impact Evaluations on World Bank Group Strategies

A body of evidence from IEs is more influential for institutional strategies than evidence from a single evaluation. IEs tend to provide assurance that certain interventions will work, but individual IEs have limited potential to influence institutional strategies of development agencies. The views from interviewed senior management regarding the influence of IEs on sector strategies are mixed: 7 of 17 people rated the extent to which IEs were used for this purpose as above average. Their view is also that syntheses of multiple IEs are more valuable for strategic planning than individual IEs.

In areas where a large number of relevant and good quality IEs have been conducted across different contexts, such as CCTs, early childhood development, school feeding, or agricultural adaptations, the accumulated evidence can raise the profile of these categories of programs, increase confidence in their effectiveness across varied contexts, and contribute to the Bank Group's knowledge agenda and development strategies. For example, IE evidence has contributed to the Bank's acceptance of CCTs as an effective instrument for dealing with a range of poverty-related issues. In contrast, when there are few IEs in certain areas (such as institutional reform and urban development), the critical mass to make a difference at a strategic level is not available.

The World Bank has contributed to synthesizing and disseminating available evidence and identifying underresearched topics. At the World Bank, DIME, the Chief Economist's Office, anchor units, and IEG have been making efforts to synthesize IE evidence, disseminate the knowledge, and encourage more IE work through metareviews, regular seminars, repositories with IE reports, publications, cluster learning, thematic blogs, and annual network weeks by issues.[18] These works seem to attract a large audience and stimulate lively discussions about lessons learned in program effectiveness. Yet most of these efforts are concentrated in areas where there are many completed IEs and demand for new evaluations is high (for instance, human development sectors).

Although IFC has not had many IEs and adoption is low, there have been efforts to synthesize IE evidence to influence business line strategies. These efforts have been more systematic in some business lines, for example, on investment climate (business registration), and reveal other areas where evaluative evidence is scant. A recent agribusiness metareview examined the effectiveness of various service delivery models for IFC and external agribusiness projects. The review included findings from IFC's agribusiness project evaluations, including several IEs. This metareview is expected to inform the new agribusiness strategy.

IFC IEs are not published in research outlets and have been mostly presented to the key stakeholders and staff. The RMU has also published several monitor notes and video clips with findings and lessons from evaluated advisory services. However, there is no central platform that facilitates the sharing of IEs or synthesizing findings by business line or theme to close global knowledge gaps or to the publishing of results in research outlets.

IEs have contributed to developing sector or institutional strategies in areas where there is a large body of evidence, such as in human development. A review of all sector strategies of the World Bank produced in the last decade found that IE was mentioned more often in education and social protection and sporadically in the financial and private sector development network; governance; health, nutrition and population; infrastructure; transport; urban development; and water and sanitation; and not at all in other sector strategy documents.

Most of the time, the sector strategies pointed out IE as an evaluation tool or an area to which more resources could be devoted, the potential use of IEs, and factors that constrain their production in the sector. Few strategies cited lessons learned from IEs or their influence on framing strategic priorities. The education sector strategy in particular, where IEs were cited the most, has been significantly shaped by learning from IEs (box 5.4). The fact that IE is more likely to be cited in the strategies of sectors with large IE evidence suggests that IEs have the potential to make a larger contribution to influencing strategic priorities when there is a critical mass of credible evidence available.

Forty percent of the Country Assistance Strategies developed in 2007–10 referred to IEs, compared with 25 percent in earlier years. In addition, World

Box 5.4   Influence of Impact Evaluations on Education Sector Strategy

Strategic priorities reflect a consensus built up from an earlier set of issues and one that is being constantly modified and challenged based on emerging findings from IEs and other forms of research. By the very nature of strategic priorities, which are based on institutional consensus that takes longer to form, the research and IE agenda will lead to filtering the findings into a broader formulation of priorities.

The strategic priority of learning as an objective in the Education Sector Strategy of 2010–20 has been the result of the production of considerable evidence on what children are learning in school and several researchers highlighting that enrollment did not imply learning. It took almost a decade from the first papers on learning to the current strategic focus on learning to be articulated as a goal in the priorities of the World Bank. By then, a large body of evaluations had already built up (in addition to the 44 supported by the World Bank, there are close to 100 from outside the Bank) showing that a host of different interventions was producing small effects on learning (much smaller than what would be required) and these effects faded quite quickly.

Meanwhile, researchers were documenting that enrollment itself had surprising effects on wages, fertility, and a host of other outcomes that were difficult to look at in short-term studies. Although the consensus is still being developed, there is increasing evidence that schooling produces non-cognitive skills that are important for later life outcomes and that keeping children in school longer helps. Research has moved in two parallel tracks: a recent book summarizes precisely the impact of programs looking at information, local accountability, pay for performance, and contracting (Bruns and others 2011), and another track has started looking at enrollment, long-term outcomes and non-cognitive skills.

Source: IEG, based on discussions with World Bank management.

Bank country strategies that made a reference to IEs mostly correspond to countries in Latin America and the Caribbean and Africa Regions, where the IE agenda is active. For instance, Brazil is the one of the countries with the highest number of IEs; in fact, around one-fourth of all investment operations approved in 2009–10 in Brazil were subject to an IE. More recently, this IE effort has been highlighted and identified as one of the essential pillars of the Country Partnership Strategy for Brazil (FY12–FY15). The contribution of IEs to Brazil's knowledge agenda, operational work, and policy dialogue is also reflected in the Country Management Unit's decision to create a multisector group of regional IE experts, responsible for ensuring adequate technical quality of the activities, providing guidance to task team leaders, and supporting the operational and knowledge dialogue on the topic.

Influence of Impact Evaluations on Evaluation Capacity and Culture

The direct contribution of conducting an IE to building local capacity has been limited because of the modest engagement of local researchers and government staff in the analytical stage of the evaluations. Thirty-two percent of completed World Bank IEs were considered by the surveyed team leaders and evaluators to help improve World Bank staff/client (or other institution) capacity in the conduct or analysis of IEs. As pointed out in chapter 2, in less than one-third of completed IEs, local researchers have been involved in the analysis stage; similarly, government staff have been involved in the analytical stage for only 8 percent. Data collection is the only part of these completed IE that was predominantly carried out by local researchers or government.[19]

Local research institutions have a comparative advantage in local knowledge and costs, but they may have more limited technical skills in designing evaluation strategies or analyzing data. Indeed, there is a tradeoff between capacity building and quality assurance when using local researchers, and increasing the engagement of local researchers has to take into account the base from which local counterparts start and the need for a guarantee of objective and independent analysis. As a result, evaluators may lack the incentives to engage and train their local counterparts (box 5.5).

World Bank IEs initiated in 2009–10 have significantly higher expectations of building local capacity than IEs initiated in the years before. According to surveys, IEs initiated in 2009–10 (58 percent) are expected to improve World Bank staff/client (or other institution) capacity in the conduct or analysis of IEs more than IEs initiated in 2007–08, 2005–06, or earlier (35–40 percent). The comparison of 2009–10 with all other cohorts is statistically significant. This is consistent with the adoption of the programmatic model by many more IE programs during this period.

Box 5.5	Impact Evaluations and In-Country Evaluation Capacity Building: The Case of Vietnam Hand Washing and Indonesia Sanitation Projects

The hand-washing and sanitation projects in Vietnam and Indonesia, respectively, are part of the Global Water and Sanitation Program, which aims fo improve the hygiene and sanitation practices in rural communities and create global knowledge from the experience of these and similar interventions to apply in other parts of the world. Both evaluations have finished collecting data and are now undergoing analysis.

For both projects, Bank staff and international academics are commissioned to design and analyze the data. Only the data collection was contracted to local institutions (the survey firm Survey Meter in Indonesia and the research institutes National Institute of Hygiene and Epidemiology and Mekong Economics in Vietnam), which already have capacity for conducting surveys. They would like to play a bigger role in designing the questionnaires and analyzing the survey data but were not given the opportunity. Because capacity building is not one of the mandates of the projects or IEs, and the program has to adhere to strict guidelines from the donor (the Gates Foundation) to ensure quality, the evaluation program of the two projects did not create opportunities to train local survey firms on evaluation techniques.

Sources: IEG country case studies.

Because this approach emphasizes a coordinated learning agenda and capacity building, the clients, staff, and local teams connected to the IE that is embedded in this framework also benefit from IE programmatic activities like training workshops and engagement with researchers throughout the IE process (see box 2.1). Therefore, a possible explanation for this trend is that the shift in how IEs are coordinated under this model has led to changing expectations about the capacity building benefits of doing an IE.

To reduce constraints to IE capacity in developing countries, the dedicated efforts at the World Bank to build local capacity need to be sustained. DIME, HDN, SIEF, and other trust funds, including the Health Results-Based Financing IE program and Russia Financial Literacy, are pursuing capacity building through formal training, networking with a large community of practitioners, publishing guidance notes, conducting periodic workshops that provide clients and Bank staff with a forum to compare and benchmark their results and learn from the experience of others, and, as noted above, learning-by-doing through joint government-Bank evaluations. DIME and SIEF organize field-based workshops for government officials, development practitioners and evaluation experts in client countries, and World Bank task teams (box 5.6). These workshops aim to equip the teams with the knowledge and technical skills needed to build rigorous IE into project design.[20]

Networks and units such as HDN, SDN, PREM, and DEC are also very active in setting up workshops to build capacity among government officials and to share IE results and experience. For instance, SDN has organized (together with HDN) a number of IE workshops in Latin America and the Caribbean and South Asia. The World Bank has also published a series of technical guidance notes, including two comprehensive publications that cover conceptual and practical issues related to conducting IE (Gertler and others 2011; Khandker, Koolwal, and Samad 2010). IFC is not active in capacity building, partly because IE has not been taken up in IFC as much as in the World Bank and, perhaps more importantly, because there is limited IE capacity in house (most IFC IEs were done on a contract basis by external researchers). Overall, these efforts require significant and long-term investment from the Bank Group because IE is a complex tool that requires continued coaching, obtained through both theoretical training and practice with actual projects.

In some cases IEs were found to increase interest in strengthening the M&E of activities linked to the projects evaluated. As project teams and governments experience firsthand what IEs can and cannot do, they become more aware of their applicability. An indication of this is that in a large proportion (65 percent) of follow-on projects of evaluated World Bank interventions, an IE was planned for either similar or complementary interventions. Although far from conclusive, country-level experience indicates that several evaluations have contributed to encouraging governments and project teams to adopt more robust M&E strategies. This was the case for 5 of the 19 case study projects with completed IEs, which include Peru's Rural Roads project, the Kecamatan Development Program in Indonesia, the Reaching Out-of-School Children

SIEF workshops are training workshops with broad and diverse participation that involves no prior commitment and that are not sector specific. SIEF does not systematically organize support for IE implementation after these workshops. In contrast, DIME workshops are sector specific only and target a different audience—teams and their counterparts that express interest in conducting an IE. Discussions are held with all teams before the workshop. Each government team has a required minimum composition (policy maker, program manager, and economist/statistician) to secure decision power, knowledge, and follow-up capacity. The presence of a task team leader or senior project team member is required. Each team is assigned at least one researcher and develops an IE design and presents it at the workshop. DIME organizes follow-up implementation support for all teams.

IEG interviewed participants of the 2010 DIME workshop in Dubai focusing on fragile states, the 2010 SIEF Workshop in Kathmandu, the 2010 SIEF workshop in Seoul, and the 2009 SIEF workshop in Lima on different aspects of their experience. At these workshops, the participants were exposed to different IE techniques and applications, including technical sessions for people with relatively advanced knowledge of the methods and more applied sessions that cater to policy makers. By and large, there was high appreciation among all participants for the technical skills and understanding of IE applications that they acquired, the relevance and clarity of the sessions and materials used during the workshops, and the connections made with a wider community of practice. Participants who already had a clear idea of which project they would like to evaluate said that the knowledge they gained was sufficient to initiate, supervise, and contribute to the production of IEs. In fact, this study found four IEs in Africa whose design was conceived by participants at the workshop, and their implementation was later facilitated by DIME.

In contrast, for participants without a planned IE, the workshops appear to have had little effect (beyond providing the skills) on their subsequent work. However, even in such cases, the workshops helped the participants improve their M&E structure, especially in terms of more accurate indicator measurement, more acceptance of the need for collecting baseline, and more focus on results.

In general, interactions with the instructors and fellow participants were highly valued as a way to learn about other IE efforts and their results. However, there was also consensus among participants that technical capacity constraints in local institutions remained large and that sustained and broader efforts, including partnerships with local research institutions and continued engagement with previous workshop participants, would be necessary to address these limitations. Many of these observations have been corroborated by a recent HDN tracer study, drawing on the views of 181 former participants who responded to a structured survey, that sought to assess the performance of past SIEF IE workshops.

Sources: Country case studies; World Bank 2010; discussions with World Bank management.

Project in Bangladesh, *Familias en Accion* in Colombia, and *Bono de Desarrollo Humano* in Ecuador.[21]

Although this is difficult to assess, some IEs help promote and institutionalize an evidence-based policy-making culture. At a broader institutional level, influence on evaluation culture can happen if IEs emphasize the importance of sound data collection plans, comparable and well-measured indicators, analytical rigor, and capacity into local evaluation systems. Yet identifying this type of contribution is difficult because IE is not the only determining factor.

Examples of projects with this influence, such as the Southwest Poverty Reduction Project in China and the Life Enrichment Project in India, are illustrative. In the former case, the outcomes of the IE included a significant increase in the government's poverty monitoring and analysis capability and an unusually good database for detailed project monitoring and evaluation. In the latter, the IE helped the client start to understand the benefits of such evaluation, because it was the first of its type on the topic of HIV/AIDS prevention and other development programs for migrant workers.

There are at least two other cases where IEs contributed substantially to the development and institutionalization of results-oriented evaluation systems for policy making. One is the IE of *Progresa/Oportunidades* in Mexico; this was argued to be a major catalyst to the redesign and renewed focus on results of the M&E system of the Ministry of Social Development that housed the program (Franco and Fernandez-Ordonez 2010). The other example is the positive influence that a set of IE activities, including some supported by the World Bank, had on SINERGIA, Colombia's national results-based management and evaluation system (Castro 2008).

Factors Affecting Use and Influence of

Impact Evaluations

The effectiveness of IEs for enhancing development practice depends on many factors inherent in their production that vary by how they are perceived. IEG has found many cases where IE use and influence depend on the active engagement of clients, the relevance of the evaluation, the timeliness of its results, and its perceived quality. Use also often depends on dissemination, the type of policy the evaluation is useful for, the people who commission the study, and the policy environment in which the IE is conducted.

IEs are more likely to be used in development policy if they focus on the issues that are of interest to future users. The low usage rate of IEs for project assessment, as pointed out in the previous section, can be partly explained by the lack of alignment between the outcomes assessed in the IE and the project's results framework. At the World Bank, 59 percent of IEs aligned with the results framework merited a substantive discussion in the ICR, compared with 20 percent of IEs not aligned. Similarly for IFC, around 80 percent of IEs were adequately mentioned in the PCR, compared with 17 percent of nonaligned IEs.[22]

There are some encouraging signs that World Bank IEs are starting to be more closely linked with operations. DIME is promoting a results-based model for the Bank's operations, which includes collaborating with Bank operations to introduce prospective evaluations. This allows for better alignment between IE questions and project design, results framework and implementation plans, and vice versa.

In addition, intermediate IE products, such as baseline data analysis, can be used to adjust project design and implementation and identify other constraints that have to be addressed to ensure effectiveness (World Bank 2010). It is too early to capture the use of the IEs conducted under this model because many of them are still ongoing. However, there is evidence that IEs are becoming better integrated in projects over time: 52 percent of IEs initiated in 2009–10 are part of project M&E, compared with 38 percent initiated in 2007–08; this indicates that IEs can be expected to be more used. Survey data for completed IEs suggest that IEs that have been initiated later are better used: 47 percent of World Bank completed IEs initiated before 2005 were used to inform design of follow-on projects, compared with 60 percent of completed IEs initiated between 2005 and 2010.

Closely linked with relevance, the timeliness of results is an important determinant of IE usefulness. Even if the questions are relevant, IEs can still fail to influence the evaluated projects if their results come too late to be incorporated into decision making. Limited use of IEs in assessing project impacts in ICRs because of lack of timeliness of IE outputs was evident in three World Bank IEs examined in the case studies: the Female Secondary School Education Assistance Project in Bangladesh, the Nutrition Enhancement Project in Senegal, and the Nutrition and Early Childhood Development Project in Uganda. In the Senegal Nutrition Project, the IE was still in progress at the time of the ICR, even though the IE was not assessing outcomes extending beyond life of the project.

Another type of timeliness issue that limits use of IEs in design of follow-up projects is when the follow-up project is conceptualized/appraised before the current project closes and before IE results are likely to be available (for example, the Second Rural Transport Project in Vietnam). This impedes IE use in informing new project design. However, in the case of an IE assessing outcomes that manifest themselves much later after the project closes, synchronization with the project cycle is not realistic.[23] There is some evidence that, at IFC, timeliness is not perceived as a significant problem: for seven of eight IEs for which survey responses were available, transaction leaders said that the IE was timely enough to be useful for the project.

At the World Bank, there are signs that IEs are increasingly synchronized with the project cycle. For instance, 54 percent of completed IEs that were initiated since 2005 disseminated a baseline report to the project team, and 68 percent shared results on project implementation. Comparatively, 34 percent and 43 percent of completed IEs initiated before 2005 shared a baseline report and implementation progress report, respectively, with the project team.

IEs of sound quality whose findings are credible and robust are more useful from an operational perspective. IEG found suggestive evidence that high-quality World Bank IEs were more likely to be used in project reviews than low or average quality IEs. Meanwhile, the difference between the reported contributions of IEs of high versus medium quality on informing the decision to stop/continue/expand the evaluated project, or the design of new/follow-on projects, was not statistically significant. Nine of thirteen low-quality IFC IEs were substantively referenced in completion documents, compared with one of four good-quality (that is, medium to high quality) IEs. In the same vein, based on the small survey sample, three of three low quality IFC IEs were reported to have influenced operational decisions about evaluated project compared to one of five high-quality IEs.

It is important to note that the perception of quality is not always objective. In fact, the actual quality of an IE is not necessarily understood to the users, who are often unfamiliar with the technicalities of different methods. Furthermore, as discussed, there is no formal and standardized mechanism to review quality, which applies to all IEs across the World Bank and IFC. Without effective quality controls, IEs that are of unsound quality can be used for policy dialogue and decision making.

Not all World Bank IEs are disseminated to their potential users, which limits the likelihood of use. At the World Bank, 54 percent of completed IEs were shared with counterparts in the government. According to the survey, 76 percent of completed World Bank IEs whose findings were disseminated to the government influenced policy dialogue, compared with less than 20 percent of IEs that were not disseminated to counterparts. Similarly, IEs that were disseminated to the government were more likely to be used to affect operational decisions and to inform the design of follow-on/new projects (46 percent and 52 percent, respectively) than IEs whose findings were not shared with the counterpart in government (19 percent and 33 percent, respectively). Furthermore, the emphasis on methods and overreliance on the technical language in the communication of IE findings by evaluators is a recurring issue raised by operational staff and counterparts.

Finally, there was also consensus among people interviewed that more brief communications of preliminary findings (including in the local language) is necessary to provide results in time for decision making. This keeps stakeholders engaged and ensures that the results, if controversial, could be gradually introduced and accepted. In recent years, there has been much more emphasis on dissemination of results to specific clients and communities of practice at the World Bank (the SIEF policy and dedicated funding to share results being a notable example).

Active involvement of counterparts in the government in the IE process improves the uptake of evaluation findings and lessons. Active engagement of the client/government in the initiation, design, and conduct of IEs will affect how they are used. Client/government involvement in the IE process leads to greater ownership of the final product, better adaptation of the design in time for changes in the project implementation, and more likely reflects client/government priorities (box 5.7).

Findings from the survey corroborate the impression that client participation is central to IE use. According to the survey of evaluators, 58 percent of completed World Bank IEs that had client involvement in the design stage were also used to inform the design of follow-on or new projects, compared with 40 percent of

Box 5.7	Partnership with Project Teams and Clients: Vietnam and Central America

Vietnam Rural Energy Project

The Vietnam Rural Energy Project aimed to expand rural access to electricity in Vietnam through grid extension. The desired outcomes were to improve welfare, enhance earning capacity, and help alleviate poverty.

The IE found significant impacts on households' income, expenditures, and educational outcomes. The impacts are higher during the first few years after a household receives electricity, and incremental benefits eventually level off after about nine years of electricity use. The IE was sent to the project team and country office but was never presented to the government. It was not available for the project ICR or decisions regarding the follow-on project. The Bank team found the language of the IE too technical to understand. As a result, the project team felt little ownership of the IE findings. The government was eager to partner with the World Bank in evaluating similar projects because it lacked the capacity to do so and the energy sector had not been widely evaluated. The government expected the evaluation to answer many questions that were important but beyond its scope. Because of a lack of partnership, no dissemination, and different expectations, the IE was not used by the government or project team.

Central American Coffee Project

The project partners in the Coffee Value Chain Project in Central America were interested in conducting a credible evaluation to assess the impacts of the project since its beginning. The project was a public-private partnership between IFC, the Nestlé Group, and ECOM. The objective of the project was to increase the income (shared value) of coffee farmers in the Central American and Southern Mexican region included in the ECOM-Nestlé Value Chain. It sought to do this by improving their social and environmental standards to gain premium prices, and by decreasing their operating costs and enhancing their productivity.

IFC contracted IEs for two components of the project, productive investments and improving sustainable investments. The goal of the IEs was to assess the impacts of the project and to test certain design features. The key facilitating factor in these evaluations was client buy-in. Partners invested time in collecting the data and reviewing the final drafts and were interested in using the findings.

Stakeholder interviews revealed that the reports need to be clear and more readable. In response to the stakeholders' demands to understand IE findings better, the project team hired a consultant to prepare a summary note of these evaluations and triangulate findings with qualitative data.

Sources: IEG country case studies.

completed Bank IEs that did not engage the government at the design stage. In some contexts, the involvement of a national statistical agency can increase a government's trust, and the results and the process may be better accepted when overseen and presented by the statistics agency (World Bank 2009). For instance, completed World Bank IEs that involved the government in the fieldwork and analysis stages were more likely to be used to inform the design of follow-on projects (67 percent and 83 percent, respectively) than IEs where the government was not involved in these stages (table 5.1).[24]

The political environment and a culture of using M&E evidence in decision making also affect IE use and influence on policy making. The country case studies and interviews with World Bank Group staff reveal that the policy makers' acceptance of IEs depends on the culture of evidence-based policy making, the appreciation of the decision makers for technical analyses, the agenda of the party in power at that time, and other political economy aspects. Relevant and credible findings of IEs sometimes go against the ideology or belief of the policy makers and thus are less welcome or are ignored. In addition, a change in government often results in a shift of direction in policy, with the new government rejecting programs endorsed by the previous one, either to separate itself from the legacy of the previous government or to put more

Table 5.1	Comparison of IE Utilization between IEs with Client Involvement versus No Client Involvement (percent of completed World Bank IEs)					
Client involvement in different stages of the IE process	IE used in the project's decision to continue, stop, reduce, expand assistance or change project design		IE used to inform the design of a follow-on or new project		IE used to influence the policy dialogue with the government	
	Client participation	No client participation	Client participation	No client participation	Client participation	No client participation
Design	45	37	59	43	77	47
Fieldwork and implementation	45	38	65	42	70	51
Analysis	50	39	83	45	83	54
Review	45	36	65	36	68	8

Source: IEG.

Note: Based on evaluator survey of 64 completed World Bank IEs. The difference between client and nonclient participation is statistically significant for IE influence on design of follow-on/new project (all four stages of the IE process) and in policy dialogue (three stages, not including the fieldwork stage). In terms of IE influence on decisions related to the evaluated project, the difference—though positive—is not statistically significant at the 10 percent level between client and non-client participation.

emphasis on its own signature programs, even if there are robust IE findings that confirm their effectiveness (box 5.8).

Similarly, IE users accustomed to the culture of evidence-based policy making are more likely to be receptive to IEs and use them to make policy decisions. For instance, the report "Making Results Count" on M&E for India (Fiszbein and Shah 2008) shows that in Implementation Status Reports for 11 projects, the sector manager made at least one comment related to data analysis in 3 cases (for example, "What did the data say?") and on data quality in none of the 11 cases.

The Country Management Unit made no comments in the Implementation Status Reports for these projects on (i) progress toward Project Development Objectives that made reference to actual data; (ii) implementation of M&E activities; (iii) data analysis; and (iv) data quality. This is consistent with reported uses of IE findings in India: Of the 8 completed World Bank IEs for which survey responses were available (of a total of 11 completed IEs), the use of IE findings to validate project impacts or inform the design of a follow-on or new project was reported for around one-third of IEs or less, even though the

---

Box 5.8 Political Context for Using Impact Evaluations: The Case of *Atención a Crisis* in Nicaragua

The CCT component of the *Atención a Crisis* pilot, modeled on an existing CCT in Nicaragua—the *Red de Protección Social*—was implemented for one year in 2005–06. The goal was to learn the impacts of a CCT scheme with some enhanced features, including skill promotion and productive investment. Hence, the pilot was accompanied by a rigorous IE program, initiated mainly by the World Bank, with some involvement of government counterparts, to inform the social protection strategies of the country.

This IE effort resulted in a number of papers showing that the pilot had significant positive effects on consumption, utilization of health care, and early childhood cognitive outcomes and helped protect vulnerable households from the adverse effects of negative shocks. In addition, the program had significant social spillover effects and improved households' attitudes about—and hence investments in—the future.

The ICR stated that the IEs were being used extensively. However, the findings of these IEs actually were not used for policy making. This was mainly because of the change of government in 2008, when the Sandinista National Liberation Front came into power. This led to a massive change in public officials across ministries and agencies involved in *Atención a Crisis*.

Despite the evaluation results, the new government associated social protection programs such as *Atención a Crisis* with the previous regime and thought of them as typical cash handouts that perpetuate passive aid receiving and populist agendas. In undermining the reputation of *Atención a Crisis*, the new government also argued that these programs increased domestic violence against women and failed to help empower them. As a result, they switched the focus of social policies away from CCT schemes to others types of interventions.

Sources: IEG country case studies.

---

same respondents for three-fourths of the evaluations perceived the IE to be useful for filling a knowledge gap. [25] These factors—political environment and culture of evidence based policy making—are not within the control of the World Bank, but they highlight the importance of promoting results orientation and use of evidence in policy decision making.[26]

Notes

1 The literature on theory of evaluation utilization identifies many uses (see appendix G for details).

2 For instance, six of eight transaction leaders of completed IFC IEs (who responded to the question) found IEs more useful than or as useful as midterm reviews; seven of eight found them more useful than or as useful as client surveys; and all found them more useful than or as useful as PCRs and before-after studies. The response rate for World Bank Group IEs for this question was low, and results cannot be generalized. However, interviews with World Bank Group management supported the viewpoint that IEs are perceived as useful.

3 The coding of impact description on ICRs was not conservative. As long as the direction of impact on any outcome(s) in the IE was mentioned in the ICR (not necessarily in the discussion to validate the results framework) without any meaningful discussion or documentation of size of impact, or even if preliminary results were mentioned, the IE was coded to have been used in the ICR to show that the project was effective. The difference in numbers between surveys and desk-based review, although not very large, might be because the respondents were more conservative in their interpretation of use.

4 Excluding IEs that are still under discussion and not yet designed or taken up by the client (and therefore less likely to be integrated in the project M&E), the difference in expectations about IE use becomes slightly larger: 62 percent of ongoing IEs initiated in 2009–10 are expected to be used in project reviews, compared to with 54 percent of IEs initiated in 2005–08. Whether respondents' expectations are realistic cannot be determined. However, survey results for completed IEs show a statistically significant relationship between IE use in project completion reports and the involvement of project teams at the concept stage. Evidence from surveys also shows that ongoing IEs are more likely to involve project teams. In tandem, these findings suggest that ongoing IE input to future completion reports may be higher than has been the case for completed IEs.

5 Surveys of task leaders and evaluators of ongoing IEs show that half of ongoing IEs are expected to influence operational decisions regarding evaluated projects, and two-thirds of ongoing IEs are expected to inform decisions about follow-on or new projects. In addition, no discernible differences were observed in expectations about the use of ongoing IEs initiated in 2009–10 versus 2005–08.

6 *Plan Jefes y Jefas* in Argentina, *Familias en Accion* in Colombia, *Atención a Crisis* and *Fondo de Inversion Social de Emergencia* in Nicaragua, Punjab Female Secondary

School Stipend Program in Pakistan, the Early Childhood Development Program in the Philippines, the Nutrition Enhancement project in Senegal, the Local Initiatives project in Russia, the Jalswarajya project in India, and the Safe Water Systems project in Afghanistan.

7 Life Enrichment Project in India, Business Simplification Project in Peru, and Corporate Development Project in Ukraine.

8 It is important to acknowledge that IE is one tool among many that decision makers use, and the ICR/PCR would not necessarily single out any one source of information as attributing to operational decisions. The ICR/PCR may single out the IE as the source of such decisions if the IE had a huge bearing on these decisions, and it is this "influence" that the ICR/PCR review was able to capture. It may also not necessarily be the case that operational decisions occur so early after project closure (the ICR is submitted six months after project closure), in which case the ICR/PCR will not provide evidence of IE use and influence on operational decisions.

9 Around 70 percent of the evaluated Bank lending operations have a follow-on project—this does not include subsequent phases in which the Bank is not involved.

10 The programs for each country are the following: Kecamatan Development Program (Indonesia), Reaching Out-of-School Children (Bangladesh), *Familias en Accion* (Colombia), Community Nutrition (Madagascar), Early Childhood Development (the Philippines), Nutrition Enhancement (Senegal), and Business Simplification and Rural Roads (Peru).

11 Two of the follow-on project documents only described impacts from the IE of the previous project, one made a passing reference to the IE, and two explicitly cited use of IE findings in project design.

12 Fifteen of the 24 programs for which project managers cited the influence of other IEs are also part of the desk review, yet the PADs/PDSs of only six cite the influence of other IEs.

13 It is important to note that the first wave of IEs of *Progresa* was neither linked to a Bank operation nor funded by the Bank.

14 In contrast, the CCT adoption curve has the S shape that one would expect for any new technology; one can even say that there is no discontinuity around the point where the *Progresa* IE was published (apart from many more people working on it). It is possible that if the supporting evidence showed negative or zero effects, the programs would not have taken off in the way they have, but without a counterfactual, this is hard to assess. For instance, teacher training programs consistently show little effect in most evaluations, but probably follow the same S-shaped diffusion curve as CCTs. Typically people stop funding and encouraging IEs rather than allow negative evidence to accumulate. Although the data are not available to provide a good answer to the second-order question of whether IEs

are more or less active in areas where IEs show negative or low impacts, this is perceived as an issue: in interviews, 7 of 21 Bank managers and directors explicitly voiced the need for more space tolerance for IEs that report failures.

15 *Red de Protección* Social Program.

16 The Education Quality Improvement Program and the Japan Fund for Poverty Reduction Scholarship.

17 Among team leaders and evaluators of ongoing World Bank IEs, the expectation is that 67 percent of these IEs will contribute to policy dialogue, which is consistent with the high use of completed IEs initiated in 2005 or later to inform policies. However, no discernible differences were observed in expectations about use in policy dialogue of ongoing IEs initiated in 2009–10 versus in 2005–08.

18 Examples include Office of the Chief Economist, DIME, and HDN seminars; the Development Impact blog; SIEF and DIME training workshops; and syntheses of the literature (Fiszbein and others 2009; Bruns, Filmer, and Patrinos 2011; Mansuri and Rao 2010).

19 At IFC, eight of eight IEs for which survey response was available were perceived to improve staff/client capacity. However, only one of the six IEs for which survey response on stakeholder involvement is available mentioned local researcher involvement at the analysis, two involved the client, and two involved the contracted company/institutions for survey. Because these findings are inconsistent, they are not reported.

20 See SIEF website (http://go.worldbank.org/Q2XYY39FW0); see also World Bank (2010).

21 Plans for a comprehensive M&E framework of the follow-on project of *Bono de Desarrollo Humano* were not implemented because the operation associated with the follow-on project was cancelled by the new government of Ecuador.

22 Because ICRs/PCRs are intended to report on program progress on indicators defined in the results framework, the absence of IE references in cases where IE questions are not aligned with the results framework is less surprising.

23 The timeliness of evaluation depends on many other factors, some of which are beyond the control of the evaluators. These factors include delays in data collection, agreement on an evaluation design, complications in procurement, unexpected changes in project implementation, funding running out, and political changes, among other things.

24 Apart from clients, a deeper engagement with other stakeholders (for instance, project teams in country) during the IE process may also increase IE usage. According to the survey, almost 40 percent of team leaders and evaluators said that IE relevance and usefulness can be increased if they are an integral part of the project and involve collaboration with stakeholders during their conduct.

Also, in the survey, stakeholder involvement is coded yes for one out of six IFC IEs. The number of responses is not sufficient to make any inferences about IFC.

25 Expectations about use of ongoing IEs to validate project impacts or influence design of follow-on or new projects is somewhat better (around half of IEs for which survey responses are available), but this is still modest, although virtually all of these IEs are perceived by the same respondents to be useful for filling a global knowledge gap. Of the 12 ongoing IEs that have been designed or that are further along in implementation, survey responses are available for 7 IEs.

26 Indeed, as mentioned elsewhere in the report (box 3.4), there are instances where the conduct of IEs has strengthened M&E frameworks and/or promoted the use of more IEs.

References

Bruns, B., D. Filmer, and H.A. Patrinos. 2011. "Making Schools Work: New Evidence on Accountability Reforms." Human Development Perspectives, World Bank, Washington, DC.

Castro, M.F. 2008. "Insider Insights: Building a Results-Based Management and Evaluation System in Colombia." ECD Working Paper Series, no. 18, World Bank, Washington, DC.

Fiszbein, A., Shah, S. 2008. *Making Results Count: A Strategy for World Bank Monitoring and Evaluation Work on India*. Washington, DC: World Bank.

Fiszbein, A., N. Schady, F.H.G. Ferreira, M. Grosh, N. Keleher, P. Olinto, and E. Skoufias. 2009. *Conditional Cash Transfer: Reducing Present and Future Poverty*. Washington, DC: World Bank.

Franco, G., and X. Fernandez-Ordonez. 2010. "Toward a Results-Based Monitoring and Evaluation System in the Ministry for Social Development." Quality of Public Expenditure, no.11. http://siteresources.worldbank.org/EXTLACREGTOPPUBSECGOV/Resources/Note_11.pdf.

Gertler P.J., S. Martinez, P. Premand, L. Rawlings, and C.M.J. Vermeersch. 2011. *Impact Evaluation in Practice*. Washington, DC: World Bank.

Grosh, M., C. del Ninno, E. Tesliuc, and A. Ouerghi. 2008. "For Protection and Promotion: The Design and Implementation of Effective Social Safety Nets." World Bank, Washington, DC.

Khandker, S., G.B. Koolwal, and H.A. Samad. 2010. "Handbook on Impact Evaluation: Quantitative Methods and Practices." World Bank Training Series, Washington, DC.

Lindquist, Evert. 2001. "Discerning Policy Influence: Framework for a Strategic Evaluation of IDRC—Supported Research." School of Public Administration, University of Victoria, Victoria.

Mansuri, G., and V. Rao. 2010. "Policy Research Report on Community Driven Development and Local Governance." World Bank, Washington, DC.

Rawlings, L., and G. Rubio. 2003. "Evaluating the Impact of CCT Programs: Lessons from Latin America." World Bank Research Policy Working Paper No. 3119, Washington, DC.

Soares, Y. 2011. "The Practice and Use of Impact Evaluation in Development: Reflections for the Evaluation Cooperation Group Meeting in Manila." Mimeo.

World Bank. 2010. "Development Impact Evaluation Initiative: A World Bank-Wide Strategic Approach to Enhance Developmental Effectiveness." World Bank, Washington, DC.

———. 2009. "Making Smart Policy: Using Impact Evaluation for Policy Making—Case Studies on Evaluations that Influenced Policy." Doing Impact Evaluation No. 14, Thematic Group on Poverty Analysis, Monitoring and Impact Evaluation, World Bank, Washington, DC.

Chapter 6

Conclusions and Recommendations

The World Bank and IFC have expanded their efforts in IE in the past decade. At the World Bank in particular, IEs have received special corporate attention, starting with the creation of DIME in 2005. More recently, the importance of institutionalizing IE at the World Bank under a strategic framework has been emphasized in IDA16 replenishment discussions. IEs are assumed to have benefits for improving development practices, yet that expected contribution has not been systematically assessed. In this report, IEG addresses this gap by examining the relevance of World Bank Group IEs in relation to operational needs and institutional and broader knowledge priorities; their technical quality; their use and influence on operations and institutional strategies; and their contribution to building evaluation capacity.

IEG recognizes that the World Bank and IFC are at different phases in their adoption of IE as an evaluation tool: At the World Bank, IE is recognized as a unique AAA product line and there are several advanced initiatives, but in IFC, IE has been used relatively recently, with limited technical capacity and resources. In spite of this, IEG identifies a set of common elements for both institutions that characterize the relevance and use of their IEs.

The findings indicate that although most of the evaluations are relevant and meet acceptable standards of quality—particularly those supported by the World Bank—there are interventions in some key areas and aspects of impacts that IEs can but have not addressed. The findings also point to an "underutilization" of IEs. There is no comprehensive evidence to quantify the benefits of IE, but many sources reviewed for this report point to how IEs have influenced aspects of development practice with real benefits, as well as a belief in their potential to yield much greater benefit. Yet overall the utilization of IEs is much less than generally expected within the World Bank Group. These results call for improvements in strategic IE selection and funding, as well as strengthening operational linkages, to fully leverage IE knowledge.

Conclusions

RELEVANCE OF IEs FOR OPERATIONAL, INSTITUTIONAL, AND KNOWLEDGE PRIORITIES

World Bank Group IEs are relevant for operations, institutional strategies, and knowledge purposes, but there are interventions in key areas and aspects of impacts that IEs have not addressed.

- Most Bank Group IEs are relevant to the objectives and outcomes articulated in project results frameworks and respective sector/business line strategies. In particular, at the World Bank, recent IEs are more likely to be integrated with project M&E and better aligned with global knowledge priorities than earlier ones.

- With few exceptions, completed Bank Group IEs did not examine supplementary questions of operational relevance, such as the following: Are impacts sustained over time and generalizable? What are the channels of transmission from interventions to outcomes? Which form of intervention is most beneficial? Are the interventions worth the cost? Many recent IEs at the World Bank have begun to test the impacts of alternative treatment strategies on development outcomes, and some efforts are being undertaken to encourage the use of cost-benefit analysis in IEs.

- Although there are more World Bank Group IEs in some sectors than others, recent IE initiatives—especially at the World Bank—have led to more IEs being undertaken in sectors that did not have an IE or that were scarcely evaluated. Even in sectors where IE presence before 2005 was strong, World Bank IEs in recent years have been initiated in strategic priority areas with fewer IEs in the past. However, IE activities in a few sectors and sector priority areas, where IEs are not traditionally used but where IEs can have significant learning potential, remain to be further developed.

- At the World Bank, the roll-out of SIEF has led to strategic selection and financing of IEs, most widely in human development sectors. Meanwhile, other IE initiatives—such as the creation of thematic programs and the adoption of the programmatic model by a growing number of IE programs—has improved strategic prioritization of IE topics as well as coordination between DIME and project teams in the conduct of IEs. However, opportunistic IE selection remains a concern, particularly in non-human development sectors. At IFC, IE selection to date has not been guided by any strategic framework; however, the recent IFC evaluation strategy, approved in FY12, intends to take identification of evaluation opportunities, including IEs, in a more strategic direction.

- In both the World Bank and IFC, opportunistic IE selection, where it occurs, is characterized by weak coordination and selection based on evaluation methods and topics that do not respond to strategic and/or knowledge priorities, or driven by readily available funding. In recent years, strategic coordination in IE selection and the integration between IEs and the operations they evaluate has improved in the World Bank; yet issues related to staff incentives, capacity, and funding are still perceived as key constraints to the production and relevance of IEs in the World Bank, as well as at IFC.

QUALITY OF WORLD BANK GROUP IMPACT EVALUATIONS

The majority of World Bank IEs meet medium or high quality standards, but some aspects of quality require deeper and more rigorous technical analysis. In contrast to this, IE work in the IFC has had design weaknesses, particularly in the construction of counterfactuals, compromising their quality.

- The majority of World Bank IEs used high-quality data; measured well-defined outcome indicators; checked, discussed, or at least acknowledged the most fundamental assumptions underlying the preferred estimate; and conducted some form of robustness check. However, the scope and quality of the tests used to validate the assumptions and findings vary.

- With a few exceptions, there are presently no formal and standardized mechanisms at the World Bank to ensure that all evaluations go through similar quality controls. Recent IE initiatives like SIEF have established formal quality review procedures, which are applied uniformly to all SIEF IEs. It is too early to assess these IEs for their quality, but IEG finds that IEs initiated under this approach are more likely to be subject to specialist review at the concept stage. A more formal process could therefore help ensure that individual evaluations get the feedback they need.

- Around half of completed IFC IEs meet high or medium standards of IE quality. Most IEs of low technical quality do not adequately address methodological problems such as weak construction of counterfactuals and selection bias and/or the statistical inference in these IEs rely on very small samples.

- The weakness in the technical quality of IEs is explained in part by lack of quality controls. In IFC, in particular, the lower technical quality of IEs reflects that the IFC IE agenda is still in its early developmental stage, with inadequate staff capacity and weak quality assurance mechanisms.

Use in Operational Decisions, Policy Dialogue, Institutional Strategies, and Evaluation Promotion

Although there is no comprehensive evidence to quantify the benefits of IEs, many sources point to how IEs have influenced aspects of development practice and had real benefits, and many people believe in their potential to yield much greater benefit. Yet overall, the use of IEs is much less frequent than generally thought within the World Bank Group.

- When influential, World Bank Group (mostly World Bank) IEs chiefly contributed to project assessment and decisions to design and sustain evaluated and future projects; they also raised the profile of certain types of interventions, substantiated the Bank Group's knowledge and position in policy dialogue, and promoted the appreciation for M&E. In addition, in areas where there is a critical mass of IEs, they have contributed to the formulation of strategic priorities at the World Bank.

- In earlier years, stand-alone IEs had limited influence on increasing local capacity, which requires a concerted and sustained engagement. Recent IEs initiated under the programmatic approach, which emphasizes a coordinated learning agenda and capacity building, are more likely to contribute to capacity building of staff and clients. In addition the World Bank has been undertaking systematic efforts to improve IE capacity, including formal training, guidance notes, periodic workshops, and linkages with communities of practice.

- Factors that strengthen the usefulness of IEs for enhancing development effectiveness include their relevance, timeliness, dissemination, engagement with potential decision makers, political environment, and a culture of using M&E evidence in decision making.

Recommendations

The objective of this report is to provide some insights on strengthening the value, relevance, and use of IEs to enhance development outcomes. Compared with other types of evaluation, IEs are more expensive, require specialized skills, and cannot be applied universally to all modalities of development assistance. Given these resource constraints, issues of selection and allocation are particularly relevant for IEs. IEG's recommendations focus on the IE tool, although they are also applicable to other forms of evaluations.

In light of the findings on IE relevance, quality, and utilization, IEG makes five major recommendations, recognizing that the World Bank and IFC are at different stages of IE adoption; therefore, the findings, conclusions and recommendations are separated for both institutions.

IEG findings and conclusions	IEG recommendations
1. Application of a strategic approach to identify IEs **In the World Bank:** Rapid growth in IE activity in the World Bank has been accompanied by efforts to improve strategic selection and coordination of IEs, led by DIME and SIEF. There is emerging evidence that IEs initiated under more strategic and better coordinated approaches over the last three to four years have better quality assurance mechanisms and greater engagement of clients and project teams and are aligned with a broader set of sector and knowledge priorities. However, in some sectors, particularly non-human development sectors, a strategic framework for IE selection from an operational and knowledge perspective is less prevalent. These IEs were more often selected opportunistically, often because of skills and funding availability and ease of evaluation The importance of strategic IE selection has been further underscored during the IDA16 replenishment, in which IDA deputies requested that the World Bank increase the number of IEs and deploy a more strategic approach to selecting projects for IE. **In IFC:** Efforts to conduct IEs, mainly to supplement Advisory Services project-level assessments, started in 2005 with modest resources, and 26 IEs of IFC Advisory Service operations have been completed to date. IE selection at IFC has been generally opportunistic, and not guided by a strategic framework. IEs were initiated mostly based on staff interest; results measurement team's initiatives; and availability of funding. Through a recent general evaluation strategy, approved in FY12, IFC plans to move toward a more strategic approach to identification and prioritization of evaluation opportunities, including IEs.	Apply mechanisms for strategic identification and prioritization of IEs at the World Bank and IFC to balance learning and results measurement objectives: • At the **World Bank**, develop a strategic approach to guide IE selection across sectors and Regions. Introduce guidelines to implement the strategic framework, building on a framework developed in the context of IDA16. • At **IFC**, prepare and apply a strategic selection framework, in consultation with relevant stakeholders, to guide selection of IE topics that are of strategic relevance for results measurement, global learning, and deployment of limited IE resources.

(continued)

IEG findings and conclusions	IEG recommendations
2. Coordination of fragmented funding **In the World Bank and IFC:** IEs increasingly depend on donor support through trust funds. Although access to multiple sources of financing eases the budget constraint, their fragmentation adds to staff transaction costs. Reliance on trust funds is not necessarily detrimental to IE relevance, but there is less flexibility over allocation and strategic planning.	Coordinate fragmented external funding with core funds at the World Bank and IFC to strategically finance the production of IEs: • At the **World Bank**, explore options for consolidation of external funding for IEs, including pooled trust fund facilities (umbrella funds), as IEG recommended in the 2011 evaluation of trust funds, to better coordinate and mobilize trust fund resources along with internal funds to support IE production within the strategic priority areas agreed by management and clients. • **At IFC**, explore options to coordinate IE funding from different sources (that is, donor, business line/Region budget), including possible financing window(s) under the monitoring and evaluation budget for the conduct of IEs in the Development Impact Department.
3. Integration of IEs into project design **In the World Bank:** Overall, there is a modest feedback loop among IE production, project operations, and learning. There are notable examples of IE influence on development practice, including project assessment, decisions to design and sustain evaluated and future projects, raising the profile of certain types of interventions, informing policy dialogue and institutional strategies, and building local M&E capabilities. Such examples indicate that, overall, IE is regarded as a valuable tool to increase development effectiveness through better evidence. But in some instances, even when IEs have been relevant and of good quality, they appear to have had limited use and influence for varying reasons: poor timing, failure to engage project teams and decision makers, or lack of dissemination. However, there are signs of improvement, including, for example, dedicated SIEF support for results dissemination as well as closer collaborations with operations and clients in design of ongoing IEs. **In IFC:** The evidence indicates that IFC IEs were often used by the project teams, but their use beyond the project has been less common. In particular, the link between IEs and learning has not been fully established. The evidence indicates that there is a limited awareness of IE applicability to operational work and policy, which constrains wider uptake and use of IEs.	Improve the integration of IEs into the design and review of projects at the World Bank and IFC to sharpen the focus of project operations on results by: • Stating clearly in the implementation design of the IE how it will achieve operational usefulness, serve the key decision points of the project, engage operational teams and local counterparts, and disseminate the findings to the relevant audience, in particular local counterparts. • Strengthening the use of IE evidence in the appraisal and ex post assessment of World Bank and IFC projects, wherever such information is available. • Effectively communicating IE evidence to the global audience by maintaining a central repository of IEs and undertaking thematic syntheses of existing IE evidence. • Building capacity of project teams and other local counterparts to understand and integrate IE evidence in program and policy decisions.

(continued)

IEG findings and conclusions	IEG recommendations
4. Adoption of quality standards **In the World Bank:** More than half of completed IEs were of high quality, and another two-fifths met medium quality standards. World Bank IEs go through varying degrees and types of quality assurance processes, especially IEs not initiated under IE initiatives, such as SIEF, which has formal and standardized quality review controls. In addition, little IE data are available for replication, which can help ensure quality. **In IFC:** Around half of 26 IFC IEs met the medium or high quality standards. The main limitations of the low-quality IEs were low sample sizes and the weak reliance on evaluation designs that affect the credibility of IEs to claim causal results. The absence of peer review standards and processes to ensure high technical quality is a contributing factor. IE data for replication to ensure high quality are not publicly available.	Adopt and consistently apply good practice quality standards to the conduct of all IEs at the World Bank and IFC, including independent peer review protocols. Additionally, ensure data availability for replication.
5. Incorporating analytical elements that enhance operational relevance **In the World Bank and IFC:** There has been mixed coverage of analytical elements relevant for operational needs, such as analysis of distribution of program impacts; cost-benefit or cost-effectiveness analysis of interventions; mapping of the causal chain from program inputs to outputs to outcomes; and measuring the contribution to impacts of individual components of program design. At the World Bank, IEs initiated in recent years appear to pay greater attention to some of these dimensions, and this trend should be sustained in future IE efforts. Similarly, these elements should be included in the design of future IFC IEs.	Regularly incorporate, where feasible, analytical elements, such as analysis of heterogeneous program impacts and cost-benefit analysis, in the design of all World Bank and IFC IEs.

Appendix A

Glossary of Terms

Impact Evaluation Methods

Impact evaluation (IE) assesses the causal effects (impacts) attributable to specific interventions, where the outcomes of interest of program participants are compared with a *counterfactual* situation.

The **counterfactual** is an estimate of what the outcome (Y) would have been for a program participant in the absence of the program (X). For example, if X denotes a vocational training program and Y denotes income, then the causal impact of the vocational training program is the difference between a person's income (Y) after participating in the vocational training program (in other words, when X = 1) and the same person's income (Y) at the same point in time if he or she had not participated in the program (in other words, when X = 0). Yet measuring the same person in two different states at the same time is impossible. This is called "the counterfactual problem": how to measure what would have happened if the other circumstance had prevailed.

To address this, evaluators typically use comparison groups (also called "control groups"). A key goal of an IE, therefore, is to identify a group of program participants (the treatment group) and a group of nonparticipants (the comparison group) that are statistically identical in the absence of the program. If the two groups are identical—except that one group participates in the program and the other does not—then any difference in outcomes must be caused by the program (Gertler and others 2011).

Ensuring that the two groups are nearly the same—establishing a credible counterfactual—is often difficult. Those in the treatment group may differ from those in the control group because programs often target different populations or because people with certain characteristics may self-select for participation in the program. Moreover, many factors other than the program may change over time. Various methods, each with its own underlying assumptions, can be employed to generate a control group that minimizes these biases and can serve as a counterfactual. The construction of a credible counterfactual is essential in establishing internal validity. These methods include the following.

EXPERIMENTAL METHODS

Randomized assignment of the intervention among eligible beneficiaries at the individual, household, or community level is considered the strongest method for evaluating program impact. It creates treatment and control groups that are, on average, statistically similar in both observable and unobservable characteristics. The difference between the average outcome for the treatment and control groups shows the impact of the program.

Potential threats to this method are crossover between the treatment and control groups (that is, those who are supposed to receive the treatment end up not getting it, or vice versa) and errors in implementing the randomization. Randomized assignment is also used often as an instrument in experimental evaluations with imperfect compliance/take-up as well as in non-experimental

IEs to encourage program take-up among participants. These uses are discussed under instrumental variable methods.

As noted in Karlan (2009), randomized assignment may not be suitable everywhere. The key criterion for randomized controlled trials is sample size, in separable enough units such that spillovers and general equilibrium effects can be measured. If planned properly and if the effects are not overly aggregated, then careful randomized controlled trial designs can measure both the direct impacts of the intervention as well as the positive and negative spillovers onto groups other than the direct beneficiaries (Karlan 2009). (Note that random assignment is not the same construct as random selection: The former assigns treatment and control and is related to internal validity; the latter selects those under observation from a larger population and is related to external validity.)

Non-Experimental Methods

Regression discontinuity design offers an alternative to constructing a counterfactual, taking advantage of discrete changes often present in the selection criteria used to establish eligibility for social programs. The idea behind this technique is to estimate (local) average impacts (that is, applicable only to a subset of the beneficiaries) of the program by comparing participants and nonparticipants with similar characteristics who are just above and below the cutoff point that determines eligibility. Concerns with this approach include the possibility that the eligibility index is not fully enforced, that covariates do not balance, or that estimates of program impact could be sensitive to the functional form used in modeling the relationship between the intervention and the outcome of interest.

The difference-in-differences method estimates program impacts by comparing changes over time in the outcomes of interest between a treatment group and a control group. The underlying assumption of this approach is that both groups would have progressed similarly over time without the intervention and that any unobserved heterogeneity is time invariant and therefore differenced out. This method, however, does not account for time-variant characteristics that affect the outcomes of one group but not the other.

The instrumental variable method involves using a variable (or instrument) that helps predict participation in the program but that is uncorrelated with unobservable characteristics that influence the outcomes of interest or affect such outcomes directly. This design estimates impacts through statistical econometric models in two steps. The first is to predict program participation based on the instrumental variable. The second is to calculate the program's impacts by drawing on the predicted value of the equation estimated in the first step.

Finding a sound instrumental variable (especially one that is defined ex post) is often difficult, however, and concerns remain about the possibility of exacerbating the bias if it is not selected carefully. In experimental evaluations with imperfect compliance/take-up, the ex ante randomized assignment is often used as an instrument. In some non-experimental IEs, an ex ante randomized encouragement design has been used, in which subjects are randomly assigned to receive either encouragement to accept the treatment or no such encouragement, such that only the treatment itself, not disregarded encouragement alone, will affect the outcome. The ex ante randomized assignment of incentive to participate in the program is then used as an instrument to estimate local treatment effect.

Matching methods pair program beneficiaries with nonbeneficiaries based on similar preprogram observable characteristics (simple matching) or on the predicted probability of receiving the treatment, given a set of observable preprogram characteristics (propensity score matching). Program impacts are measured as the difference in mean outcomes between program beneficiaries and matched controls. This method does not account for unobservable characteristics that could affect program participation. An additional concern of matching techniques is the size of the common support, that is, the overlap in the probabilities of participation across the two groups. Variants of this approach include a combination of matching and double-difference methods to account for time-invariant heterogeneity across treatment and comparison groups.

Structural modeling seeks to assess the impacts and different aspects of a program (for example, targeting, size, and timing of benefits) or other mechanisms of transmission based on models of economic behaviors that underlie the most relevant decisions for the program evaluated—for example, whether to send children to school in the context of a scholarship program. Empirical estimates of the structural parameters of the model are then used to simulate counterfactual outcomes of no program scenarios or modifications to the design of the program. However, estimation of structural models is not easy, as assumptions about the relationship between factors in the model and the functional forms of equations affect estimates.

Control functions are a class of structural modeling in the sense that they take into consideration the participation decision in the estimation process, more specifically the type of selection that is determined by unobservables. The idea is to incorporate the decision to participate in the program in the estimation of the impact of the program to fully control for endogenous selection and treat it as a traditional selection bias caused by omitting variables that can affect the outcome in the estimation. This approach is just an application of an estimator developed by Heckman (1979) to correct selection bias. A difficulty of this approach is modeling the control function so that conditional on this function, the treatment is uncorrelated with the error term.

Other Impact Evaluation Terms

Internal validity refers to the property of estimation of an effect being attributable solely to the reputed cause. In other words, if there is a causal relationship between X and Y, an estimation of that relationship has internal validity to the degree that it isolates the sole contribution of X to Y independent of any other (confounding) factors. IE methods are used to establish internal validity of an estimated causal relationship.

External validity is the ability to generalize findings from one context to another which differs in population, scale, or time. External validity across populations is often a function of sampling: If a sample is representative of a larger population (the **sample frame** or **universe**), then characteristics and internally valid relationships established between interventions and outcomes in the sample population are externally valid to the larger population from which the representative sample was drawn. Randomization is often used to select the observation sample from the sample frame to ensure representativeness and thereby realize a high level of external validity; this process is termed **random selection.**

Internal validity and external validity are independent constructs: one need not imply (or preclude) the other. They also vary along a continuum from high, in which an effect is fully identified or fully generalizable, to low, in which an estimated effect is not credible or generalizable.

Bias is a term that refers to how systematically different the average statistic is from the population parameter of interest. Sample selection bias and endogeneity bias refer to two distinct concepts, both entailing distinct solutions. Sample selection bias refers to problems where the dependent variable is observed only for a restricted, nonrandom sample. For example, one observes an individual's wage within a union only if the individual has joined a union. Conversely, one observes an individual's nonunion wage only if the individual does not belong to a union. Endogeneity refers to the fact that an independent variable included in the model is potentially a choice variable, correlated with unobservables relegated to the error term. The dependent variable, however, is observed for all observations in the data. For example, when assessing the impact of unionization on wages, union status may be endogenous if the decision to join or not join a union is correlated with unobservables that affect wages.[1]

Prospective versus Nonprospective Impact Evaluations

IEs can be divided into two categories: prospective and retrospective (nonprospective).

Prospective evaluations are developed at the same time that the program is being designed and are built into program implementation. Baseline data are collected prior to program implementation for both treatment and comparison groups.

In general, prospective IEs are more likely to produce strong and credible evaluation results, for three reasons (Gertler and others 2011). First, baseline data can be collected to check if treatment and comparison groups are similar and establish preprogram measures of outcomes of interest. Baselines can also be used to assess targeting effectiveness, that is, whether the program is going to reach its intended beneficiaries. Second, defining measures of a program's success in the program's planning stage focuses the evaluation and the program on intended results. Consequently, the IE design can be fully aligned to program operating rules, as well as to the program's rollout or expansion path. Third, in a prospective evaluation, the treatment and comparison groups are identified before the program is implemented. At the design stage, alternative ways to estimate a valid counterfactual can be considered; therefore, many more options exist for carrying out evaluations with robust counterfactuals when the evaluations are planned from the outset and informed by a project's implementation. Prospective evaluations can have either an experimental or quasi-experimental design (Gertler and others 2011).

Retrospective (or nonprospective) evaluations assess program impact after the program has been implemented, generating treatment and comparison groups ex post. Generally, options to obtain a valid estimate of the counterfactual are more limited in those situations. The reason is partly that many programs do not collect baseline data unless the evaluation was built in from the beginning, and once the program is in place, it is too late to collect the data. Furthermore, these evaluations are dependent on clear rules of program operation regarding the assignment of benefits. It is also dependent on the availability of data with sufficient coverage of the treatment and comparison groups both before and after program implementation. As a result, the feasibility of a retrospective evaluation depends on the context. When feasible, retrospective evaluations often use quasi-experimental methods and rely on stronger assumptions to estimate causal impact (Gertler and others 2011).

Aspects of Interventions

According to Ravallion (2009), the art of good evaluation is to ask the right questions at the outset and to tailor the data and analysis to answering those questions. One such question has to do with understanding the specific program setting, as it is critical to determining the appropriate IE design. For instance, is it a uniform intervention or a collection of disparate initiatives? Is the intervention tightly specified and standardized or does it vary in different locations? Are the impacts likely to be the result of a "silver bullet" intervention that achieves results irrespective of context or a "ducks lined-up" intervention that achieves results only in conjunction with other interventions (Rogers 2009)?

These different characteristics of development interventions have been summarized in the literature in terms of a three-part typology—simple, complicated, or complex (table A.1). According to Rogers (2009), the typology is particularly useful when it is used to classify aspects of interventions rather than the whole intervention.

Simple aspects of interventions are discrete, standardized interventions that are intended to be implemented in the same way in different locations (for example, conditional cash transfers [CCTs] have some aspects that can be characterized as simple). However, CCT interventions can have *complicated* aspects as well (Rogers 2009).[2] For instance, CCTs may be accompanied by a package of other interventions to achieve the intended outcomes (for example, the evaluation capacity development-CCT pilot in Nicaragua or the CCT school attendance monitoring program in Morocco), or the size of the cash transfer (for example, the Sindh Differential Stipend Program) or the recipient of the cash transfer (for instance, the CCT program in the Nahouri Province in Burkina Faso).

Complicated aspects of interventions have multiple components, are part of a larger multicomponent intervention, or work differently as part of a larger causal package, for example in particular implementation environments, for particular types of participants, or in conjunction with another intervention (Rogers 2009).

Complex aspects of interventions are dynamic, adaptive, and responsive to emerging needs and opportunities. Complex interventions are not standardized interventions, nor do they appear to be tightly prescribed in advance. Instead, the specific objectives of the program, and the means of achieving these, are likely to emerge as the program proceeds and a better understanding of the priorities and possibilities is developed (Rogers 2009).

Table A.1	Simple, Complicated, and Complex Aspects of Interventions		
	Implications for		
Aspects	**Implementation of the intervention**	**Causal processes**	**Reporting and use of IE findings**
Simple	Single organization	Single causal strand needed to produce the impacts	Single message—what works
Complicated (multiple components)	Multiple organizations in contractual relationship with clearly defined roles	Multiple causal strands needed to produce the impacts; Multiple sequential interventions or multiple levels of intervention or different causal mechanisms operating in different contexts	Contingent message—what works for whom in what situations
Complex (dynamic and emergent)	Multiple organizations in developing partnership relationship	Causality is recursive, with feedback loops; Emergent outcomes—the whole is more than the sum of the parts	Dynamic, emergent message—what is working

Source: Rogers 2009.

Notes

1 http://www.stata.com/support/faqs/stat/bias.html.

2 This is also illustrated by the considerable heterogeneity in terms of outcomes seen in evaluations of CCTs. For instance, a CCT may be successful in achieving the initial objective of school attendance but not when it comes to achieving longer-term impacts such as learning, graduation, and employment outcomes, or the CCTs may be more effective in certain implementation environment and for certain participant characteristics (Rogers 2009).

References

Gertler P.J., S. Martinez, P. Premand, L. Rawlings, and C.M.J. Vermeersch. 2011. *Impact Evaluation in Practice*. Washington, DC: World Bank.

Heckman, J. 1979. "Sample Selection Bias as a Specification Error." *Econometrica* 47(1): 153–61.

Karlan, D. 2009. "Thoughts on Randomized Trials for Evaluation of Development: Presentation to the Cairo Evaluation Clinic." 3IE Working Paper No. 4, pp. 8–13. 3IE, New Delhi.

Ravallion, M. 2009. "Evaluating Three Stylized Interventions." 3IE Working Paper No. 4, pp. 14-23. 3IE, New Delhi.

Rogers, P. 2009. "Matching Impact Evaluation Design to the Nature of the Intervention and the Purpose of the Evaluation." 3IE Working Paper No. 4, pp. 24–33. 3IE, New Delhi.

Appendix B
Methodology

Sampling for Desk Review

A sampling exercise was undertaken for the desk review of completed or ongoing IEs that had any Bank engagement (financing or authorship) but were not linked to a lending or an operation of analytical and advisory activities (AAA). The universe of International Finance Corporation (IFC) IEs is small (26 completed, 4 ongoing), so they were not subject to sampling, and all were included in the desk review.

The universe of World Bank IEs (completed or initiated since 2000 and having World Bank Group involvement—funding, authorship, or financing of the intervention being evaluated through a lending or AAA project) was drawn from two sources:

- The database of IEs from the Development Impact Evaluation Initiative (DIME), which started in the past few years to document IEs across the World Bank.

- The list of IEs covered by literature reviews conducted for nutrition and social safety nets, or other IEs that were referred to the team by World Bank staff. This list is complemented by the IE list from IFC.

This limitation in data sources and coverage may introduce biases in the trends reported in this evaluation, but it does so in known ways: under-reporting of IEs at the World Bank means that estimates of IE frequency at the Bank Group are a lower bound; similarly, because the DIME database comprises a large share of the sample evaluated in this report and because DIME and the Spanish Trust Fund for Impact Evaluation (SIEF) are so engaged in experimental work, estimates of the frequency of experimental versus non-experimental IEs represent an upper bound. Finally, IEG is limited in the depth of coverage for supplemental data in sectors beyond nutrition and social safety nets.

The compiled Bank Group IE database, although not comprehensive, covers the majority of IEs with Bank Group involvement. This includes 460 IEs (198 completed and 262 ongoing), of which 309 evaluated World Bank lending or IFC advisory service projects.[1] Each IE report constituted a single unit of observation.

Of the 43 completed IEs with World Bank support *but not linked to a lending or AAA operation,* 21 were randomly selected for review. The results for a sample of this size are significant at a 95 percent confidence level with a ±10 percentage point margin of error.

Of 172 ongoing IEs linked to a World Bank lending or AAA operation (whose description was verified by a survey),[2] 59 were selected for the random sample, significant at a 95 percent confidence level with a ±10 percent margin of error. During the review stage, five of these IEs were dropped, as they corresponded to dropped or duplicate IEs. Forty-four of the 54 ongoing IEs were of World Bank lending operations; 10 corresponded to AAA operations.

Table B.1.	Information Sources and Collection Methods for Evaluation Questions

Evaluation questions/chapters	Information sources and collection methods
Chapter 2 (IE Experience at the World Bank Group)	• Structured interviews with World Bank Group management • Electronic surveys of IE evaluators and team leaders of World Bank Group-evaluated projects • Desk review of relevant project documents (PADs/PDSs, ICRs/PCRs, PPARs) of all 117 completed IEs and a sample of 46 of 182 ongoing IEs of World Bank Group lending projects
Chapter 3 (Relevance of IEs): *To what extent and why (or why not) are IEs relevant to close knowledge gaps and aligned with the World Bank Group's and clients' priorities and strategies?*	• Structured interviews with Bank Group management • Electronic surveys of IE evaluators and team leaders of Bank Group-evaluated projects • 12 field-based and 7 desk-based country case studies • Desk review of relevant project documents (PADs/PDSs, ICRs/PCRs, PPARs) of all 117 completed IEs and a sample of 46 of 182 ongoing IEs of Bank Group lending projects • Desk review of all World Bank sector strategies and a sample of CAS since 2000 • Desk review of all World Bank education projects closed in 2009 • One sector case study in the education sector
Chapter 4 (Quality of IEs): *To what extent and why (or why not) do IEs meet the expected quality standards and address the questions of interest?*	Desk review of all completed evaluations of World Bank lending and nonlending (117 IEs) and IFC advisory service projects (26 IEs) and a random sample of 21 of 43 completed evaluations of non-World Bank projects
Chapter 5 (Use and Influence of IEs): *To what extent and why (or why not) are IEs used to influence development practice?*	• Structured interviews with World Bank Group management • Electronic surveys of IE evaluators and team leaders of Bank Group-evaluated projects • 12 field-based and 7 desk-based country case studies • Desk review of relevant project documents (PADs/PDSs, ICRs/PCRs, PPARs) of all 117 completed IEs and a sample of 46 of 182 ongoing IEs of World Bank Group lending projects

Source: IEG.

Note: CAS = Country Assistance Strategy; ICR = Implementation Completion and Results Report; IE = impact evaluation; PAD = Project Appraisal Document; PCR = Project Completion Report; PDS = project data sheet; PPAR = Project Performance Assessment Report.

Desk Review of Sector Board Strategies and Country Assistance Strategies

To identify the contribution of IE to World Bank Group strategies, Independent Evaluation Group (IEG) staff reviewed all sector board strategies and a stratified random sample of half of all Country Assistance Strategies developed since 2000. The sampling of the strategies was done randomly, stratified by Region. In the review of strategies, a search for the keyword "impact evaluation" was conducted using Atlas TI. The team then extracted the paragraphs including the keyword and reviewed them to classify them as a reference to a specific IE, citing findings from IEs, identifying lessons learned from IE evidence, acknowledging the use and influence of IEs, and promoting more IEs in the future, or a marginal reference. The results of these searches and classification provide information for the analysis on the use of IEs for the World Bank institutional strategies.

Surveys of Evaluators and Project Task Leaders

IEG sent electronic surveys (via SurveyMonkey.com) to IE authors (including M&E officers in IFC) and team leaders of Bank Group projects that had been subjected to an IE, to collect information about their experiences and views.

The surveys asked respondents about many dimensions of IEs: what motivated the conduct of the IE, its funding, implementation, findings and dissemination, and use and influence of the findings with regard to country and World Bank Group policies. The surveys also asked general questions about the main institutional factors constraining the conduct of IEs and how the relevance and usefulness of IEs could be improved. Although some questions were asked of both evaluators and team leaders, to compare different perspectives on certain issues, team leader questionnaires focused on project matters and the usefulness of IEs for Bank Group operations; evaluator questionnaires asked more questions about the conduct of the evaluation itself. A copy of the questionnaires is available to interested parties upon request.

The list of evaluators (people involved in the IEs) was compiled from the list of evaluation authors, IE team leaders, and contact persons of all the IEs supported by the World Bank Group between 2000 and 2010 in the compiled IE database.[3] The list of team leaders was compiled from project completion reports (Implementation Completion and Results Report [ICR]/Project Completion Report [PCR]) and project design documents (Project Appraisal Document/ project data sheet, if the ICR/PCR was not available). Each project has at most two team leaders (at approval and at completion/current). These lists include more than one IE done on a single project, a number of team leaders involved in more than one project for which there was an IE in the database, and a number of evaluators who were involved in more than one IE. Because each person could only receive one survey,[4] a criterion was used for deciding which IE each respondent would be asked about. This maximized the number of surveys and thus the potential for data gathering, as well as the number of IEs and projects covered in the survey, based on information available to select survey recipients.

In some cases, more than one IE was conducted about the same project or about a similar topic, so there was a risk of confusion about the reference IE on the part of the respondents. To prevent confusion, information about the specific IE (title, description, and, when appropriate/available, project name and IE authors) was mentioned either in the email that contained the survey link or in the survey itself.[5] In the survey, the evaluators were also asked to confirm the description of the IEs. The responses to the surveys were anonymous and reported at an aggregate level.

Although the total number of possible survey recipients was 804, a number of them did not receive or complete surveys for reasons such as lack of an email address, opting out of the SurveyMonkey,[6] or lack of IE description.[7] The surveys were sent to 661 task team leaders, transaction leaders, and evaluators between March and June 2011. By the closing date for the surveys (June 30, 2011), 318 responses had been received, corresponding to a response rate of 48 percent (table B.2).[8]

BIAS CHECKS

To check for potential biases in responses, the characteristics of survey respondents (region and network affiliation) were compared with those who did not respond. The breakdown of net surveyed team leaders/evaluators across some dimensions (region, network, affiliation) was compared with the breakdown of survey responses. Other than in the regional breakdown of team leaders (further explained below), there do not appear to be major differences in the breakdowns to suggest any bias in survey responses.

- A regional breakdown shows that the Latin America and the Caribbean Region is underrepresented among survey respondents, and East Asia and

Table B.2	Survey Response Rates				
	World Bank task team leader	IFC transaction leader	World Bank Evaluator	IFC M&E	Total
Addressable	287	21	482	14	804
Dropped	88	4	47	4	143
Net survey recipients	199	17	435	10	661
Responses	78	14	218	8	318
Response rate (%)	39	82	50	80	48

Source: IEG survey data.

Note: IFC = International Finance Corporation; M&E = monitoring and evaluation.

Pacific and South Asia are slightly overrepresented. For evaluators, the regional breakdown of responses is mostly in line with the breakdown of surveys sent, with Africa showing a slight overrepresentation (figure B.1).

- A comparison across evaluator affiliation shows that although a majority of evaluators are affiliated with the World Bank, those who are not were more likely to respond to the survey (figure B.2).[9]

- Across networks, the breakdowns of team leader and evaluator responses are consistent with the breakdowns of surveys sent (figure B.3).

Country Case Studies

IEG selected five countries (Bangladesh, Indonesia, Nicaragua, Peru, and Vietnam) out of ten for an in-depth review of the of Bank Group IE experience,

Figure B.1   Regional Breakdowns

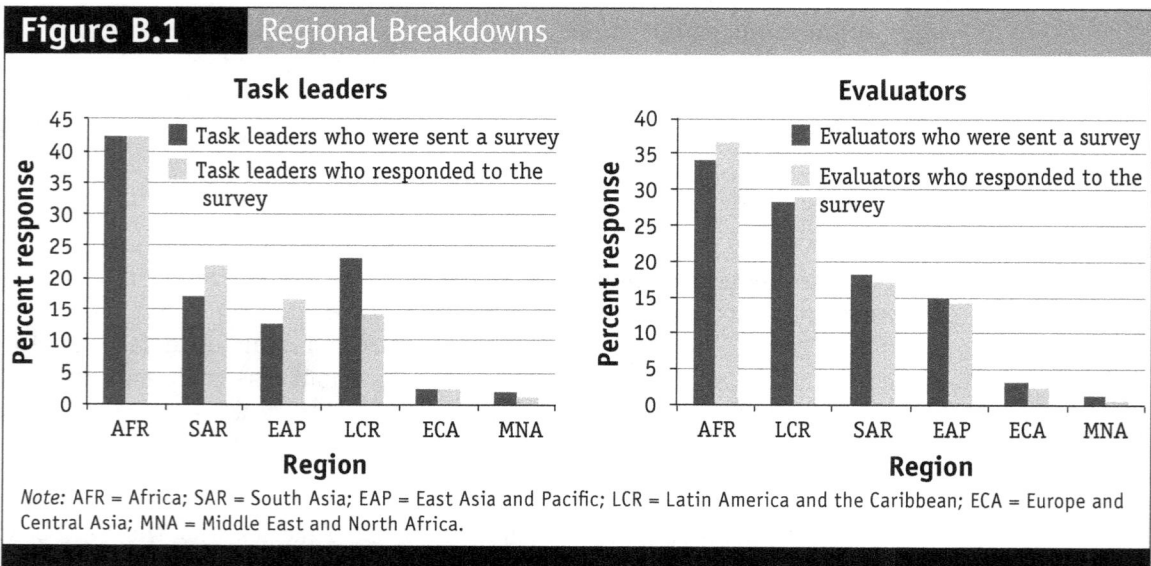

Note: AFR = Africa; SAR = South Asia; EAP = East Asia and Pacific; LCR = Latin America and the Caribbean; ECA = Europe and Central Asia; MNA = Middle East and North Africa.

Figure B.2   Evaluator Affiliation Breakdowns

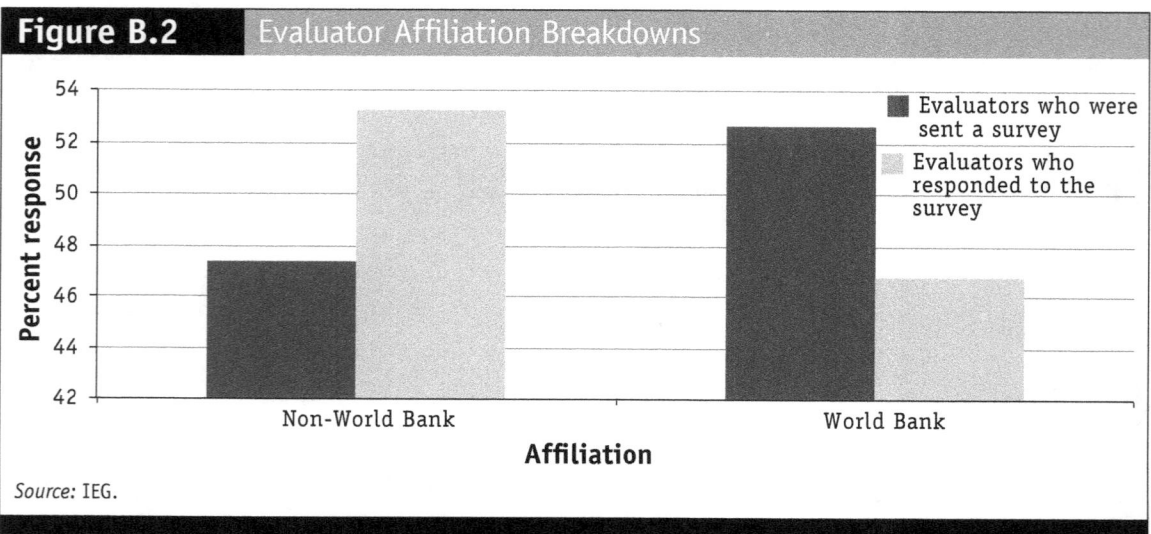

Source: IEG.

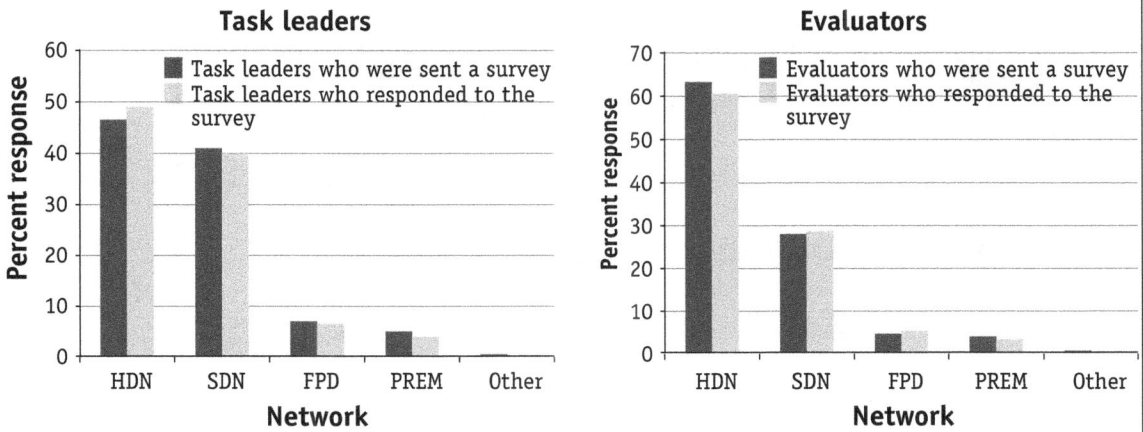

Figure B.3   Network Breakdowns

Task leaders

Task leaders who were sent a survey
Task leaders who responded to the survey

Evaluators

Evaluators who were sent a survey
Evaluators who responded to the survey

Source: IEG.

Note: FPD = Finance and Private Sector Development; HDN = Human Development; PREM = Poverty Reduction and Economc Management; SDN = Sustainable Development.

from initiation to dissemination and uptake stages. The selection is purposive and not representative of client countries of the World Bank Group; it includes those countries with a high number of completed IEs while maintaining regional and sectoral balance. Completed IEs were of greater interest because it allows IEG to document how the IE process works, from conception to use. This would not have been possible by focusing on ongoing IEs.

Once the five countries were selected, two to three case study projects were selected in each country, based on considerations for whether a project with an IE is active or when it closed. Country-level reviews entailed desk reviews of the IEs and project documents as well as structured interviews (including in the field) with internal and external stakeholders involved in the IEs and evaluated projects. IEG reviewed a total of 22 completed and ongoing IEs covering 10 Bank projects and 2 IFC projects. Eighty-five stakeholders were interviewed: 34 were Bank Group staff, 29 were staff of the government or affiliations, 8 were from the private sector, and 14 were from academia or research institutions. The list of interviewees is available on request.

Additionally, IEG encountered constraints to including Africa in the sample of field-based country case studies as originally intended. Instead, secondary case studies from a previous systematic review of IEs in nutrition (Madagascar, Senegal, and Uganda)—and following the same format as the case studies in the present report—were used to make sure that IE experiences in Africa were not left out. IEG also incorporated the findings from four additional country studies done for a nutrition study (Bolivia, Colombia, Ecuador, and the Philippines).[10] The projects in the country case studies are listed in table B.3.

Table B.3	Country Case Studies
Country	**Project**
Bangladesh	Female Secondary Education Assistance Project
Bangladesh	Reaching Out-of-School Children
Bolivia	Integrated Child Development
Colombia	Familias en Accion
Ecuador	Bono de Desarrollo Humano
Indonesia	Kecamatan Development Project
Indonesia	Scaling up Sanitation
Madagascar	Community Nutrition II
Nicaragua	Coffee Value Chain in Central America and Mexico (IFC)
Nicaragua	Atención a Crisis
Peru	Rural Roads Rehabilitation and Maintenance
Peru	Business Simplification in Lima (IFC)
Philippine	Early Childhood Development
Senegal	Nutrition Enhancement
Uganda	Nutrition and Early Childhood Development
Vietnam	An Trach Irrigation Scheme
Vietnam	Rural Energy
Vietnam	Scaling Up Hand Washing

Structured Interviews with World Bank Group Senior Management

The team conducted interviews with sector managers, sector directors, and chief economists at the World Bank and with business line leaders and M&E officers at IFC to capture the perspectives of World Bank Group management regarding IEs (see table B.4). The questions pertained to such issues as the motivation and selection of IEs, the process of producing IEs, and the use of IEs within their respective departments, as well as their views about the influence of IEs for the World Bank Group and its clients (and recommendations to improve IE usefulness). The list of interview questions is available upon request. The interviewees (21 from the World Bank and 13 from IFC and the joint IFC-World Bank Finance and Private Sector Department) were selected randomly from the list of all World Bank sector managers, sector directors, and chief economists and IFC business line leaders and M&E officers with representation at the sectoral and regional levels. The team conducted the interviews during May and June 2011.

Table B.4 — People Interviewed

Name	Title	Unit
Alan Johnson	Product Leader (Global)	Sustainable Business Advisory
Alexis Diamond	Evaluation Officer	Development Impact Advisory
Ariel Fiszbein	Chief Economist	HDN
Augusto de la Torre	Chief Economist	Latin America and the Caribbean
Cecile Fruman	Sector Manager	Investment Climate - FPD
Chiaki Yamamoto	M&E Officer	Public Private Partnership
David Crush	Regional Business Line Leader	Access to Finance
Dietrich Fischer	Consultant	Sustainable Business Advisory
Elizabeth King	Sector Director	Education - HDN
Emmanuel Y. Jimenez	Sector Director	East Asia and the Pacific Human Development
Gerardo M. Corrochano	Sector Director	Europe and Central Asia FPD
Gilles Galludec	Product Leader (Global)	Access to Finance
Hans Timmer	Director	DEC Prospect Group
Jesko S. Hentschel	Sector Manager	Europe and Central Asia Human Development Economics
John Henry Stein	Sector Director	South Asia SDN
Juergen Voegele	Sector Director	Agriculture and Rural Development - SDN
Karen McConnell Brooks	Sector Manager	Africa Agriculture
Laurence Carter	Director	Public Private Partnership
Lily L. Chu	Sector Manager	Latin America and the Caribbean Finance and Private Sector
Luba Shara	M&E Officer	Development Impact Advisory
Lucio Monari	Sector Manager	Africa Energy
Mansoora Rashid	Sector Manager	South Asia Social Protection
Manuela V. Ferro	Sector Director	Middle East and North Africa PREM
Marcelo Giugale	Sector Director	Africa PREM
Martin Ravallion	Director	DEC Research Group
Monika Weber Fahr	Senior Manager	Sustainable Business Advisory
Paramita Dasgupta	Regional Business Line Leader	Investment Climate
Peter D. Thomson	Director	Europe and Central Asia SDN
Rita Ramalho	Program Manager	Enterprise Analysis—FPD
Robin S. Horn	Sector Manager	Education—HDN
Sanweree Sethi	M&E Officer	Sustainable Business Advisory
Shantayanan Devarajan	Chief Economist	Africa Region
Xian Zhu	Sector Director	South Asia Strategy and Operations
Xiaoqing Yu	Sector Manager	East Asia and the Pacific Social Protection

Source: IEG.

Note: DEC = Chief Economist's Office, World Bank; FPD = Finance and Private Sector Development Network; HDN = Human Development Network; M&E = monitoring and evaluation; PREM = Poverty Reduction and Economic Management Network; SDN = Sustainable Development Network.

Notes

1 This number does not include some of the IEs that were dropped because of low project take-up and data issues, among other reasons. IFC has five IEs conducted for non-IFC projects but with IFC financial support.

2 There are 259 ongoing World Bank IEs in the database. Of these, 172 were randomly selected for the survey and their description verified and subsequently updated/amended. Because the description of the remaining IEs was not validated, it is not included for sampling purposes.

3 Because IFC IEs are mostly conducted by external companies, it was not possible to reach to evaluators directly; M&E officers who are responsible for the coordination of the evaluations were contacted instead.

4 Only a few evaluators received more than one.

5 Evaluators/team leaders linked to one IE received an email with the IE description contained in the text of the email. For evaluators/team leaders linked to multiple IEs, the SurveyMonkey questionnaire contained the description of the multiple IEs (up to three). If the leader/evaluator indicated that he or she was not aware of the first IE based on its description, he or she would be directed to the description of the second IE. If the team leader/evaluator indicated that he or she was aware of this second IE, he or she would be directed to the third questionnaire.

6 These are persons who received the survey but chose to unsubscribe from the SurveyMonkey mailing list.

7 Information such as email addresses was pulled from the World Bank Directory, another internal Bank database, and the Bank directory for retired employees.

8 Response rates were quite low at first, so the team followed up with team leaders, M&E officers, and evaluators by sending reminder emails. Team leaders who are still World Bank Group employees were contacted by phone as well.

9 A possible reason for this discrepancy may be that those not affiliated with the World Bank tend to be academics and may be more willing to participate in surveys and voice their opinions/views. Also, Bank affiliates may already be overwhelmed with Bank surveys and therefore be less willing to answer another one.

10 Primary country case studies for countries in Africa could not be undertaken as originally intended. In lieu of that, secondary case studies from a previous IEG evaluation on nutrition following the same format as the case studies in the present report, were used to make sure that IE experiences in Africa are not left out.

Appendix C

Assessing the Potential Coverage of
Impact Evaluations in Education

The World Bank estimates that IE covers around 13 percent of the portfolio of active International Bank for Reconstruction and Development/International Development Association lending (World Bank 2010). In this study, IEG sought to estimate how widespread the opportunities are for IEs in education, a sector where the production of IEs is relatively strong, based on technical grounds and without radically changing the nature of the intervention.

This appendix summarizes results from this assessment, that is, how many Bank-supported education projects that closed in 2009 would have been amenable to an IE without radically changing the nature of the intervention. As of January 2011, 35 projects in the education sector were listed as having closed in fiscal year 2009. Of these, seven were either cancelled or closed and did not have available documents describing the original project (one closed project did have documents available and was assessed). This left 28 projects, all of which were used in this assessment.

The criteria applied to assess suitability of the intervention for an IE are as follows:

- Interventions must be *sufficiently measurable*. Admittedly, measurability is a matter of degree, as some errors are inevitable in any observation, so some judgment is involved in determining when measurability is sufficiently high. If an intervention can be "observed to happen" in a reliable way, it is taken to be measureable for the purposes of an IE (for example, whether a student received training, whether a school was built, whether a class used a new textbook).

- Interventions must be *sufficiently excludable*. It must be possible to tell when a group or individual got the intervention and when it did not. Related to this, spillovers from the treatment group to the control group must be low.

- The outcomes of interest have to be *sufficiently measurable*.

- The outcomes of interest have to be *sufficiently different* from the interventions. For example, if the intervention is to "decentralize" something, the outcome to be achieved should be something other than "decentralization." Otherwise testing for impact would be too close to simply confirming whether the interventions were delivered. The greater the separation in the causal chain between interventions and outcomes is, the greater is the potential learning from the evaluation.

- There must be *multiple observations or experimental units*. An IE cannot be conducted if an intervention is indivisible or designed for a single national government agency, because there would be no scope for multiple experimental units (this will also be referred to as the n = 1 issue).

Interventions Amenable to Impact Evaluation

This exercise finds that a relatively high proportion of interventions in recently closed education projects would have been amenable to an IE of some kind.[1]

Of the $2,041.6 million in project expenditures, $1,612.1 million, or 79 percent, was estimated to be amenable to an IE. Of the 85 project components assessed, 42 (49 percent) were estimated to be amenable to an IE.

It is plausible that a higher proportion of expenditures than project components was judged amenable to IEs because expensive interventions tend to be amenable to them. A high proportion of expenditures in education projects include construction or rehabilitation of schools, acquisition of textbooks and equipment, teaching, teacher training, tutoring, and scholarship programs; all of these are excludable and therefore inherently amenable to IEs. The interventions in the education sector that are inherently unsuitable for IE are things like curriculum design, which are not large expenditure items, however important they are for overall education quality.

Among the five criteria applied to determine whether a project was amenable to an IE, the first criterion, measurability of the intervention, is almost always satisfied. The second—excludability of the intervention—is usually satisfied: most interventions can, strictly speaking, be excluded for some groups. The third criterion proves problematic for several interventions—in part because the outcomes are unmeasurable, but also because the anticipated outcomes are not articulated clearly in the project documents. In some cases where the objectives are vague, a measureable outcome could safely be imputed to the project even though the project documents are not explicit.

Examples where objectives are judged not clear enough for an IE included capacity building, management assistance, and leadership training. When the intervention is decentralization of management, the objective is essentially decentralization; therefore, such interventions fail the fourth criterion, separation between the intervention and the objective.

In addition to measureable objectives, several projects were deemed not amenable to an IE because they were national programs for a single entity. In some cases, such as a diagnostic study of the education system, the intervention itself could not be applied to multiple units; in other cases, there was only one national agency to receive the intervention. This was also deemed not amenable to an IE.

Impact Evaluations Conducted

IEs are being conducted or have been conducted for 3 of the 28 projects examined, or 4 of the 42 project components considered amenable to IE.[2] The Lifelong Learning and Training Project in Chile commissioned three IE studies: one on the impact of secondary school completion on incomes and employment probabilities; one on the impact on income and formal employment of having skills that workers had learned on the job formally certified; and one on the impact of career counseling on employment rates. There is also an ongoing IE associated with the Basic Education Project in Niger to measure the impact of the introduction of basic information management systems on "school outcomes" to promote effective management of schools. However, this intervention is not listed as one of the components of the project, which instead includes literacy training, school construction, and teacher training, so the IE is not assessing a project. A final IE was planned for the Rehabilitation of Basic Education Project in Sierra Leone. However, the project was cancelled.

In sum, of these three projects with some IEs, the Chile project is the only one where the evaluations were used constructively to shed light on questions critical to the effective performance of the project. It also used the estimated impacts from the evaluation to refine and validate the economic analysis of the project, demonstrating the potential of well-chosen IEs to shed light on issues that are central to the justification of the project.

However, a related question is whether all IEs that are technically feasible *should* be conducted. Given existing resource constraints and knowledge priority, a better strategy would likely apply IE to a much smaller subset than the feasible set identified above. Criteria for determining this could include the extent of previously established scientific knowledge, number of likely replications in the future, value of the information yielded, number of previously funded IEs, likely internal validity and external validity, availability of skills and resources, the clients' demands for knowledge and ability to absorb the message, and time constraints. The exercise does not explore these issues in detail, but this exercise identifying projects in the education sector amenable to an IE based on technical considerations still suggests that the potential to apply this tool is greater than is perceived. [3]

Notes

1 Applying the same technical criteria to projects approved in 2009, as opposed to projects closed in 2009, actual coverage would likely be much higher. Since 2005 and with the creation of DIME, the incidence of IEs has risen substantially. For instance, the database of IEs compiled by the team indicates 33 ongoing education IEs versus 27 completed ones (excluding IEs of cash transfer, evaluation capacity development, or health and nutrition programs that also evaluate education outcomes).

2 Applying these criteria to recently approved projects will likely show a higher proportion of education projects being subject to IEs than the number presented in the exercise, which is based on a review of projects closed in 2009. This is because there has been a substantial growth in IEs being produced by the World Bank in recent years.

3 When some of these normative assumptions (namely, whether bias is expected to be a major issue and existing knowledge gaps) are applied to projects that could have been assessed based on technical grounds, the exercise identified around 20–25 percent of education interventions where IEs, if done, would have been valuable.

Reference

World Bank. 2010. "Development Impact Evaluation Initiative: A World Bank-Wide Strategic Approach to Enhance Developmental Effectiveness." World Bank, Washington, DC.

Appendix D
Analysis of Impact Evaluation and Intervention Costs

The cost analysis exercise compares IE costs to intervention costs. Ideally, such an exercise requires using actual cost information. Although the cost of the intervention can be obtained from project documents, it is far more difficult to trace IE cost. This is because IEs are not generally funded from a single source. As described in chapters 2 and 3, IEs at the World Bank mobilize resources from multiple sources: government, donors, trust funds, Bank budget, and so forth. Meanwhile, documentation on consolidated outlays is difficult to obtain for the whole range of IEs subject to review.[1]

Because it is difficult to find the cost of each IE (for instance, funding coming from multiple sources that are not always recorded and several components of the evaluation such as data collection financed directly by the client), three cost scenarios are assumed based on the costs of different types of IEs:[2]

- Low IE cost, equivalent to $0.25 million
- Medium IE cost, equivalent to $0.5 million
- High IE cost, equivalent to $1 million.

Some of the interventions have been subject to multiple IEs, and later IEs may use the same evaluation design and data as the first in the intervention. In such cases, the costs of later IEs are not likely to be the same as the first IE— the first IE bearing the full cost of data collection, which is often the largest cost. Therefore, a later IE of the same intervention was assigned a differential cost based on whether it used existing data or the same data as the previous IE of the same intervention. For example, if an IE corresponds to a unique IE activity, it is assigned the full cost ($0.25–$1 million, depending on the scenario).[3]

For interventions subject to multiple IEs, the first evaluation is assigned the full cost (presumably including the cost of data collection), and later IEs using the same data sets (whether or not they evaluate the same intervention) are assigned a cost of $0.1 million. Similarly, if the later IE uses only existing data (for example, administrative data), it is also assigned a cost of $0.1 million. However, if this later evaluation collected additional data to estimate impacts, it is assigned the full cost ($0.25–$1 million, depending on the scenario). The costs of IEs are then aggregated up to the intervention level to allow for comparison against intervention costs.

Intervention costs are based on cost estimates in the ICR (or the Project Appraisal Document if the ICR is not available). Therefore, the cost analysis is limited to IEs linked with World Bank lending operations.[4] Also, the intervention cost is inclusive of Bank, government, and other donor financing, to the extent that these numbers are available in the documents reviewed.[5] There are, however, some estimation errors, because the intervention costs are not always listed explicitly in the documents. In cases where the difference between the observed and actual intervention cost is perceived to be large (for instance, a small subactivity of a bigger component for which cost is available) or cannot be reliably measured (for instance, budget support operations for which the budget amount for a program being implemented by the government is not given), the interventions and their associated IEs are excluded from the cost analysis.

Once the costs are assigned to the IEs and aggregated to the intervention level and intervention costs are documented, the cost is estimated as a proportion of intervention costs for the three (high, medium and low) cost scenarios.

The analysis presented in the report is based on a sample of 102 interventions corresponding to 124 IEs. Thirteen interventions corresponding to 16 IEs were not included in the sample for cost analysis, as they could not be accurately estimated (for reasons cited above).

Notes

1   The outlays on recent IEs are better documented, especially among those that have been assigned an IE code. Nevertheless, not all Bank IEs have been assigned an IE code, and tracing cost information remains a difficult exercise and cannot eliminate noise (World Bank 2010).

2   According to the DIME strategy report, "For the programs coordinated by the DIME Secretariat, average cost per impact evaluation is $526,198 divided between the Bank's internal funds ($25,638), donors ($273,785), and government ($225,224)" (World Bank 2010).

3   Several IEs may evaluate the same intervention, but if they use separate data, they are considered unique IE activities.

4   When the duration of the intervention being subject to an IE spans two operations, the intervention cost is taken as the sum of intervention costs given in the respective ICRs (PADs if ICRs are not available).

5   Note that it is cost of intervention being subject to an IE that is being captured, not the cost of all components/interventions covered by a lending operation.

Reference

World Bank. 2010. "Development Impact Evaluation Initiative: A World Bank-Wide Strategic Approach to Enhance Developmental Effectiveness." World Bank, Washington, DC.

Appendix E

Criteria for Scoring Spanish Trust Fund
for Impact Evaluation Cluster Proposals

Cluster proposals for the Spanish Trust Fund for Impact Evaluation (SIEF) are scored using five criteria, two pertaining to the cluster and the three to individual projects. Using these criteria, the technical committee scores each cluster and project. The score is assigned equally to all projects within a cluster, whereas the project scores are assigned to individual projects. The total points accumulated by each project determine the amount of funding requested to the SIEF Steering Committee. The criteria are as follows:[1]

Criteria 1: Policy Relevance (30%): What is the strategic importance of the cluster in relation to the World Bank's operations? How important are the results in informing future World Bank policies? *Scores range from 0–10.*

Criteria 2: Cluster Depth (10%): How well developed is the cluster? How many rigorous examples of country cases are currently under way? *Scores range from 0 to 10.*

Criteria 3: Technical Quality (25%): What is the overall technical rigor of the evaluation? How rigorous is the identification strategy, given the constraints of the intervention? How robust is the sample frame? *Scores range from 0 to 10.*

Randomization	Maximum score of 10
Quasi-experimental	Maximum score of 7
Non-experimental/other	Maximum score of 4

Criteria 4: Timeline for Result (25%): How soon will results be available for publication and dissemination? What is the current stage within the evaluation cycle? *Scores range from 0 to 10.*

Stage	Status	Score
Follow up Survey	In field or beyond	10
Planned		9
Under discussion		8
Baseline Survey	In field or beyond	7
	Planned	6
	Under discussion	5
Discussion/Design	Completed design	4
		3
	Concept note	2
		3

Criteria 5: Capacity for Delivery (10%): How capable is the evaluation team? What is the likelihood of successfully implementing the evaluation? How technically sound is the principal investigator? *Scores range from 0 to 10.*

Note

1 Based on information provided by SIEF.

Appendix F
Quality Review Framework

The framework used to review the quality of World Bank Group IEs originates from a well-developed literature on this tool. The team referred to theoretical and practical guidelines that mandate how IEs should be conducted to fulfill its scope and adapt to the available resources (Gertler and others 2011; Khandker, Koolwal, and Samad 2010; NONIE 2009; Duflo, Glennerster, and Kremer 2006; Imbens and Wooldridge 2008; Imbens and Lemieux 2008; Blundell and Costa Dias 2008). The assessment framework follows objective standards that cover the bulk of the aspects that make up the quality of IEs. It was developed and validated with guidance from an IE expert. The review focuses on four aspects/criteria of quality:

- Data quality and characteristics
- Relevance of outcome analysis and measurement
- Quality of evaluation design
- Robustness of findings.

Data Quality and Characteristics

Information in IE reports is insufficient to fully assess data quality, because information on potential data problems (missing data, measurement errors, and sampling errors) is not consistently presented across these reports. However, this review looks at select data characteristics that have a bearing on the quality of IE findings:

- *Use of baseline data* to compare pretreatment characteristics and outcomes of the treatment and control groups and/or estimate program impacts.

- *Use of retrospective data:* For the purposes of the quality assessment, data on outcomes and/or treatment indicators that were collected based on a "long" recall period were classified as retrospective. The study did not define a recall period as "long" based on some universal measure of elapsed time. Instead, the coding was based on a review of several factors: (i) how the recall period for a certain question is usually defined in other surveys (for example, in labor force and standard living measurement surveys, it is usual for questions on number of hours worked to be based on a seven-day recall period. Hence, if the IE uses data on hours worked based on a seven-day recall period, the study does not consider it as use of retrospective data); (ii) how the data were collected (for example, data on household food consumption in the past three months based on the diary method is more reliable but less so if it is based on recall); (iii) the uniqueness and/or frequency of the event (for example, a three- or five-year recall period for questions on births and deaths in the family is acceptable, as these are memorable events, but the same recall period for a question on number of visits to the doctor could lead to large measurement error); and (iv) if the data collected were discrete or continuous (for example, was the respondent ever employed during the past year versus how many days did the respondent work in the past year?).

In addition, the study also documented information on the type of data used (longitudinal, pooled cross-section, single cross-section) and the sources of data (administrative data, data collected through regular surveys, data collected through surveys conducted especially for IE), not as intrinsic measures of data quality but to understand key attributes of data collection instruments used in Bank Group IEs.[1]

Relevance of Outcome Analysis and Measurement

This criterion assesses the quality and relevance of outcome indicators, as this will indicate if the IE is accurately evaluating what it set out to assess. Three subquestions under this criterion determine the relevance of the outcome measurement and analysis:

- Does the IE provide evidence that all or some outcomes are *measurable*?
  - Are all or some of the outcome indicators *well defined* in the report?
  - Is the basis for selecting outcome indicators discussed in the report (only applies to indicators whose selection basis ought to be explained)?
- Are all or some outcome indicators *achievable,* given the length of exposure to the program?
- Are all or some outcome indicators *separate* from the intervention being evaluated?

Quality of Evaluation Design

The quality of evaluation design is the most critical determinant of IE quality; it is the linchpin for estimating the share of the change in outcomes attributable to the intervention. The starting point for this exercise is identifying the evaluation design (randomized/quasi-experimental) and methods (single difference, difference-in-difference, matching, instrumental variables, and regression discontinuity) used to identify program impacts. The next step is determining the quality of design, with special emphasis on whether the report provides a discussion of the assumptions/conditions under which the estimation methodology is valid:

- ***Assumptions under randomized experiment:*** Balanced treatment and control groups (the two groups having no statistically significant difference in main baseline or time-invariant characteristics) and noncompliance and/or attrition (minimal incidence of beneficiaries not receiving treatment or leaving the program, and vice versa).

- ***Assumptions under single difference:*** Balanced treatment and control groups (if the two groups are not randomized, there should be a discussion of potential confounders, especially regarding differences in unobservable or time-variant characteristics).

- ***Assumptions under double difference:*** (i) Parallel trending (the treatment and control groups progress similarly in terms of the outcomes of interests) and (ii) time-varying confounders (there are no time-variant variables that may affect the progress of the outcomes other than the intervention).

- **Assumptions under matching:** (i) Common support (the overlap in terms of propensity scores or matching variables between the treatment and control group); (ii) balancing checks on propensity score (the treatment and control groups having no statistically significant difference in main characteristics); (iii) matching on outcomes or covariates (the variables used to match are not affected by the intervention); and (iv) selection on unobservables (there should be a discussion of potential selection bias from unobservable differences between the treatment and control).

- **Assumptions under instrumental variables:** (i) First stage tested (the relationship between the intervention and the instrument is statistically significant) and (ii) exclusion restriction (the instrument affects the outcome only via the intervention).

- **Assumptions under regression discontinuity:** (i) Sorting around the assignment rule (beneficiaries tricking the rule to be eligible for the treatment) and (ii) balanced covariates at discontinuity (the two subgroups above and below the eligibility cutoff have statistically similar characteristics).

Robustness of Findings

An important element of quality is the strength and credibility of findings usually achieved through various types of robustness checks. The subquestions developed to capture this aspect of IE quality are the following:

- Did the IE use multiple estimation methods/evaluation designs?
- Did the IE use multiple specifications?
- Did the IE perform other robustness analyses (for instance, falsification tests; alternative ways to measure the treatment; multiple control groups; subsample analysis; sensitivity analysis and bounds; and so forth)?

IEG reviewed and coded each IE according to the extent that it satisfied these four quality dimensions. Once the coding exercise was finished, the documented evidence on the different quality dimensions (that is, both the coding and the extensive notes explaining the available evidence on which the coding was based) was reviewed to rate the IEs as being of *low* (not meeting most of the criteria outlined above), *medium* (meeting some, but not all, of the criteria), or *high* (meeting most of the criteria) quality.

Note

1 A repeated or single cross-section may be better in terms of data quality than a panel survey. However, IEG does not have the information available to make this assessment.

References

Blundell, R., and M. Costa Dias. 2008. "Alternative Approaches to Evaluation in Empirical Microeconomics." CEF.UP Working Papers 0805, Universidade do Porto, Faculdade de Economia do Porto.

Duflo, E., R. Glennerster, and M. Kremer. 2006. "Using Randomization in Development Economics Research: A Toolkit." MIT Department of Economics Working Paper No. 06-36, Cambridge, MA.

Gertler P.J., S. Martinez, P. Premand, L. Rawlings, and C.M.J. Vermeersch. 2011. *Impact Evaluation in Practice.* World Bank, Washington, DC.

Imbens, G., and T. Lemieux. 2008. "Regression Discontinuity Designs: A Guide to Practice." *Journal of Econometrics* 142(2): 615–35.

Imbens, G., and J. Wooldridge. 2009. "Recent Developments in the Econometrics of Program Evaluation." *Journal of Economic Literature* 47: 1, 5–86.

Khandker, S., G.B. Koolwal, and H.A. Samad. 2010. "Handbook on Impact Evaluation: Quantitative Methods and Practices." World Bank Training Series, Washington, DC.

NONIE (Network of Networks for Impact Evaluation). 2009. *Impact Evaluations and Development: NONIE Guidance on Impact Evaluation.* Washington, DC: NONIE.

Appendix G

Conceptualizing Use and Influence
of Impact Evaluation

The literature on *theory of evaluation utilization* in general identifies four types of uses: *instrumental use* (making decisions about programs based on evaluation results), *conceptual use* (affecting how people think about development issues), *strategic use* (persuading others or using evaluation findings to reach particular outcomes), and *process use* (promoting evaluation activities) (Cummings 2002; Shadish, Cook, and Leviton 1991; Worthen, Sanders, and Fitzpatrick 1997). Because *conceptual use,* that is, the effects of IEs in knowledge generation, is even more difficult to measure than the other three types of use, this evaluation assesses the relevance of IEs to knowledge priorities (see chapter 3) and focuses on the other three types of uses as they are relevant to the context of the World Bank Group.

Operational Decisions (Instrumental Use)

Within the evaluated project: IEs are a tool that can be used by various actors, inside and outside the World Bank Group, to assess whether a project produces its intended effects. Incorporating a prospective IE into a program may affect decisions regarding the design of a project in aspects such as targeting of beneficiaries, type of benefits, delivery mechanisms, and timing and quality of data collection, among other things. IEs may also help identify other related development issues to be addressed, evaluate pilot projects, and test different design features to improve subsequent phases of the project. The results from IEs could then demonstrate the impacts (or lack thereof) of the program, which could be central to operational decisions to continue, modify, expand, or terminate the evaluated project. In addition, if combined with information about costs, IE could provide an opportunity to assess the cost-effectiveness of programs, contributing to more efficient resource allocation.

Beyond the evaluated project: Evidence from IEs may also contribute to knowledge generation for enhancing development practices. As IEs are being conducted on an increasing number of sectors and countries, the evidence from them could contribute to building the stock of knowledge, which may be argued to help inform decision makers of future projects and the development community in general (Sandison 2005). When designing and implementing a new project, managers and/or policy makers may take into consideration lessons learned from IEs of other projects (for example, what approaches have worked in similar settings).

World Bank Group's Strategies, Dialogue, and Policy Decisions (Strategic Use)

As the results of IEs are disseminated, they add to the general pool of knowledge of development challenges and solutions. This pool of knowledge can then be drawn upon to, which may help motivate debates and dialogue, establish best practices, influence Bank strategies (including resource allocation), and promote evidence-based policy making.

Evaluation Promotion (Process Use)

IE has the potential role of contributing to develop capacity for and institutionalizing evidence-based evaluations, both within the World Bank Group and at the country/sector level. IEs are supposed to help narrow the gap between the demand for and supply of knowledge on development effectiveness, both directly and indirectly by supporting and supplementing the production of other evaluations (CGD 2006; Ravallion 2009). Conducting IEs could promote the capacity for evaluations, including the collection of systematic high-quality data, specialized skills, and demand for follow-up or new evaluations (World Bank 2009, 2010).

Within the World Bank Group: As the number of IEs of Bank-supported projects grows, it is expected that a higher fraction of staff will learn the skills needed to carry out sound IEs.

At the country/sector level: The Bank's promotion of IEs produced in a collaborative manner with local counterparts such as policy makers, the private sector, local researchers, and development institutions (as well as nongovernmental organizations and civil society) may help transfer the necessary technical skills, internalize the value of IEs, understand their limitations and costs, align M&E and data collection strategies, and build and strengthen evaluation capacity at the country/sector level.

References

CGD (Center for Global Development). 2006. *When Will We Ever Learn? Improving Lives through Impact Evaluation*. Washington, DC: Center for Global Development.

Cummings, R. 2002. "Rethinking Evaluation Use." Australasian Evaluation Society International Conference, Wollongong Australia, October/November.

Ravallion, M. 2009. "Evaluation in the Practice of Development." *World Bank Research Observer* 24(1): 29–53.

Sandison, P. 2005. "The Utilization of Evaluations: Review of Humanitarian Action." Active Learning Network for Accountability and Performance, London.

Shadish, W.R., T.D., Cook, and L.C. Leviton. 1991. *Foundations of Program Evaluation: Theories of Practice.* Newbury Park, CA: Sage Publications.

World Bank. 2010. "Development Impact Evaluation Initiative: A World Bank-Wide Strategic Approach to Enhance Developmental Effectiveness." World Bank, Washington, DC.

———. 2009. "Making Smart Policy: Using Impact Evaluation for Policy Making—Case Studies on Evaluations that Influenced Policy." Doing Impact Evaluation No. 14, Thematic Group on Poverty Analysis, Monitoring and Impact Evaluation, World Bank, Washington, DC.

Worthen, B., J. Sanders, and J. Fitzpatrick. 1997. *Program Evaluation: Alternative Approaches and Practical Guidelines.* New York: Longman.

RECENT IEG PUBLICATIONS

The World Bank Group's Response to the Global Economic Crisis, Phase II

World Bank Country-Level Engagement on Governance and Anticorruption: An Evaluation of the 2007 Strategy and Implementation Plan

Assessing IFC's Poverty Focus and Results

Capturing Technology for Development: An Evaluation of World Bank Group Activities in Information and Communication Technologies

IEG Annual Report 2011: Results and Performance of the World Bank Group

Earnings Growth and Employment Creation: An Assessment of World Bank Support in Three Middle Income Countries

Growth and Productivity in Agriculture and Agribusiness: Evaluative Lessons from the World Bank Group Experience

MIGA's Financial Sector Guarantees in a Strategic Context

Social Safety Nets: An Evaluation of World Bank Support, 2000–2010

Timor-Leste Country Program Evaluation, 2000–2010

Trust Fund Support for Development: An Evaluation of the World Bank's Trust Fund Portfolio

Peru: Country Program Evaluation for the World Bank Group, 2005–09

Water and Development: An Evaluation of World Bank Support, 1997–2007

Climate Change and the World Bank Group, Phase II: The Challenge of Low-Carbon Development

Cost-Benefit Analysis in World Bank Projects

To see all of IEG's work, please visit our web site: http://ieg.worldbankgroup.org/publications

www.ingramcontent.com/pod-product-compliance
Lightning Source LLC
Chambersburg PA
CBHW080611270326
41928CB00016B/3009